BRITISH AND AMERICAN PLAYWRIGHTS
1750–1920
General editors: Martin Banham and Peter Thomson

James Robinson Planché

OTHER VOLUMES IN THIS SERIES

Already published

TOM ROBERTSON edited by William Tydeman
W. S. GILBERT edited by George Rowell
HENRY ARTHUR JONES edited by Russell Jackson
DAVID GARRICK AND GEORGE COLMAN THE ELDER edited by E. R. Wood
WILLIAM GILLETTE edited by Rosemary Cullen and Don Wilmeth
GEORGE COLMAN THE YOUNGER AND THOMAS MORTON edited by Barry Sutcliffe
ARTHUR MURPHY AND SAMUEL FOOTE edited by George Taylor
H. J. BYRON edited by J. T. L. Davis
AUGUSTIN DALY edited by Don Wilmeth and Rosemary Cullen
DION BOUCICAULT edited by Peter Thomson
TOM TAYLOR edited by Martin Banham
A. W. PINERO edited by George Rowell

Further volumes will include:

CHARLES READE edited by M. Hammet
HARLEY GRANVILLE BARKER edited by Dennis Kennedy
SUSAN GLASPELL edited by C. W. E. Bigsby

Plays by
James Robinson Planché

THE VAMPIRE
THE GARRICK FEVER
BEAUTY AND THE BEAST
FORTUNIO AND HIS SEVEN GIFTED SERVANTS
THE GOLDEN FLEECE
THE CAMP AT THE OLYMPIC
THE DISCREET PRINCESS

Edited with an introduction and notes by

Donald Roy

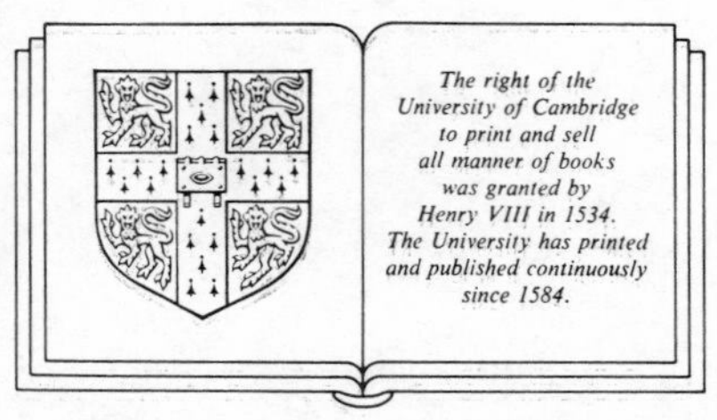

CAMBRIDGE UNIVERSITY PRESS

Cambridge
London New York New Rochelle
Melbourne Sydney

Published by the Press Syndicate of the University of Cambridge
The Pitt Building, Trumpington Street, Cambridge CB2 1RP
32 East 57th Street, New York, NY 10022, USA
10 Stamford Road, Oakleigh, Melbourne 3166, Australia

First published 1986

Printed in Great Britain at
the University Press, Cambridge

British Library cataloguing in publication data

Planché, James Robinson
Plays. – (British and American playwright 1750–1920)
I. Title II. Roy, Donald III. Series
822′.7 PR5187.P2

Library of Congress cataloguing in publication data

Planché, James Robinson, 1796–1889.
Plays.
(British and American playwrights, 1750–1920)
Bibliography: p.
Contents: The vampire – The Garrick fever – Beauty and the beast – [etc.]
I. Roy, Donald, 1930– . II. Title. III. Series
PR5187.P2A6 1985 822′.8 85-13232

ISBN 0 521 24111 1 hard covers
ISBN 0 521 28441 4 paperback

CE

GENERAL EDITORS' PREFACE

It is the primary aim of this series to make available to the British and American theatre plays which were effective in their own time, and which are good enough to be effective still.

Each volume assembles a number of plays, normally by a single author, scrupulously edited but sparingly annotated. Textual variations are recorded where individual editors have found them either essential or interesting. Introductions give an account of the theatrical context, and locate playwrights and plays within it. Biographical and chronological tables, brief bibliographies, and the complete listing of known plays provide information useful in itself, and which also offers guidance and incentive to further exploration.

Many of the plays published in this series have appeared in modern anthologies. Such representation is scarcely distinguishable from anonymity. We have relished the tendency of individual editors to make claims for the dramatists of whom they write. These are not plays best forgotten. They are plays best remembered. If the series is a contribution to theatre history, that is well and good. If it is a contribution to the continuing life of the theatre, that is well and better.

We have been lucky. The Cambridge University Press has supported the venture beyond our legitimate expectations. Acknowledgement is not, in this case, perfunctory. Sarah Stanton's contribution to the series has been substantial, and it has enhanced our work.

Martin Banham
Peter Thomson

FOR
ARLETTE

CONTENTS

ILLUSTRATIONS

ACKNOWLEDGEMENTS

I should first, perhaps, record a debt to the benign chance that brought me into active contact with Planché's work when, in 1970, my search for a suitable production with which to inaugurate the Drama Department's new theatre culminated in a triple bill originally presented at Hull's Theatre Royal in December 1820. That typically generous evening's entertainment had included *The Vampire*, and it was the experience of directing this melodrama that led me to an interest in other plays by Planché and some of his contemporaries.

Where the present volume is concerned, I am indebted to the general editors of the series, Martin Banham and Peter Thomson, for the patience they showed and the encouragement they gave me during its preparation. To Lady Ursula Bellew, great-great-granddaughter of the playwright, and her husband Sir George I wish to express my gratitude for their hospitable kindness in making family records available to me. Other individuals helped materially with my enquiries: at the Garrick Club Mr Geoffrey Ashton was a model cicerone to the Club's library and priceless gallery of theatrical portraits, while Mr R. C. Yorke, archivist to the College of Arms, and Mr John Hopkins, librarian to the Society of Antiquaries of London, provided valuable assistance with texts and memorabilia relating to Planché in their respective collections. I am also grateful to Mr George Rowell for advice, to Mr Phillip Gilbert for some musicological guidance and to Mrs Barbara Carmichael for hours of dedication at the typewriter. The staff of the Theatre Museum and of the Brynmor Jones Library at Hull University proved unfailing sources of support. Finally I am aware of a keen, if imponderable, sense of indebtedness to my departmental colleagues for the forbearance which enabled me to take a term's study leave and thereby complete the volume.

University of Hull, July 1985 — DON ROY

I Planché aged 63, at the time of *Love and Fortune*.

INTRODUCTION

James Robinson Planché is a prime casualty of the vagaries of dramatic taste. Although he was a formidable presence on the English theatrical scene for over fifty years and still occupies a secure, not to say significant, niche in the history of theatre practice, his work as a playwright is now almost totally forgotten. The fate is not an uncommon one for nineteenth-century dramatists, but, unlike peers and near-contemporaries such as Tom Taylor and John Maddison Morton, Planché has not even been paid the compliment of an occasional modern revival. The descent into obscurity had begun even before his death in 1880, and after 1900 it rapidly became complete: there appears to have been not a single professional performance of his work in the present century, apart from the periodic 'adaptations' of a handful of his fairy extravaganzas staged as Christmas entertainments by the Players Theatre in London.[1]

Yet at the time of his death he was the acknowledged grand old man of English drama, esteemed no less for his personal qualities than for his achievements. Palgrave Simpson called him 'one of the brightest and most genial writers that ever shed sunlight on the British drama'; Squire Bancroft characterised him as a 'courtly veteran . . . ever cheery'; while to Percy Fitzgerald he was 'an excellent, amiable, brilliant and most interesting man'.[2] Tom Taylor, a professional rival of Planché's for many years, perhaps best summed up the consensus of feeling when he wrote: 'I wish I could unload myself of my debt of gratitude to that kind, good man, and delightful writer, that I had room to express here my sense of the graceful and harmless amusement he has afforded to so many generations of play-goers, combining in one entertainment pretty story, humorous action, pointed and graceful dialogue, sweet music, beautiful scenery and tasteful costumes, as no man ever before combined them.'[3] The foundations of this universal regard were laid in the course of a long career in the London theatres and strengthened by the sheer scope of Planché's interests and activities. Though no Renaissance man, he was far more than the dramatic journeyman that so many purveyors of entertainment in the nineteenth century were called upon to be.

As playwright he was the author of approximately 180 pieces, intended for a whole range of theatres which embraced the Olympic, Sadler's Wells, the Adelphi, the Lyceum, the Haymarket and others, as well as the two patent houses. Many of them were supplied to order while he was employed as stock author at one theatre or another, and still more contained roles written expressly for the talents of a succession of leading players from T. P. Cooke, William Farren, Charles Kemble, Ellen Tree and Frederick Yates in the early years of his career via Robert Keeley, Madame Vestris, Mrs Glover, John Liston, Charles Mathews, James Bland, Benjamin Webster and Priscilla Horton, to J. B. Buckstone and Frederick Robson at the end. He worked with several managements as costume designer, adviser on scenic design and stage manager, and for short periods was himself manager of the Adelphi, Vauxhall Gardens and (as deputy for Madame Vestris) the Olympic. He was an active campaigner for theatrical causes like Bulwer-Lytton's Dramatic Authors Act of 1833 and for what became the Theatre Regulation Act of 1843, though he subsequently came to deplore the shortsightedness and unfortunate results of this piece of legislation. He was much concerned with the actual workings of the principle of dramatist's (and librettist's) copyright which had been established in theory by the 1833 act, successfully entering into litigation against John Braham over his libretto for *Oberon* at the time of the opera's revival in 1837, and joining the Dramatic Authors' Society, which sought to regularise copyright control and to exact royalty fees on behalf of its members. Towards the end of his life he published a pamphlet and wrote to the press championing the idea of a national theatre 'not wholly controlled by the predominant taste of the public' and with the threefold aim of 'the restoration to the stage of the masterpieces of the great dramatists of the last three centuries . . . the production of original plays of the highest class . . . and the general cultivation and encouragement of histrionic art and the welfare and respectability of its professors'.[4]

Planché was also the author of collections of verse, travel books, several volumes of French and German fairy-tales in translation, and he wrote extensively and authoritatively on historical costume, armour and antiquities, both in his own right and as editor or annotator of the work of others. That he became a genuine scholar in these fields is attested by his election to fellowship of the Society of Antiquaries in 1829 as 'a Gentleman very conversant in the History and Antiquities of this and other countries' and by his leading part in the foundation in 1843 of the British Archaeological Association, of which he became the honorary secretary for nearly twenty years and ultimately vice-president. These pursuits led quite logically to an interest in genealogy and heraldry, where his expert knowledge was officially recognised by his appointment to the College of Arms as Rouge Croix Pursuivant in 1854 and Somerset Herald in 1866, in which capacity he performed ceremonial duties and accompanied Garter missions to Portugal, Austria and Italy. In 1868 he was responsible for arranging the important Samuel Meyrick collection of armour and weapons for exhibition at the South Kensington Museum, and in the following year he was invited by the War Office to reorganise and catalogue the armoury of the Tower of London, an object he had long canvassed. In fact, public and scholarly activities of this kind came increasingly to dominate the last two decades or so of his life and it is doubtful whether he would have returned to writing for the stage after the mid-1850s had it not been for severe financial difficulties, compounded by the need to support a widowed daughter and her numerous family until the award of a Civil List pension in 1871, 'in recognition of his literary services', brought some measure of relief.

In reviewing Planché's *oeuvre*, then, one is disregarding all but one aspect of a many-sided, yet curiously organic career – and even within this one aspect the diversity of his output is striking. G. H. Lewes was not alone in making the comparison with an equally prolific contemporary: 'Planché . . . may be called the Eugène Scribe of England, if we look to the amazing quantity and variety of his dramatic productions',[5] a comparison which is apt, too, on the grounds of his avowed admiration for and not infrequent indebtedness to the French *vaudevilliste* and master of the well-made play. Planché's 'variety' embraces dramas, melodramas, comedies, farces, burlettas, pantomimes, interludes, vaudevilles, burlesques, extravaganzas, 'dramatic reviews', masques and several assorted spectacles, and he collaborated on a goodly number of operas or operettas with composers like Henry Bishop, Tom Cooke, Giovanni Liverati, Vincent Wallace and (on one occasion) Weber, as well as providing English libretti to operatic scores by other foreign composers.[6] Faced with such a miscellany the critic's impulse to discover patterns or phases of development asserts itself and, at the risk of imposing on his dramatic work a rather more self-conscious order than Planché himself may have been aware of at the time, it is possible to trace certain trends. As might be expected of a working playwright whose livelihood depended on his ability to respond to the needs of acting companies and theatrical seasons, these are linked, for the most part, to his relationships with particular managements.

Planché's début as a dramatic author appears to have happened by chance. As a young man he did a good deal of amateur acting and for a time reportedly harboured a desire to turn professional. His first piece, *Amoroso, King of Little Britain* (1818), described as a 'Serio-Comick, Bombastick, Operatick Interlude' and clearly inspired by Rhodes's *Bombastes Furioso* (1816), was intended for performance by an amateur company at Greenwich but was seen in manuscript by the then popular comedian, John Pritt Harley, who arranged for it to be staged at Drury Lane, where it was well received and given seventeen performances. Planché duly became an habitué of the theatre's green-room and, encouraged by Harley, Stephen Kemble and Elliston, he turned to playwriting as a career. His early work for the minor theatres, mostly burlettas and melodramas, is largely unremarkable, though *The Vampire, or the Bride of the Isles* (1820) already shows clear signs of his skill as an adapter and his sure dramatic instinct. Using as his source a melodrama staged in Paris barely two months earlier, Planché reduced the original's three acts to two, trimmed much of the dialogue while adding several songs, withheld the pathetic fallacy elements of storm and thunderclap until the closing scene, and made some interesting changes in characterisation: the fearful, superstitious servant Scop of the French version becomes the bibulous ne'er-do-well M'Swill, thus infusing a contrapuntal strain of comedy and providing an ideal role for Harley; the heroine's brother is altered to a father who has lost his only son and therefore welcomes her vampirical fiancé with the extra emotional warmth due to a son-surrogate; and the Ossian-like bard Oscar is omitted altogether as too improbable for English (and certainly Scottish) audiences. In fact, throughout the action Planché has marginally improved plausibility and motivation as well as accentuating the sense of temporal urgency, though he remained dissatisfied with it, having pleaded in vain with Arnold, the manager, to let him translate the scene of the action to some place in eastern Europe authentically associated with legends of the undead.[7] Nonetheless the play was extraordinarily successful at the Lyceum in August 1820, had reached Stephen Price's theatre in New York by the end of September and was quickly taken up by the provincial circuits, opening at Hull in December and at Bath in January 1821 before reopening the Lyceum summer season in June. Years later the actor–manager John Coleman still remembered seeing a revival in Derby in his youth: 'When I recall that gruesome Scottish horror feeding upon the blood of young maidens and throwing himself headlong through the solid stage, and vanishing into the regions below amidst flames of red fire, I protest I shudder at it now.'[8] It was of course for the first production of this play that the famous 'Vampire trap' was devised.

The majority of these early pieces, including a popular melodrama adapted from Scott's *Kenilworth* and presented in February 1821, only a few weeks after the publication of the work itself, were written for the James and Rodwell management at the Adelphi, and Planché did in fact become stock-author there shortly after his marriage in April of that year. This arrangement he terminated after two months and four plays, rather than, as he put it, 'soil the stage' with an adaptation of Pierce Egan's *Tom and Jerry* – an early instance of the tone of self-satisfaction and complacency that is seldom far away from his memoirs. (In Moncrieff's adaptation this burletta went on to run for a hundred consecutive performances at the Adelphi in the 1821–2 season.) Planché's first really successful engagement as stock-author, however, was with Charles Kemble at Covent Garden between 1822 and 1828, successful in terms not only of the writing, but also, and more particularly, of the mounting of plays. In 1823, apparently at Planché's own suggestion – though the contemporary press understandably attributed it to the manager – it was decided to present *King John* in historically accurate costume in direct defiance of the customary practice of dressing all Shakespeare's plays in a conventional or fancifully picturesque fashion. Knowing little about costume at the time, Planché took it upon himself to do the necessary research, seeking advice from the distinguished antiquaries

Samuel Meyrick and Francis Douce, and found himself entrusted not only with design but with the overall superintendence of the production as well.

His account of what happened makes revealing reading. There was hostility from Fawcett, the normal stage manager, and from Farley, 'the recognised purveyor and director of spectacle' at the theatre, who could not conceive of such expenditure except for an Easter or Christmas holiday show, while the actors were deeply suspicious of their 'new and strange habiliments', nicknaming the flat-topped twelfth-century helmets 'stewpans'.[9] Even Kemble was sufficiently apprehensive to instruct Planché to prepare a booklet, outlining his plans to make 'the dresses and decorations of Shakespeare's plays, if possible, worthy of them' and providing notes on the costumes themselves, which was intended for publication shortly before the opening in order to stimulate public interest and condition audience expectations. The outcome, however, was triumphant: roars of approbation greeted the first sight of King John 'dressed as his effigy appears in Worcester Cathedral', his subsequent appearance attired for battle in accordance with the design of his Great Seal, his barons 'sheathed in mail' with correct armorial shields, his courtiers in the long tunics and mantles of the period, and the various other costumes drawn from 'indisputable authorities' all listed in the playbill.

The immediate effect was to reimburse the Covent Garden management amply for its pains, the long-term consequence to bring about a revolution in stage practice. Kemble followed up the success of *King John* with a similar approach to performances of *King Henry IV, Part I*, *As You Like It*, *Julius Caesar*, *Othello* and *Cymbeline* in subsequent seasons, preparing the way and helping to create a favourable climate for the Shakespearean productions of Macready, Phelps and, most remarkably, Charles Kean. Planché was not slow to claim the credit for initiating the whole 'antiquarian' movement, at least in stage costume, but in fairness to him it must also be said that he recognised the 'excess and abuse' to which it at times led. It is demonstrable, too, that he did not hesitate to modify the historical sources in his actual designs, either for theatrical considerations or in response to prevailing fashion in dress.[10]

The same antiquarian principle was extended to other plays which Planché wrote during his engagement at Covent Garden and of which he also oversaw the production. These included his 'historical drama' or opera *Cortez* (the published version of which is laden with footnotes testifying to the authenticity of Mexican names, customs and articles as well as incidents mentioned in the text and offers a historical justification for the use of Ducrow's horses on stage) and several adaptations of seventeenth-century comedies. Interpolated into his version of Rowley's *A Woman Never Vext*, for instance, was 'a pageant of the Lord Mayor's Show as it appeared in the reign of Henry VI'. A contemporary event, the coronation of Charles X of France in 1825, provided the subject for another exercise in decorative ceremonial and costume, Planché being despatched to Paris and Rheims to make drawings on the spot as a basis for his designs and his direction of the spectacle. His usual rationale for these spectacular displays was their audience appeal and their informational value for the uneducated, 'whose instruction as well as amusement is the bounden duty of the stage'; though he also argued that historical research could be a source of creative inspiration to the designer.

Throughout his six years at Covent Garden, Planché was supplying scripts to other theatres, amongst them the Adelphi, where in 1828 his comedy *Paris and London* was performed, a musical romp affording multiple opportunities for authentic scenic display – real locations in Paris, London and Calais, the deck of a cross-channel packet, a 'Moving Panoramic View from Calais to Dover', to the accompaniment of a storm at sea, the interior of the English Opera House with a domino ball in progress, and 'a diagonal view of the Stage of the Odéon', with characters singing the finale of *The Barber of Seville* to an off-stage audience. In the same year he terminated his association with Covent Garden and entered into a similar agreement with Stephen Price at Drury Lane. Here too Planché's taste for historical plays in period costume found ample scope, notably in *Charles XII*, derived from Voltaire's life of the Swedish monarch and set in eighteenth-century Pomerania, which the *Literary Gazette* went so far as to call 'a genuine picture of the times'; *The Partisans, or The War of Paris in 1649*; *Hofer, or the Tell of the Tyrol*, a 'historical opera' with music adapted by Henry Bishop from Rossini; and *The Brigand*, which made interesting use of stage tableaux drawn from Charles Eastlake's series of Italian 'banditti' pictures, then at the height of their popularity. In 1830 Stephen Price's tenancy of Drury Lane succumbed to its crippling rental, but in the offing for Planché was another collaboration with management which was to prove by far the longest and most productive of his career.

Planché's association with Madame Vestris lasted, with two brief interruptions, for over twenty years, from 1831 until her retirement from the stage in 1855, and spanned her management of three London theatres: the Olympic, Covent Garden and the Lyceum. It became a genuine partnership, one which brought the best out of both parties; and, as has been said of Robertson and the Bancrofts, it is doubtful whether the two – or indeed Charles James Mathews who became the actress's second husband and co-manager of the Olympic in 1838 – would have developed in quite the way they did without each other. In his memoirs Planché is suitably gracious in recording his indebtedness to Vestris for 'many of the most gratifying of my successes', while on the other hand Edmund Yates, who described Planché as the 'staunchest supporter of Madame Vestris, and founder of her fortunes in her early managerial career', was not alone in emphasising her debt to him.[11]

Moreover, their association effected several innovations which left a strong imprint on the development of nineteenth-century theatre, and in Planché's case it supplied a unique stimulus to his literary and visual imagination.

It began with the presentation of *Olympic Revels*, a 'classical burlesque' which Planché had apparently written earlier and which he and Charles Dance now refurbished for the opening night of the new management in January 1831. Its remarkable success was due in no small measure to 'the charm of novelty imparted to it by the elegance and accuracy of the costume; it having been previously the practice to dress a burlesque in the most *outré* and ridiculous fashion'. Once again, as at Covent Garden, the suggestion had come from Planché, but here it was for the purpose of comic incongruity, 'to try the effect of persons picturesquely attired speaking absurd doggrel'.[12] For *Olympic Devils*, another burletta in the same vein, which Planché and Dance hastened to provide for Christmas of the same year, more money was spent to ensure that the décor was as 'picturesquely' Greek as the costumes. Henceforward period accuracy and elegance, whether in the interests of realism or comedy or sheer enchantment, were to become a hallmark of the Vestris–Planché collaboration.

A much-quoted passage in Charles Mathews's autobiography indicates clearly the break with the tradition of conventional staging that was effected: 'Drawing-rooms were fitted up like drawing-rooms, and furnished with care and taste. Two chairs no longer indicated that two persons were to be seated, the two chairs being removed indicating that the two persons were not to be seated. A claret-coloured coat, salmon-coloured trowsers, with a broad black stripe, a sky-blue neckcloth with large paste brooch, and a cut-steel eye-glass with a pink ribbon no longer marked the "light comedy gentleman", and the public at once recognised and appreciated the change.'[13] But this conveys little idea of the lengths to which scenic realism was taken at the Olympic or of the attention that might be lavished on the smallest detail, irrespective of the importance of the play. Matthew Mackintosh, who was Madame Vestris's stage carpenter for most of her Olympic management, records that for another of the opening-night pieces, *Mary, Queen of Scots*, the curiosity shops of London had been ransacked in search of period furniture and properties and in the setting of the queen's room at Lochleven Castle everything on stage – table, chair covers, cutlery, drinking goblets, even the floor carpet – bore the arms or emblazonment of Stuart.

Even greater pains were taken a few years later with Planché's *The Court Beauties* (1835), set in Charles II's London. Special permission was obtained to copy eight full-length portraits by Sir Peter Lely in the picture gallery at Hampton Court; the curtain which had once draped these portraits, a crystal chandelier and a piece of bona fide seventeenth-century tapestry were purchased at some expense 'to contribute to the *vraisemblance*' as stage-dressing; and for the scene in Bird Cage Walk a long passage at the rear of the stage was opened up to represent the Mall in perspective, complete with trees and real singing birds, through which the monarch himself entered leading a number of King Charles spaniels and accompanied by his attendants 'all in gorgeous and scrupulously correct costumes'.[14] Footnotes in the printed text draw attention to such period details, not least the use of contemporary madrigals, and the epilogue mock-modestly comments in Restoration pastiche:

> Scene, music, dress, all cull'd the time to fit.
> You have lack'd nothing of it but the wit.

Whetted by costume design, Planché's historical interests had evidently moved into other areas as well. To make such elaboration possible the new Olympic manager had installed a much larger, sectionalised stage for her second season. It was of novel design, each lateral section measuring four feet in depth and incorporating six independent traps, 'up which were sent', Mackintosh tells us, 'all the properties for each scene, thus avoiding any awkward changes of this sort in sight of the audience'.

In his writings Planché often has occasion to congratulate Vestris on her visual taste and her willingness to spend money on costume and scenic design, which frequently ran to re-dressing a Christmas piece twice in the course of its run in order to preserve its initial brilliance, and he compares this policy favourably with that of a manager like Alfred Bunn, whose attitude to such things was cavalier in the extreme and limited to the contrivance of spectacular effect, not always successfully. It is obvious, not least from his eloquent dedication to her of *The Two Figaros* (1836), that Planché and Vestris were of like mind in this regard, and their co-operation flourished accordingly, though their priorities may have been subtly different. For Vestris, realistic staging seems to have been above all a matter of visual elegance, refinement and attention to detail. She was, for instance, not averse to appearing on stage as a lady's maid attired and bejewelled at least as decoratively as, if not more so than, her mistress, and further evidence of her fashion-consciousness is provided by an interesting anecdote of Mackintosh's, who remembers purchasing from a Cheapside warehouse a seventeen-guinea Kidderminster carpet chosen by the manager herself 'out of about twenty samples' for a scene set in a chamber of a lady's residence at Naples, 'the entire appointments of which were beyond challenge by any lady among the audience'.[15] Planché's concerns, historical and antiquarian in bent, supplied the necessary impetus towards period realism.

Indeed, the whole series of comedies, farces, vaudevilles and burlettas that Planché wrote for Vestris and Mathews to perform at the Olympic, and later at Covent Garden and the Lyceum – so many of which were set in the late seventeenth or eighteenth century, in France, Spain and other foreign climes as well as England – could well have represented a working compromise between elegance and authenticity, allowing both parties to indulge their divergent, but complementary, predilections in the field of stage-dressing. John Coleman, writing in 1888, had no doubt that the Vestris–Mathews management, with Planché, 'had anticipated all, and more than all, that is done today, in regard to taste and elegance in the mounting of dramas of society'.[16]

Almost throughout the 1830s Planché was also writing for other theatre managements, notably Covent Garden, where his operas *The Romance of a Day*, *Gustavus the Third* and *The Challenge* were staged in 1831, 1833 and 1834 respectively, and Drury Lane, which presented no fewer than six operas and one operetta with an original or adapted libretto by Planché: *The Love Charm* (1831), *The Students of Jena* (1833) – for Maria Malibran – *The Red Mask* (1834), *The Jewess* (1835), *The Siege of Corinth* (1836), *Norma* (1837) and *The Magic Flute* (1838). In two of these he had to submit to the kind of indignity with which dramatic authors were all too familiar at the time. Fearful of upsetting audience sympathies, Bunn, the Drury Lane manager, obliged a very reluctant Planché to rewrite the final scene of *The Red Mask* to allow for a happy ending, thus completely perverting the moral drift of the story on which it was based, Fenimore Cooper's *The Bravo*, and a similar 'adjustment' was made to the original text (by Scribe) of *The Jewess* before it even reached the stage. Nevertheless he accepted a contract as stock-author for Bunn during the season 1835–6 and continued to write for Drury Lane for another two years. But increasingly his fortunes came to be identified, in the latter half of the decade and thereafter, with those of Vestris and Mathews, and he achieved many of his greatest successes as their accredited purveyor of extravaganzas.

It is significant of the almost universal popularity they enjoyed that these extravaganzas were gathered together by two of Planché's friends into a five-volume testimonial edition which was published on a subscription basis in the year before his death. Though some of the earliest were first announced as burlettas, in accordance with the required playbill parlance of the day, they can all more or less conveniently be grouped into three categories: those which make use of figures from Greek or Roman mythology or parody the forms of classical drama, those derived from fairy-tales, and those which Planché dubbed *revues*.

The first of the 'classical' extravaganzas, *Olympic Revels, or Prometheus and Pandora*, originated in a burlesque that he had written some years earlier, shortly after *Amoroso*, but had been unable to place. Borrowed from George Colman's story *The Sun Poker*, which, Planché says, furnished him 'not only with a subject, but suggested a mode of dealing with it', and perhaps inspired by Madame Vestris's recent appearance in a revival of Kane O'Hara's *Midas*, it is a lively, if slight piece, replete with word-play and puns, topical allusions to English life, and a prevailing mood of comic bathos that arises from the incongruity of such utterances in the mouths of classical gods and demi-gods. The dialogue, in rhyming couplets, is liberally punctuated with good-humoured travesties of popular songs or of airs and choruses from operas with which the theatre-going public was familiar, such as *Masaniello*, *Der Freischütz*, *The Marriage of Figaro*, *Guillaume Tell* and *Midas* itself, and it culminates in an appeal to the audience from Vestris in the character of Pandora:

> Smile, ye kind gods, on our Olympic Revels;
> Ye gay gallants, come, banish my blue devils,
> Let not my grapes be sour as the fox's
> But fill with patrons all Pandora's boxes . . .

The extravaganza ran until the end of the season, its reception having much to do with the firm establishment of Vestris as the first woman theatre manager, and, thus successfully launched, the *Olympic Revels* recipe was re-employed with increasing ingenuity, verve and visual display in an annual series of 'classical' extravaganzas, each written with Charles Dance and expressly for performance as a Christmas holiday piece: *Olympic Devils* (1831), *The Paphian Bower* (1832), *The Deep, Deep Sea* (1833) and *Telemachus* (1834).

After an interval of ten years, in 1845, Planché returned to Greek mythology in *The Golden Fleece*, but with a rather different purpose. He had intended to write a straightforward *revue* for Easter, but the interest lately aroused at Covent Garden by the production of Sophocles' *Antigone* in something approaching the original manner, 'on a raised stage and with a chorus' and to music by Mendelssohn, prompted him to make his own comment on that style of presentation – 'to burlesque', as he says in his preface, 'not the sublime poetry of the Greek dramatist . . . but the *modus operandi* of that classical period, which really illustrates the old proverbial observation that there is but one step from the sublime to the ridiculous'. By this time Planché was attached as stock-author to Benjamin Webster at the Haymarket, where he remained from 1843 to 1847, another period of intense collaboration which yielded seventeen plays in four seasons, including comedies, farces and above all extravaganzas, which he was specifically contracted to produce at each Christmas and Easter. But Madame Vestris and Charles Mathews were members of the company there, their three-year tenancy of Covent Garden and a brief spell with Macready at Drury Lane having both come to grief, and the subject of *The Golden Fleece* was chosen so as to capitalise on their individual talents, Vestris's early experience as *diva* in Italian opera giving a rhetorical edge to her Medea and Mathews's characteristically relaxed, nonchalant manner as the Chorus enabling him to confide in the audience in an amused and amusing fashion. The effect proved to be well calculated; the play was revived many times, becoming a regular part of Mathews's repertoire, and its treatment even earned Planché something of a reputation among academics as a classical scholar.

The following Easter he went a stage further with *'The Birds' of Aristophanes*, which he sub-titled a 'Dramatic Experiment' and conceived not as a burlesque but as 'an humble attempt to imitate or paraphrase . . . such portions of the Comedy of "The Birds" as were capable of being adapted to local and recent circumstances', his ambition being to open 'a new stage-door by which the poet and the satirist could enter the theatre without the shackles imposed upon them by the laws of the regular drama' and thereby 'lay the foundation for an Aristophanic drama, which the greatest minds would not consider it derogatory to contribute to'.[17] Though only a *succès d'estime*, it is an accomplished piece of work, decidedly free in its paraphrase of the original and more decorous in tone, but nonetheless vigorous and idiomatic throughout and quite trenchant in those passages that offer contemporary comment or satire. Take, for instance, the Chorus's parabasis:

> What in men turned to birds, is too strange to be funny,
> When they make every day ducks and drakes of their money?
> Why should not the fowls in the air build a palace,
> When there's hope of a submarine railway to Calais? . . .

or Jackanoxides' exchanges with the Architect:

ARCH: . . . My quarrel is with the new Building Act:
I feel my genius cramp'd, sir, upon land.
They stipulate that houses now should *stand*!
A fallacy exploded long ago,
As ruinous to architects, you know;
For if your dwellings are to last for ages,
The half of us wiil not get workmen's wages.
JACK: Sir, to be frank with you, I think a swallow,
Would beat the best half of your builders hollow.
To talk of architecture is a joke,
Till you can build a chimney that won't smoke!

and the Poet:

POET: . . . Of course you'll build a theatre – and there
I'll satirise them all.
JACK: Apply elsewhere,
I build a theatre *above* – no, no!
There are too many to be let below.

Air – CHORUS – *"Lucy Neal"*

In dust, at Covent Garden,
The mourning Muses sit,
Misfortune floored the management,

And Jullien floored the pit.
The Northern Wizard conjures,
And reckless maskers reel,
On boards so oft by Kemble trod,
By Siddons, and O'Neill.
Kemble, Young, and Kean,
Siddons and O'Neill!
If now ye graced the Drama's side,
How happy she would feel.

Even the final admonition given by Jupiter, warning men not 'to be something they are not' and of the confusion that would ensue if 'wild theorists' were heeded and if 'fools could follow whither knaves would lead' is, for all its safe conservatism, salutary.

After this, the two remaining 'classical' extravaganzas add little of substance. Evidently an attempt to repeat the success of *The Golden Fleece* and written for the Easter following Vestris and Mathews's assumption of control at the Lyceum, *Theseus and Ariadne* (1848) has a rather more fragmentary, adventitious air and lacks some of the earlier play's wittily tongue-in-cheek manner, despite three virtuoso patter-songs for Mathews as a choric Daedalus and a memorable punning of 'baccy' with 'Bacchae'. *Orpheus in the Haymarket* was adapted from Offenbach and Crémieux's *Orphée aux enfers* at Buckstone's request for the first appearance of Louise Keeley at his theatre in 1865.

Planché clearly disliked the *opéra bouffe*, not so much because of its 'utter subversion of the classical story' but rather 'the inartistic mode in which it was carried out, the unmeaning buffoonery forced upon it', so he took it upon himself to make extensive alterations and felt he had 'succeeded in elevating the tone and imparting to the Drama generally a more definite purpose' – a quality which emerges most clearly in tableau 3, when Public Opinion, acting as Chorus, interferes in the action to restore Eurydice to earth and Orpheus, asserting in the process a strong sense of Victorian morality and reproving the deities for their lack of it. There are some good theatrical jokes and, as Planché says in the preface, 'with the addition of pretty scenery, pretty dresses, and some pretty faces . . . the piece went merrily with the audience'; but he was obviously not entirely satisfied with it.

More distinctive still, and buoyantly original throughout his career, were Planché's so-called 'fairy' extravaganzas. Their initial conception owed something to the French *féerie*, which flourished so spectacularly in the early years of the nineteenth century, but in adapting the genre to English taste Planché naturalised it so thoroughly as to make a lasting contribution to the English theatre. His first essay in it was *Riquet with the Tuft*, produced at the Olympic for Christmas 1836, with Charles Mathews as the deformed Prince

Riquet and Madame Vestris as the beautiful but foolish Princess Emeralda [*sic*], who in return for the gift of sense bestows on him the gift of love which magically removes his deformities. In view of the known popularity of Planché's classical extravaganzas with the Olympic audience, both performers had grave reservations about this new departure. The form of the piece, too, was unfamiliar. Nursery tales like *Mother Goose*, *Aladdin* and *Little Red Riding Hood* were of course long established on the English stage as the subject-matter of Easter entertainments and the openings of Christmas pantomimes, but by and large they had been handled in a straightforwardly dramatic (or melodramatic) fashion and, more often than not, as a pretext for spectacle, whereas the *féerie* proper was a more refined confection of whimsy, badinage and delicate satire, retaining much of the charm of the early eighteenth-century 'contes de fées' by Charles Perrault, the Comtesse d'Aulnoy and others, on which so many of them were based.

In the event, fears about the piece's viability proved totally unfounded: *Riquet with the Tuft* played to crowded houses from Boxing Day until the end of the season and initiated a tradition of fairy extravaganzas which were to come annually from Planché's pen for the next twenty years, all intended for either the Christmas or the Easter holidays – on three occasions, in 1843, 1850 and 1851, there was one for each of the holiday seasons – and produced successively at the Olympic, Covent Garden, Drury Lane, the Haymarket, the Lyceum and, to complete the circle, finally the Olympic again. Increasingly Planché became personally associated with the genre, and in his hands it came to occupy a special place both in the affections of holiday audiences and in the memories of regular theatre-goers. Writing half a century later, Frank Burnand, destined to be a prolific and successful exponent of a related entertainment, recalled that 'the pit of the Lyceum at Christmas time, when Madame Vestris produced one of Planché's extravaganzas preceded by a couple of farces of which Charles Mathews was the life and soul, was something marvellous to see, so jammed and crowded was it'.[18]

Riquet with the Tuft was the only one of these extravaganzas for which Planché was directly indebted to a *féerie*, *Riquet à la Houppe*, in which he had seen the French comedian Potier years before at the Porte Saint-Martin theatre in Paris. For the remainder he preferred to draw his inspiration from the original fairy-tale itself, following its story-line closely almost without exception but tailoring characterisation and business to fit the special gifts of his actors. The first group, *Puss in Boots* (1837) and *Blue Beard* (January 1839) at the Olympic, followed by *The Sleeping Beauty in the Wood* (1840), *Beauty and the Beast* (1841) and *The White Cat* (1842) at Covent Garden, were all written for the Vestris–Mathews company and contained suitable heroines or breeches roles for Madame Vestris, a succession of burlesque kings or other notables for James Bland (a specialist in this 'line') and a couple of 'gagging' clowns for John Harley. At Drury Lane in *Fortunio* (1843), the first of Planché's extravaganzas not connected with the name of Vestris, the transvestite Miss Myrtina was entrusted to a rising newcomer, Priscilla Horton, who then went on to play similar roles alongside Bland in the four fairy extravaganzas produced at the Haymarket, *The Fair One with the Golden Locks* (1843), *Graciosa and Percinet* (1844), *The Bee and the Orange Tree* (1845) and *The Invisible Prince* (1846). After Vestris and Mathews became lessees of the Lyceum, Planché proceeded to write nine fairy extravaganzas for them in seven seasons, beginning with *The Golden Branch* at Christmas 1847 and ending with *Once Upon a Time There Were Two Kings* in 1853, for which Bland rejoined the company to play King Periwigulus the Proud. Opposite him as King Placid the Easy was Frank Matthews, who had been a regular in these roles since 1849, while most of the breeches parts were taken first by Kathleen Fitzwilliam and later by Julia St George; for Madame Vestris, in deference to her advancing years (and declining health), Planché devised a number of matrons and confidantes. Julia St George reappeared in tights in two of the final group of three fairy extravaganzas presented at the Olympic – *The Yellow Dwarf* (1854), *The Discreet Princess* (1855) and *Young and Handsome* (1856); but here the dramatic interest centred upon the series of grotesques he fashioned for Frederick Robson, an actor equally at home on the music-hall stage, who possessed such passionate intensity of feeling to match his comic brilliance that he was capable of controlling the whole mood of a piece.

In the preface to *The Queen of the Frogs* (1851) Planché listed his criteria for a good fairy extravaganza, all of which he had found in its source, *La Grenouille bienfaisante* by the Comtesse d'Aulnoy: 'A plot, the interest of which is sustained to the last moment, and is not in the least complicated; a series of startling and exciting events, the action in which required no verbal explanation, and numerous opportunities for scenic display and sumptuous decoration – what more could be desired?' Evidently he felt that audiences would desire more, for to this basic formula he invariably added the same kind of embellishments as had been used to enliven his classical extravaganzas: elaborate and inventive play on words, spirited or plaintive songs to the music of drawing-room ballads, traditional airs, nursery rhymes and well-known operas (often enough those – such as *Guillaume Tell* and *Norma* – to which Planché had already supplied a 'straight' libretto), and a good deal of witty allusion to topics of a literary, theatrical or social nature, which contrive, as it were, to domesticate the fairy world and assimilate it to the familiar actuality of London life.

The guiding principle behind these references – either incongruity or anachronism, or both at once – is fairly simple, but they certainly presuppose the existence of a cultivated and intellectually alert audience. So much is clear even from such 'throwaway' lines as:

I've looked for you through all the château, Margot;

and

The lock upon the door at the first landing,
The only Lock upon my understanding.[19]

Elsewhere the allusiveness can be more extended and potentially more serious in tone. The railway mania of 1845, for instance, the feverish speculation in bubble companies which ruined hundreds of investors for every one it enriched, is dealt with at length in *The Bee and the Orange Tree*, which also unburdens itself of some fairly outspoken comment on the evils of industrial capitalism in general in the song of the ogre, Ravagio:

. . . And why I'm so plump the reason I'll tell,
Who lives on his neighbours is sure to live well.
What sharper, or swindler, or usuring Jew,
But lives much the same as the Ogres do . . .
The sempstress wasted by slow decay,
Has her bones but picked in another way;
To the weary weaver with sleep o'ercome,
The factory bell sounds like 'Fee Fo Fum' . . .
And better swallow infants, fast as pills,
Than grind their bones to dust in cotton mills.

Again, in *The King of the Peacocks*, performed at Christmas 1848, the burden of the opening scene between the rival fairies Faith and Fickle, who champion the relative merits of tradition and change fuelled by scientific progress, is a commentary on the revolution which had agitated France for most of that year. Twelve years later, on the occasion of the revival of *The Fair One with the Golden Locks* in 1860, a second stanza was appended to the closing song in order to accommodate a reference to the recent annexation of Nice by Napoleon III.

By far the most consistent subject for reference, however, is Shakespeare, whose work Planché plunders for material with a reckless abandon born at once of an obvious love and knowledge of the plays and a certainty of their familiarity with audiences. Frequently he provides the briefest of echoes, single lines or phrases quoted (or misquoted) in passing, as it were, and without the least dramatic emphasis, though some of the puns, such as this in *Once Upon a Time There Were Two Kings* (1853), are irresistible:

. . . a piano you're not born to play.
Oh, there be misses, I have here and there heard,
Play in a style that quite out Erard's Erard.
Pray you avoid it . . .

Just as frequently, however, it is a question of full-scale, prolonged parody of key speeches, as in *The Fair One with the Golden Locks* (1843) where King

Lachrymoso contemplates taking a draught of magic elixir (which turns out to be a bottle of poisonous fly-spray) with the lines:

> Is this a corkscrew that I see before me?
> The handle towards my hand – clutch thee I will!
> I have thee not – and yet I see thee still!
> Art thou a hardware article? or, oh!
> Simply a fancy article, for show.
> A corkscrew of the mind – a false creation
> Of crooked ways, a strong insinuation! . . .

Even entire scenes are echoed, as in *Graciosa and Percinet*, which has a parody of the closet scene from *Hamlet*, and *The Island of Jewels*, where the storm scene parodies *King Lear* at some length and contains the following exchange between King Giltgingerbread the Great and his son Prince Prettiphello:

PRINCE: Are you aware, sir, you have no umbrella? (*rain*)
KING: A thought has struck me, rather entertaining,
I am a King more rained upon than reigning.
My wits are going fast!

Many similar passages could be instanced where the whole effect depends on the audience's ability immediately to recognise and savour the parallel.[20] Planché's primary object of creating an elegant, urbane kind of humour is amply realised, but it would appear that in performance the parody was susceptible of greater ambivalence of tone. In the hands of a remarkable burlesque actor like Robson, for instance – who many thought, had he lived longer, might have challenged the memory of Edmund Kean in the latter's most celebrated tragic roles – some moments could even partake of the quality of the Shakespearean original. Robson's portrayal of the monstrous Gam-Bogie in *The Yellow Dwarf* was so powerful that, in Planché's words, 'he elevated Extravaganza into Tragedy'. The way in which he handled the dwarf's proposal to the Princess Allfair, which is strongly reminiscent of the wooing scene in *Richard III*, is unfortunately not recorded, but his Othello-like lament over her dead body,

> Whip me ye devils – winds come, blow me tight!
> Roast me in flames of sulphur – very slow!
> Oh Allfair – Allfair! – Dead – O, O, O, O!

moved Thackeray almost to tears: 'This is not a burlesque', he exclaimed, 'it is an idyl!'[21]

To many contemporary spectators, however, perhaps the greatest single attraction of the fairy extravaganzas was their visual excitement. His long apprenticeship as stock-author, with a hand in the mounting of his own and other plays, had made Planché perfectly familiar with the technical aspects of staging, and this knowledge was employed to good purpose in all his work, particularly melodrama, opera and extravaganza, where he exploited the potential of changeable scenery and machines with a sure touch. It was of course an asset above all in fairy extravaganza, capable of making manifest the magic at the heart of the tales themselves and lending an air of enchantment to the entire performance. If this is already evident in the pieces written for the Olympic in the 1830s, it becomes abundantly clear in those destined for the larger stages of Covent Garden between 1839 and 1842 and the Lyceum in the late 1840s and early 1850s, where the full gamut of resources – from dioramas, gauzes and complete *changements à vue* to sophisticated trap-work, flying and mechanical artifices of all kinds – was turned to account, and the extravaganzas themselves grew from one to two acts, as if to accommodate the increased possibilities. At both these theatres Planché was appointed 'superintendent of the decorative department' and was in daily contact with the teams of scene-painters, machinists, property-makers and costumiers. The ingenious deployment of scenic effect in his work during these years betokens not only an acute awareness on his part of what could be made to happen on stage but also a willingness to exercise to the full the technical skill and imaginative powers of his colleagues, who included at one time or another the Grieves, Bradwell and Beverley.

That he had a profound respect for their achievements is borne out by generous comment in his memoirs and prefaces alike. Bradwell, who followed Vestris and Mathews from the Olympic to Covent Garden, he called an 'unequalled machinist', and one can understand why from intriguing stage directions of his which bear witness to trees which change colour, 'close upon' the presumptuous woodcutter and 'beat him with their branches' in *The Sleeping Beauty in the Wood* (1840), and to disembodied hands which appear in all parts of the stage, leading the way, carrying torches, bringing in tables and chairs, shaking the hands and being pressed to the lips of ordinary mortals in *The White Cat* (1842) 'in the most natural and graceful manner without its being possible for the audience to detect the *modus operandi*'. His most lavish praise, however, was reserved for William Beverley, the scene-painter and machinist who first joined the Lyceum company for *The Golden Branch* in December 1847 and remained to collaborate with Planché for almost six years. The extravaganzas produced during this period contain the most dazzling of effects, so dazzling in fact that Planché soon began to have reservations about their value, partly – and understandably – because they made his plays less likely to be revived, but more particularly because in the long run they 'injured the true interests of the Drama'.

Though that experienced theatre-goer, Henry Morley, could write in glowing terms in 1853 about Beverley's ability to create 'a fairy effect . . . of the completest kind' in *Once Upon a Time There Were Two Kings* 'by lengthening the silver skirts of damsels who appear to hover in the air, grouping them into festoons, and giving to their beauty something of a fantastic unearthly character',[22] Planché was later to comment sadly and at some length upon the whole phenomenon of 'unmeaning spectacle' to which that very prowess gave rise. In retrospect, he associated its onset with the sensation occasioned at the end of *The Island of Jewels* (1849) by 'the novel and yet exceedingly simple falling of the leaves of a palm tree which discovered six fairies supporting a coronet of jewels'; thenceforward, 'year after year Mr Beverley's powers were taxed to outdo his former out-doings. The epidemic spread in all directions. The *last* scene became the *first* in the estimation of the management of every theatre, where harlequinades were indispensable at Christmas.' On the Vestris–Mathews management alone the effect was deleterious enough: 'The most complicated machinery, the most costly materials, were annually put into requisition, until their bacon was so buttered that it was impossible to save it. As to me, I was positively painted out.'[23] Fortunately, this objection did not deter him from adapting fairy-tales to the stage until the very end of his full-time career as a playwright.

There remains that group of extravaganzas to which Planché refers as *revues*, or, for want of a snappier English expression, 'dramatic reviews', and defines as 'a running commentary on recent metropolitan events'. Again the model for these was French in origin, and again he claimed to have been the first to introduce the genre to this country with *Success, or A Hit if you Like it*, written for the Yates and Terry company at the Adelphi and presented there in December 1825. This *revue* treated audiences to a good-natured commentary on the main theatrical productions offered to them during the past London season. In it, Fashion, governor of the town for the Emperor Whim, instructs his daughter Success to receive all her suitors, who hail from the English Opera House, Drury Lane, Covent Garden, the Haymarket, the Adelphi and the Italian Opera at His Majesty's, before he, in consultation with the press, will decide who is to gain her hand; in the event they cannot agree, there is a riot, and she is awarded in temporary custody to Long Tom Coffin from *The Pilot*, the play by Fitzball then running at the Adelphi. This of course allowed T. P. Cooke, who was playing Long Tom Coffin at the time, to supply a free sample of his performance in a shop-window context. He also appeared briefly as Zamiel in *Der Freischütz*, a part he had created at the Lyceum in 1824, while Yates gave impressions of Charles Mathews the elder and Charles Young, and John Reeve impersonated Kean in John Howard Payne's tragedy of *Brutus* and Liston in his celebrated role of Paul Pry in Poole's comedy. This all makes for a genial affair, if rather flat-footed for today's reader – as all such pieces must be that rely for their principal effect on topicality and local knowledge.

Planché went on to write another eight *pièces de circonstance* in the same mould, half of them between 1853 and 1855, after he had finally abandoned his life of day-to-day commitment to the London theatre, and as if viewing the theatrical scene from a more dispassionate, not to say valedictory, perspective. All were written for or commissioned by the playhouses he knew best – the Olympic, the Haymarket and the Lyceum – normally as a *bonne bouche* for the holiday audience on Easter Monday, and all but one taking stock of the current state of the theatre. Inevitably ephemeral – a property freely admitted by Planché, though he numbered them 'amongst the most creditable of my original dramatic compositions' – they now present a sadly dated air and are certainly not revivable. On the other hand, they constitute a fascinating insight into their times and provide the theatre historian with a positive mine of information and quotation.

The Drama's Levée, or a Peep at the Past (1838), for instance, shows the Drama 'in a critical state of health' because of rivalry and dissension between her two sons, Legitimate and Illegitimate:

DRAMA . . . Now with their feuds they rend my feeble frame,
And rob me both of fortune and of fame. (*noise without*)
Hark! There, again! – that worse than O.P. riot;
Why won't they let the Drama die in quiet?
Go, part those children; bid them both appear!
Enter LEGITIMATE DRAMA in a Roman toga.
L. DRA. He whom they own Legitimate is here!
DRA. You naughty boy! when I'm so very poorly;
You have been fighting with your brother surely.
L. DRA. I have; because of him I can't get fed,
Whilst he is almost sick with gingerbread.
DRA. Will you ne'er cease this ruinous debate?
Where's that audacious Illegitimate?
Enter ILLEGITIMATE DRAMA in a dress half harlequin and half melo-dramatic.
I. DRA. Behold! (*striking an attitude*)
DRA. Unnatural son!
I. DRA. Is't thus I'm styled?
I always thought I was your natural child.
L. DRA. He puns! He'll pick a pocket the next minute!
I. DRA. I shan't pick yours, because there's nothing in it! . . .

Amid jokes, puns and allusions to contemporary dramatic fare there are other trenchant comments on the burletta and the abiding conflict between the Major and the Minor houses before the 1843 Theatre Regulation Act.

The Drama at Home, or an Evening with Puff (1844), written in imitation of Sheridan's *The Critic*, is an ambitious piece which takes up the story after the promulgation of this act and expounds Planché's 'humble opinions on the unprecedented condition of the English stage' following the abolition of the monopoly hitherto enjoyed by the patent houses and the occupation of Drury Lane and Covent Garden by non-dramatic enterprises. The Drama is now in extremis and wishes to die, but Puff attempts to revive her spirits with hare-brained, spectacular projects to pull in an audience, and conjures up brief fragments or tableaux from recent or current productions at a wide range of theatres, concluding with a 'grand anomalous procession' of the various exhibitions on offer in London. The final note is one of cautious optimism: although the removal of legal restrictions has as yet produced 'no rising drama worth the name', merely a collection of sensational or opportunist pieces, there is ample time for things to improve. A much slighter piece, *The New Planet, or Harlequin out of Place* (1847), for which the recent discovery of Neptune provided a convenient, if flimsy, pretext, is little more than a verbal and visual inventory of stage productions, quasi-scientific exhibitions or demonstrations and other entertainments – like the 'mysterious lady' and a troupe of Ethiopian Serenaders – then available to Londoners.

The Seven Champions of Christendom (1849), on the other hand, the only *revue* not concerned with theatrical matters, took the whole of Europe as its canvas and essayed a commentary on the state of the continent at a time of violent political and social unrest. The risk inherent in tackling such a subject for an Easter Monday audience was even greater than it had been with *The Birds*, but to ignore it, says Planché's preface with characteristic solemnity, 'was impossible, and I had always contended that the mission of the dramatist was of a much higher nature than the catering of mere amusement for the million'. To accommodate it, therefore, to audience expectations he allegorises the action and shows St George and the patron saints of Scotland, Wales, Ireland, France, Italy and Spain overcoming tyranny, ignorance, superstition 'and all the plagues of humanity, in the semblance of the gigantic ogres, witches, sorcerers, demons, dragons, serpents, and venomous vermin in the original legends, with the weapons with which modern science and "the march of intellect" had so powerfully armed them'. Smug and chauvinistic though it is to modern taste, the play was brilliantly successful, again demonstrating Madame Vestris's superiority to purely 'commercial managers' in her willingness to take chances, and subsequently being much anthologised for literary readings.

The last four *revues* all take a close look at the theatrical scene in the 1850s and do so in a mood of palpable anxiety. *Mr Buckstone's Ascent of Mount Parnassus* (1853), a title alluding to Albert Smith's entertainment *The Ascent of Mont Blanc*, which was then enjoying immense popularity at the Egyptian Hall, was commissioned by J. B. Buckstone for the opening of his management of the Haymarket. It shows the new manager pondering what to offer the public 'nightly for forty weeks' and being visited first by the Spirit of Fashion, who gives him some candid advice from the audience's point of view concerning the drama's shortcomings, and then by Fortune, who conjures up specimens of what she has recently favoured, including *The Corsican Brothers* and no fewer than six versions of *Uncle Tom's Cabin*, before he decides that none of this will do and vows to scale his own dramatic Parnassus. Though an equally occasional piece, *The Camp at the Olympic* (1853), written to introduce Alfred Wigan's management of the Olympic, furnishes a more comprehensive survey of the current resources of the Engish stage in comparison with the recent and distant past; while *Mr Buckstone's Voyage Round the Globe* (1854), which took its cue from Wyld's Great Globe, a scale model of the earth then on display in Leicester Square, presents a curious mixture of comments on the theatre and the state of the world, terminating with the goddess Cybele's advice to the manager:

> And here let all the world take up its quarters.
> Demonstrate to the town the earth's attraction,
> And so give universal satisfaction.

The conceit underlying *The New Haymarket Spring Meeting* (1855) is to equate all the shows vying for public favour in London – exhibitions, scientific and geographical displays, opera and dance as well as drama – with racehorses contesting the Great Metropolitan Handicap at 'Upsand Downs'; and, after seeing a parade of last and this year's runners, Buckstone, as the Lord Mayor's Fool, concludes that:

> The odds are fearfully against the stage . . .

This is very much the message of all these *revues*. In them, as elsewhere, Planché 'took the opportunity of promulgating opinions which might be serviceable to the best interests of the drama',[24] and by the mid 1850s his opinions seem bleak indeed. He sees a beleaguered theatre struggling to withstand massive competition from other entertainments and denied government support:

> The State no temple to the Drama gives –
> She keeps a shop, and on chance custom lives,
> From hand to mouth . . .[25]

To Alfred Wigan's complaint in *The Camp at the Olympic* that 'the Drama's perishing of inanition . . . And sadly empty the dramatic larder' the only remedy that his wife can suggest is an eclectic mixture of the fare that is currently available, in the hope that it will be enough to save their 'experimental Camp' – a stoical conclusion on the manager's part but scarcely redolent of confidence, still less of enthusiasm, on the author's.

In 1853 Planché had given up his London home in order to live in Kent, going so far as to resign his membership of the Garrick Club, and although he was to return in the following year after his appointment as Rouge Croix Pursuivant he never again haunted the theatrical establishment or attached himself to any manager. Instead he accepted occasional commissions, mostly at the Haymarket and the Olympic, for the *revues* and fairy extravaganzas already mentioned, several comedies and one opera. They show no decline in his powers. Indeed, after his sense of being eclipsed by Beverley at the Lyceum he relished the thought of having 'once more to rely upon acting rather than upon scene-painting'[26] and was never prouder of a success than in the case of the scenery-less, action-less *Camp at the Olympic*, where his dialogue had to stand alone. *Love and Fortune*, too, inspired in form by the fairground theatre performances of early eighteenth-century France and sub-titled by Planché a 'Dramatic Tableau (in Watteau colours)', is an interesting attempt to marry his own delicate style in verse and sung ditties to the more vigorous idiom of *commedia dell'arte*. While not entirely successful (and a comparative failure when staged by Augustus Harris in 1859), it has considerable charm and is a clear token of his continuing enterprise as a playwright. It is all the more ironic, therefore, that his final exercise should have proved a sad miscalculation. Invited by Boucicault in 1872 to contribute the songs for a 'fairy spectacle' called *Babil and Bijou* to be presented at Covent Garden, the veteran versifier of seventy-six set to work with elation, but in the event found his words heavily cut and finally overwhelmed in a sumptuous four-hour farrago of scenic display, complete with submarine and lunar sets and a huge cast of nearly a hundred exotically attired actors, singers and dancers, the action of which could not be followed without reference to a printed brochure summarising the argument and reproducing Planché's lyrics.[27] Thereafter he was not to be tempted back to the stage, preferring to devote himself to his duties as Somerset Herald which, coupled with his many scholarly pursuits, kept him fully occupied. His health remained good until the last twelve months of his life, and in a letter to an antiquarian friend in 1875 he had written '[I] am in my eightieth year, working harder than I did at thirty.'

So busy a round was it that his output of plays was restricted to a mere dozen in the last twenty-five years of his life, compared with more than 160 in the previous thirty-five. Long before this retrenchment, however, his reputation with contemporary audiences was secure, the product not only of native ability but of sheer professional assiduity. Bunn, for instance, described him as 'my able, industrious, and zealous friend', and a reviewer of *Faint Heart Never Won Fair Lady* at the Olympic called him 'as untiring as untired, and as indefatigable as the fair manageress herself'.[28] To industry, as a direct corollary, he added a complete grasp of the physical realities of stage performance. The opinion of Edward Fitzball, a fellow-toiler in the same theatrical vineyards, must command respect in this connection: 'Planché is a practical author, and one of our cleverest; a little too cautious *perhaps*; he would braid the sunbeams, so carefully, as not to burn his fingers. In the general parlance of theatrical business a practical author means a play writer who looks beyond his steel pen, and quire of foolscap; to the O.P. and to the P.S. . . . he will plumb the depth of his venture, and satisfy himself to the solving of a problem in Euclid, as regards the practicability and possibility of his scenic effect, on the stage, or of any original idea emanating from his own brain.'[29] Pragmatism of this order no doubt helps to explain Planché's great admiration for Scribe and for that other master-craftsman of the *pièce bien faite*, Victorien Sardou. It is perhaps in the same light, too, that one should see his readiness to alter existing 'classic' plays for performance and to collaborate with fellow playwrights or composers in the production of new work, as he did with Charles Dance on all but one of the first ten Olympic extravaganzas, with Weber so successfully on *Oberon*, with Bishop on other operas, and with Mendelssohn to the extent of being prepared to make all and any textual concessions in order to ensure that their aborted opera, *The Siege of Calais*, might see the light of day.

However, the single most obvious mark of Planché's understanding of 'the stage and its necessities' was his ability to write for actors. The weather-eye he kept at all times on the individual strengths and weaknesses of a company enabled him not only to fit parts to star players like Madame Vestris, Mathews, Liston and Bland, but also to make revisions for a new cast on the occasion of a revival, to add, change or suppress songs according to their vocal competence, to write into a given story what he unabashedly called 'introduced characters', or even to choose a whole subject for the benefit of available performers, as he did *Fortunio* for 'some of the best pantomimists of the day' at Drury Lane, or, most conspicuously of all perhaps, *The Yellow Dwarf* and *The Discreet Princess* for the uniquely tragi-comic Robson, in whose interests the former piece was designed to include two 'turns' for which he was already well known in the music-halls, a Lancashire clog hornpipe and a finale to the music of 'Villikins and his Dinah'. Clearly, then, it would be a mistake to bring literary values to bear on Planché's overall style or even to expect much concern for realism in his dialogue. Whatever importance he attached to realistic costume and décor, his plays were conceived first and foremost as scripts for actors, as vehicles for their peculiar talents or distinctive stage *personae*. He recognised his dependence on them and was generous in his praise for those who were most responsible for his success; his shrewd assessment of Charles Mathews shows that he was also a good judge of the limits of their powers.

Despite this capacity for compromise, Planché seems to have nurtured a genuine seriousness of purpose throughout his working life. At its simplest it is evident even in his attitude to source material. He persistently congratulates himself on fidelity to his originals, both in publishing accurate translations of French fairy-tales to replace the mutilated versions known to nursery children or pantomime audiences, and also in adapting these tales to the stage. It was what prompted him to restore the action of *Blue Beard* to fifteenth-century Brittany and its eponymous villain to the ranks of the French aristocracy, in preference to the 'very magnificent three-tailed Bashaw' found in 'George Colman's well-known and well-worn melodramatic opera'. His rationale is conveniently summarised for us in the preface to *The Prince of the Happy Land*, where he talks of preserving not only the wit and satire that have been lost in these garbled versions of the stories but also the 'moral lessons of the originals'. However commonplace the morals themselves, Planché leaves us in no doubt as to his sincerity in propounding them: 'Regardless of the opinion of the few self-constituted judges who contended that a moral was out of place in an extravaganza, and had evidently overlooked the fact that there is no very popular fairy tale without one, I most contumaciously persisted in my error, and on the present occasion, actually selected a subject which had *two*.'[30] This does not prevent him, however, from making his own occasional emendations when he finds those lessons too melancholy, as in the case of *The Yellow Dwarf*, where, having dutifully brought the piece to the required conclusion with the death of the two young lovers and their transmutation into palm trees, he disarmingly provides an alternative happy ending, more suitable to 'a tale of mirth . . . at such a season'.

Similarly, if for more aesthetic reasons, he adopted a conscientious attitude to the translation or adaptation of existing plays from the French. In a note to the published text of *The Jewess*, and subsequently in his memoirs, he indignantly deplored the changes forced on him in his own version of this opera and of *The Red Mask* in deference to the imagined susceptibilities of the public. When he initiated changes of his own it was for one of two, in his eyes, perfectly legitimate reasons: first, to correct historical inaccuracies in the original, as in Scribe's *Gustave III* or in *Fiesco* (where he took issue with Schiller on a point of Italian precedence!); and secondly, to adjust the original to English manners and taste. In so doing Planché not infrequently improved on his source. One of many actors with reason to be thankful for this, Frank Archer, maintained that his comedy *Secret Service* 'gave greater opportunities than the musical play from which it was taken', and the *Examiner* in its review of *The Knights of the Round Table* was merely echoing the consensus of press opinion when it commented: 'What he takes he makes his own by skill and expertness of handling. We have seen adaptations of his clearly better than the originals . . .'[31]

Moreover, in Planché's memoirs and prefaces alike, one repeatedly finds him claiming to have had the higher or long-term interests of the drama ever in mind, one particularly self-righteous passage declaring that 'whatever success I have been fortunate to achieve in the course of my literary life, I have certainly not been indebted for it to any intentional sacrifice of my own principles at the shrine of popularity'.[32] Even allowing for an understandable element of *post hoc* rationalisation here, the sense of purpose seems to be devoutly felt and it is borne out in much of his professional activity. It expresses itself in an almost obsessive desire to reanimate and strengthen English drama in general and to raise the tone of popular dramatic fare in particular. His introduction to English audiences of the *revue* and his acclimatisation of the French *féerie* could, to take a cynical view, be dismissed as acts of theatrical opportunism, but there is no gainsaying the fact that, once having established these forms, he endeavoured to take them further with *The Seven Champions of Christendom* and his adaptation of *The Birds*, for instance, in the service of higher satirical or moral ends. Likewise social satire, albeit of a fairly genial disposition, informed the elegant comedies of manners that he wrote for Vestris and Mathews, like *Hold Your Tongue* and *My Heart's Idol*. His promotion of historical authenticity in costume and realistic staging generally was a sincere crusade, so sincere as to give a sharp edge to his disappointment at their degeneration into a pretext for gratuitous spectacle. He wrote feelingly on this subject in an article published in 1861: 'That I was the original cause of this movement, I do not deny; that . . . I succeeded in the object I had honestly at heart, I am proud to declare; but if propriety be pushed to extravagance, if what should be mere accessories are occasionally elevated by short-sighted managers into the principal features of their productions, am I fairly answerable for their suicidal folly?'[33] The same article bitterly regrets the harmful influence that he has indirectly and unwittingly exercised on traditional pantomime through the 'last scenes' of his Lyceum extravaganzas, which in Beverley's hands became so spectacular as to provoke a mania for transformation scenes and induce rival managers to outdo each other by 'patching' extravaganza on to pantomime 'to the serious injury of both'.

Clearly, Planché was astute enough to be well aware of the dangers of the pictorial approach to production, however closely associated with it he had been. In his work as supervisor of design and stage management at Covent Garden and the Lyceum he certainly cultivated period realism – and there is ample evidence in stage directions and costume lists as well as in contemporary illustrations to show how detailed it could be – but it was always subordinate to the play itself: he was too much a man of the theatre to allow it to develop into heavy-handed antiquarianism for antiquarianism's sake. In fact, his keen historical sense could lead him to eschew spectacle altogether, as in his production of *The Taming of the Shrew* at the Haymarket in 1844, for which he designed sets and costumes as well as superintending rehearsals. His purpose on this occasion was to restore Shakespeare's text in its entirety, including the induction with Christopher Sly, in preference to Garrick's altered version, *Katherine and Petruchio*, which was still in common use for performance. He therefore took the logical step of abandoning scenery as such in favour of two simple locations, the exterior of the ale-house where Sly was discovered and the nobleman's bedchamber where the comedy itself was performed by the troupe of strolling players in conditions approximating to those of the Elizabethan stage and without a single curtain drop. The experiment was a bold and highly successful one, all the more remarkable in that it anticipated the Elizabethan Stage Society and the work of William Poel by a good half-century.

In his own plays the same sense of period can produce the most delicate and refreshing results, as in his *commedia*-inspired *Love and Fortune* and his spirited adaptation of Garrick's *Cymon* into a 'Lyrical, Comical Pastoral' in rococo style, with much of Arne's original music and *mise en scène* 'in perfect keeping with the time in which it was originally produced'. Both have an intrinsic verve which far transcends mere historical pastiche. Elsewhere in his work, too, whatever his dramatic purpose there is customarily a similar lightness of touch, and, where appropriate, a tremendous sense of fun. Self-sufficient jokes, as distinct from puns, are not common and seem designed to elicit a smile rather than a laugh, though they are certainly worth waiting for, as is Leona's wry comment in *The Queen of the Frogs*:

> Since Orpheus for his wife went to the deuce,
> The custom's fallen quite into dis-use;
> And if to take such journeys men are prone,
> It is for other wives – and not their own.

Even an otherwise indifferent piece can have good moments and erupt into pure comedy, as does *Grist to the Mill* when Francine, masquerading as marchioness to a miserly, atrabilious marquis, bids the latter's nephew 'embrace your uncle, who opens his affectionate arms. (*Aside to Marquis*) Open your affectionate arms.' But most of these moments need to be appreciated in context, depending as they do on the comic momentum that the action of the piece or the continuous flow of banter has built up. Many, indeed, can scarcely be savoured at all without the embodiment of performance, so inextricably geared are they to established dramatic procedures. Such a moment occurs with King Brown's interrupted enjambement in *The Golden Branch*:

> The bride is on her road! Ah, there's the bother!
> She may arrive ere I can say Jack Rob – (*flourish without*)
> – inson! – She has so! There's a pretty job!

and again with the burleseque stichomythia between Soyez Tranquille, Argus, Florizel and Rosetta in *The King of the Peacocks*:

SOYEZ. *Avancez*, miss! (ROSETTA *comes forward*.)
ARG. O heavens!
FLOR. What do I see?
You!
ROSE. I – myself –
ARG. Then she herself is –
ROSE. Me!

ARG. Rosetta!
FLOR. Sister!
ROSE. Brother! (*embraces – to* ARGUS) Husband!
ARG. Wife!
Transported I deserve to be for life!

Much of the best comedy, in fact, is self-referential, making capital out of perceived theatrical conventions and commonplaces. Planché seems not only at his most assured but at his most inventive and original when taking the theatre itself as his raw material. *The Garrick Fever* shows how much farcical business he can generate from a strictly theatrical setting, *A Romantic Idea* how adept he is at the burlesque of genre. Not surprisingly, incidental theatrical satire looms large, not only in the *revues*. The current London scene that Planché knew so well supplied him with targets in plenty, among the most favoured being animal shows and menageries, dioramas, *poses plastiques*, waxworks, the exhibition craze generally, nigger minstrel troupes, ballet and, perhaps the greatest source of competition to the legitimate stage, opera. Opera is also frequently absorbed into the fabric of the extravaganzas as a basis for lunatic spoof. *The Fair One with the Golden Locks* has a 'Grand Scena, on the most approved principle of Modern Operatic Composition', which incorporates recitative, songs and choruses to music from *Norma*, 'The Minstrel Boy' and 'The British Grenadiers'; while in *The King of the Peacocks* a group oath is sung by the king, his cooks and his guards holding rolling-pins to the music of 'Blessing of the Poignards' from *Les Huguenots*. There is also much linguistic guying, whereby the words of familiar Italian arias are replaced by English lyrics which are incongruous but have a similar ring: 'Com' e gentil' from *Don Pasquale* becomes 'Comb it genteelly'; 'La ci darem la mano' from *Don Giovanni* becomes 'Mind you don't let your ma know'; and the recitative and aria from *Tancredi* beginning 'O Patria' opens with 'Oh, pa! try her. Won't you, my great papa, try her', immediately after the singer has announced:

I will only stay
To sing a song – As opera heroes choose
Always to do, when they've no time to lose.[34]

In Planché's last extravaganza, *Orpheus in the Haymarket*, the vogue for sensational dramas in the 1860s provokes a touch of sarcasm as Pluto darkens the stage, except for a circle of limelight around Eurydice, and prepares to carry her off to the underworld:

EURY. What ails me? I am losing all sensation!
PLU. Then for the modern stage you've no vocation!

Moments later, self-conscious theatricality asserts itself quite unashamedly: Public Opinion interrupts an imminent rhyme on the grounds that 'the

Licenser' might object to it, and Orpheus strides on to the shadowy stage wondering who has 'turned off the gas in the sky borders'. There are many other such subversions of convention, as in the dual ending to *The Yellow Dwarf* and the references to Planché's own role as author or adapter. Perhaps the most interesting example of this comes in *The Good Woman in the Wood* where the Fairy Fragrant conveys Dame Goldenheart to the famous 'Cabinet des Fées', whose shelves are lined with volumes of fairy-tales beloved by children, including a section of 'stage editions'; on a desk, centre stage, lies a volume containing the present tale but as yet untitled, which the fairy opens to

> find out how the adapter
> Has worked the story up in the last chapter.

No doubt it was the same propensity that attracted Planché to a late eighteenth-century comedy by Richaud-Martelly, *Les Deux Figaro, ou le sujet de comédie*, which has among its dramatis personae a would-be playwright taking down details of the 'real-life' action, as outlined by Figaro, to form the basis for a comedy he is writing and in turn contributing to the former some inventions of his own. However, this single level of artifice evidently did not satisfy Planché, for he transformed the original into a musical comedy by interpolating songs to the music of *The Barber of Seville* and *The Marriage of Figaro* and complicated the French author's duplication of Figaro still further by introducing a Susanetta figure alongside Susanna.

Undeniably, it is in the extravaganzas that these elements of deliberate theatricality are seen at their best, but they are not sufficient in themselves to account for what Planché called the 'almost unprecedented popularity' enjoyed by the genre, particularly by the fairy extravaganza. Among his contemporaries it seems often enough to have been discussed in the same breath as burlesque, as if there were little or no distinction between the two, but Planché himself had a precise conception of their separateness. *The Sleeping Beauty in the Wood*, the first of his holiday pieces to be performed at Covent Garden, where the use of the term 'burletta' became redundant, was clearly announced in the bills as an extravaganza, 'distinguishing', the preface tells us, 'the whimsical treatment of a poetical subject from the broad caricature of a tragedy or serious opera, which was correctly termed a "Burlesque"'. There are certainly burlesque properties in Planché's work, and he provides an eloquent apologia for the form in the lines spoken by Burlesque in *The Camp at the Olympic*, but he was not primarily or, one suspects, by temperament a writer of burlesque.

Instinctively his preference, and hence the emphasis in his work, lay elsewhere. The epithets most commonly applied to the fairy extravaganzas in their day were 'delightful', 'beautiful', 'brilliant', 'graceful'; they were characterised as 'airy trifles', with lyrics 'as faultless in tone, tact and taste, as they were rhythmically perfect'.[35] For somewhat grudging corroboration from within the playwriting fraternity itself one may again turn to Fitzball, who after quoting Moncrieff's comment on Planché to the effect that 'he wrote in white kid gloves' adds: 'For my own part, I always seemed to entertain an idea that he lived on honey and nectar.'[36] Of those virtues so prized by his audiences some are still faintly detectable from the printed page: an extraordinary verbal facility and skill in versification; an absurd sense of humour held in check by a refinement inimical to excess and vulgarity; a gift for creating eccentrics and grotesques; an imaginative flair for situation and the possibilities of scenic imagery; above all a delicacy of touch which enables comedy to go hand-in-hand with pathos and even with a strain of seriousness. However down-to-earth or jokily familiar his treatment of it, however defused of supernatural menace, there remains an underlying respect for the marvellous. Percy Fitzgerald put his finger on this vital factor when he described Planché's dramatisation of the fairy-tale as 'done with a certain seriousness, very much as it would appear to a child's eye'.[37]

What cannot now be recaptured is the dimension of performance, the qualities of acting and *mise en scène* brought to bear on the written text. That they were considerable, possibly decisive, is suggested by Planché's personal responsibility for design and stage management at most of the theatres with which he was regularly associated, particularly Covent Garden, the Haymarket and the Lyceum. The enthusiasm generated by the scenic splendours of extravaganza, most notably by those from the hand of William Beverley, became legendary, but the visual contribution of precisely realised costume may have been almost as important. The theatre critic Dutton Cook[38] had occasion to recall 'that courtly conventional dress of the last century which Mr Planché often favoured in his modernised renderings of fairy stories', in other words the court dress of the later years of Louis XIV and those of Louis XV, the very period in which the stories themselves were originally published. Pictorial evidence confirms both this and the Greek dress worn in the classical extravaganzas, and shows occasional excursions into other periods of European history and other cultures. Whatever liberties Planché may have taken with sartorial detail, his costumes were always firmly anchored in a specific historical period and executed with a conscious sense of design. That this was the case from the earliest days of extravaganza at the Olympic is confirmed by his anecdote in the preface to *Olympic Revels*, recounting his cast's distress at the adoption of historically correct dress: 'Liston thought to the last that Prometheus, instead of the Phrygian cap, tunic, and trousers, should have been dressed like a great lubberly boy, in a red jacket and nankeens, with a pinafore all besmeared with lollipops; others that, as in *Midas*, the costume should be an incongruous mixture of the classical and the farcical.'

As for the style of acting he preferred, Planché's major innovation as stage manager was to insist that the characters of his extravaganzas be played 'straight'. Whatever nonsense they spoke, however absurdly or grotesquely they were called on to behave, their manner should be intent and matter-of-fact. Again, this was a strategy adopted from the very outset. The preface to *High, Low, Jack and the Game*, presented at the Olympic as early as 1833, attributes the play's success 'above all' to 'the spirit with which the performers entered into the whim of the piece – not attempting to be *funny* but acting it as seriously as possible', while that to *Fortunio*, premiered ten years later, congratulates the company on their 'apparently total unconsciousness of its absurdity'. It was the sheer perfection of this technique in James Bland that earned him the title of the 'monarch of extravaganza'. He had acquired the technique, Planché says, while playing subordinate roles 'under the best actors of the regular drama', and it had imparted to his diction and manner 'an earnestness, which, while it gave point to the epigram, trebled the absurdity of the language in which it was conveyed. He made no effort to be "funny", but so judiciously exaggerated the expression of passion indicated by the mock-heroic language he had to deliver, that while it became irresistibly comic, it never degenerated to mere buffoonery.'[39]

These considerations constrain one to give full weight to Planché's revealing phrase, 'the precise tissue of absurdity on which I had calculated'.[40] It comes in a passage regretting what he saw as an excessive employment of spectacle in the mounting of *Once Upon a Time There Were Two Kings* (with which he had not been personally involved) and it makes clear that his recipe for extravaganza was determined with precision, as much in the staging as in the writing. It was a compound of the fantastic, the poetic, the grotesque and the comic, and it was finely judged to appeal to a wide audience of playgoers, not least the cultivated among them. Henry Morley's evaluation of *Love and Fortune* as 'exquisite trifling, very fanciful to hear, and very beautiful to see' could have been applied to the extravaganzas as a whole, on which William Archer's apt comment was that they were 'to their successors as Tenniels to Rowlandsons'.[41]

Beyond doubt it was also a recipe that set the seal on his reputation as a dramatist. In his early days he was viewed with contempt by some – 'Who are your successful authors? Planché and Arnold, Poole and Kenney; names so ignoble in the world of literature that they have no circulation beyond the green-room'[42] – with indifference by many; and Horace Foote's *A Companion to the Theatres* of 1829 records him simply as one amongst many authors of 'comedies and farces'.[43] Yet for the generation of young writers who first encountered Planché's work in its heyday at the Haymarket and the Lyceum he was a master in his chosen field. John Hollingshead summed up their admiration well when he declared that Planché 'raised theatrical extravaganza and burlesque to the dignity of a fine art, and wrote verses to be sung on the stage which could be read with pleasure in the study'.[44]

Naturally, those who aspired to the same success strove to emulate his work. The suppliers of popular dramatic fare in the 1850s, 1860s and 1870s – the Brough brothers, Burnand, H. J. Byron, Robert Reece – borrowed his style of writing for their burlesques and took its word-play much further, until the puns became excruciating or so contorted as to require a bracketed gloss for the benefit of the reader. W. Davenport Adams, who published in 1891 *A Book of Burlesque*, the first attempt at a comprehensive survey of the whole phenomenon, had no hesitation in nominating Planché as 'the founder of modern burlesque'[45], a remark that might well have occasioned a sepulchral revolution in Brompton Cemetery in view of the so-called founder's public repudiation of his mid-century imitators thirty years before, along with their 'jungles of jingles and sloughs of slang'.[46] Another disciple, and the only one whom Planché recognised as a worthy successor, was W. S. Gilbert, and the similarities between the two, mentioned as early as 1870 by Dutton Cook in his review of the first performance of *The Palace of Truth*, have been the subject of much subsequent comment.[47] Gilbert's indebtedness was not confined merely to the inspiration for Pooh-Bah in *The Mikado* (who obviously derives from Baron Factotum, 'Great-Grand-Lord-High-Everything' in *The Sleeping Beauty in the Wood*) and a number of individual patter songs in *Patience*, *Iolanthe* and *The Grand Duke*, but may have extended to the overall lightness of touch that informs his early fairy comedies as well as the Savoy Operas themselves. Probably the example of Planché, no less than that of Robertson, lies behind Gilbert's tight control over the performance of his work through careful stage management and rehearsal and his rejection of outlandishly comic make-up and costume.

In this connection, too, the debt that Victorian pantomime owed to the staging of Planché's extravaganzas is manifest, above all in the evolution of the spectacular 'transformation scene', the burgeoning of the fairy element and the gradual erosion of the old-style harlequinade. Just as clearly, the 'principal boy' followed in the elegant footsteps of those handsome young princes and other blue-blooded breeches roles that Planché wrote for Eliza Vestris, Priscilla Horton, Kathleen Fitzwilliam and Julia St George. Extravaganza's influence may also be present in the pantomime's adoption of preposterous names for its worthies and villains along the lines of Planché's King Henpeckt the Hundredth, Viscount Verysoso, Killmany O'Gobble Killmore and the Fairy Baneful, and even in its increasing orientation towards audiences of children: as early as 1854, in the concluding verses to *The Yellow Dwarf*, comes the announcement that the piece is intended as a Christmas treat for

> . . . all you young folks who are home for the holidays,
> And children of all growths who hate melancholy days.

But the distaste he felt for the radical changes in pantomime which he had unintentionally abetted is transparent in Planché's testy animadversion upon 'the dull, monstrous, hybrid spectacle which has superseded the bright, lively, and laughable harlequinade of my earlier days'.[48]

Ironically, then, those very features of extravaganza which had assured Planché's reputation became the source of its subsequent undoing. The wit and delicacy of his work was overshadowed by the elephantine punning and coarse, boisterous gagging of mid-century burlesques, with their flippant songs, low dresses and energetic 'break-downs'; its charm was to be outshone by Gilbert. Planché's scrupulous, realistic approach to staging was lost sight of in doctrinaire antiquarianism on the one hand and extravagant spectacle on the other. To borrow Harley Granville-Barker's neat summation, the 'pattern of [his work] was . . . fated to be clowned as well as painted out of existence'.[49] Unfortunately he lived long enough to see it all happen, but not long enough, fortunately, to see himself consigned within a generation to a footnote in William Toynbee's edition of Macready's diaries with the terse comment: 'He was a prolific writer for the London theatres, but his plays have made no permanent reputation.' Though overtaken by events which contrived retroactively to discredit or diminish it, his achievement during his lifetime was considerable and worthy. His multiple talents, if circumscribed, were unique and original enough to raise him distinctly above the ruck of artisan writers and theatre people; he was content to exercise those talents within the commercial establishment of the theatre as he found it, because for most of his life he had no other source of income, but at the same time he endeavoured with cautious enterprise to advance the cause of theatre as an art.

His obituary in the journal of the British Archaeological Association, understandably emphasising his serious, scholarly accomplishments, offers but a limp tribute: 'In his plays there is an abundance of harmless mirth, but neither coarseness nor vulgarity.' Less respectful to the scholar, but more representative of the popular affection he inspired as a playwright, are some lines addressed to him by Edmund Yates in the 1870s, after he had quitted the theatre for good:

> Then Mr Planché, come once more and doff your herald's tabard!
> Clear your cobwebs, seize the pen which you have never plied in vain;
> For the bright sword of your wit is growing rusty in its scabbard,
> And we long to see it flashing in the gas-lamps once again.[50]

NOTES

1 *Sleeping Beauty in the Wood* in 1944, 1948, 1954, 1963 and 1971: *Beauty and the Beast* in 1949, 1955, 1973 and 1983; *Riquet with the Tuft* in 1951 and 1960; *King Charming* in 1957 (subsequently transferred to the Lyric, Hammersmith) and 1977.

2 J. Palgrave Simpson, obituary of Planché in *The Theatre*, August 1880, p. 95; *Mr and Mrs Bancroft On and Off the Stage*, 6th edn (London, 1889), p. 305; Percy Fitzgerald, *The Garrick Club* (London, 1904), p. 44.

3 'Some Personal Reminiscences of Alfred Wigan', *The Theatre*, January 1879, p. 414.

4 *Suggestions for a National Theatre* (1879), pp. 1–2. Cf. his *Recollections and Reflections*, 2 vols. (London, 1872), II, 300–6.

5 *Selections from the Modern British Dramatists*, 2 vols. (Leipzig, 1867), II, 325.

6 Admittedly, no clear-cut distinction existed in the early nineteenth century between opera and drama, especially melodrama. As E. W. White points out in *The Rise of English Opera* (London, 1951), there was a long-established tradition of spoken dialogue in English opera, and Planché conceded that even his most successful opera, *Oberon* (1826), was written as 'a melodrama with songs' since his 'great object was to land Weber safe amidst an unmusical public' (*Recollections and Reflections*, I, 83).

7 He was able to do so some years later when he returned to the subject in his English libretto for Marschner's opera *Der Vampyr* (Lyceum, 1829), set in Hungary and using 'national dresses of the Magyars and the Wallachians'.

8 *Fifty Years of an Actor's Life*, 2 vols. (London, 1904), I, 30. Cf. the puff in the original Lyceum bills: 'The effect produced on crowded audiences by THE VAMPIRE is perfectly electrical.'

9 *Recollections and Reflections*, I, 52–60.

10 For detailed comparisons, see Paul Reinhardt, 'The Costume Designs of James Robinson Planché', *Educational Theatre Journal*, 20 (1968), 524–44.

11 *Recollections and Reflections*, I, 120; Edmund Yates, *His Recollections and Experiences*, 2 vols. (London, 1884), I, 191–2.

12 *Recollections and Reflections*, I, 179–80.

13 *The Life of Charles James Mathews*, 2 vols. (London, 1879), II, 76.

14 Matthew Mackintosh, *Stage Reminiscences* (Glasgow, 1866), pp. 80–3. Cf. Planché, *Recollections and Reflections*, I, 237.

15 *Stage Reminiscences*, p. 134.

16 J. Coleman, *Players and Playwrights I Have Known*, 2 vols. (London, 1888), I, 240.

17 Preface to *'The Birds' of Aristophanes*; and *Recollections and Reflections*, II, 80.

18 F. C. Burnand, *Records and Reminiscences, Personal and General*, 2 vols. (London, 1904), I, 366. Planché even dubbed himself 'your Holiday Bard' in a passage of direct address to the audience at the end of *The Invisible Prince*.

19 *Blue Beard*, sc. 2 and *The Sleeping Beauty in the Wood*, part II, sc. 2.

20 For a detailed discussion, see Stanley Wells, 'Shakespeare in Planché's Extravaganzas', *Shakespeare Survey*, 16 (1963), 103–17.

21 Preface to *The Yellow Dwarf*.
22 Henry Morley, *Journal of a London Playgoer* (London, 1891), p. 67.
23 Preface to *The Island of Jewels*; and *Recollections and Reflections*, II, 135.
24 *Recollections and Reflections*, II, 152.
25 *Mr Buckstone's Ascent of Mount Parnassus (Extravaganzas)*, IV, 278.
26 *Recollections and Reflections*, II, 154.
27 The actual quality of the piece is a matter of dispute. Press notices agree on the 'unparalleled magnitude' of the spectacle and H. S. Wyndham, in his *Annals of Covent Garden Theatre*, 2 vols. (London, 1905), II, 266, deems it 'a considerable success', whereas for Edward Stirling 'it signally failed . . . This costly experiment of trying how much money may be lavished on production of novelty quickly squandered a fortune to no purpose whatever, save paying a host of persons a salary for six months' (*Old Drury Lane*, 2 vols. London, 1881, II, 242).
28 Alfred Bunn, *The Stage*, 3 vols. (London, 1840), III, 249, and an unattributed cutting in the British Library scrapbook devoted to the Olympic Theatre.
29 Edward Fitzball, *Thirty-Five Years of a Dramatic Author's Life*, 2 vols. (London, 1859), I, 260–1.
30 Preface to *The Discreet Princess*. This aspect of the extravaganzas is documented by Dougald MacMillan, 'Some Burlesques with a Purpose, 1830–1870', *Philological Quarterly*, 8 (1929), 255–63.
31 Frank Archer, *An Actor's Notebooks* (London, 1912), p. 302; and *The Examiner*, 27 May 1854.
32 *Recollections and Reflections*, I, 102–3. Cf. *ibid.*, p. 44: 'I can safely say that I never suffered pecuniary considerations to influence my conduct when the higher interests of the drama appeared to me at stake.'
33 'Extravaganza and Spectacle', *Temple Bar*, November 1861, pp. 526–7. He was equally distressed by the way in which realistic staging had been exploited in the service of crude sensationalism. Recalling the execution scene in the first version of *The Red Mask*, in which troops formed a hollow square completely concealing the condemned Bravo and 'the axe gleamed for an instant above the caps of the multitude' before it descended and the crowd dispersed to reveal a black cloth covering the body, he comments: 'Every thing being thus left to the imagination of the spectator, the effect was infinitely stronger than the grossest exhibition could have produced . . . Talk of the sensational dramas of the present day!' (*Recollections and Reflections*, I, 281–9).
34 *The Fair One with the Golden Locks*, sc. 3; *Once Upon a Time There Were Two Kings*, act. II, sc. 1; *The Deep, Deep Sea*, sc. 3. Although he subsequently 'regretted being obliged to introduce grand Italian arias to which it was impossible to write anything readable, and which reduced one to the poor fun of stringing together English words that sounded something like the Italian' (preface to *King Charming*), he employed the device frequently enough to indicate that his audiences knew their opera and enjoyed not only hearing it but hearing it travestied.
35 See, for example, Percy Fitzgerald, *Principles of Comedy and Dramatic Effect* (London, 1870), pp. 171–83; William Archer, 'The Drama', in *The*

Reign of Queen Victoria, ed. T. H. Ward, 2 vols. (London, 1887), II, 567; H. Barton Baker, *The London Stage, 1576–1888*, 2 vols. (London, 1889), II, 16–17, 53; Clement Scott, *The Drama of Yesterday and Today*, 2 vols. (London, 1899), I, 35, 119; II, 190, 194; W. Eden Hooper, *The Stage in the Year 1900* (London, 1901), p. 5; R. Farquharson Sharp, *A Short History of the English Stage* (London, 1909), p. 130.

36 Fitzball, II, 28.

37 Fitzgerald, pp. 171–2. Cf. Henry Morley's appreciation of 'that conscientious resolve to enter heart and soul into the spirit of fairy-lore which makes this writer's Christmas pieces always so delightful' (*Journal*, p. 90).

38 D. Cook, *Nights at the Play* (London, 1883), pp. 92–3.

39 *Recollections and Reflections*, I, 255–6. In his view Bland's distinction in extravaganza was equalled only by that of Robson, whose intensity of acting occasionally 'reversed the well-known quotation, and proved that there was "only one step from the ridiculous to the sublime"' (*ibid.*).

40 'Extravaganza and Spectacle', p. 530.

41 Morley, p. 199; Archer, II, 567.

42 Philo-Dramaticus [Rev. W. Harness], 'A Letter to Charles Kemble, Esq., and R. W. Elliston, Esq., on the Present State of the Stage', *Blackwood's Magazine*, June 1825, p. 730. The sentence continues: 'and which the very spectators of their productions regard as too contemptible to be allowed to claim a place in their recollection'.

43 Two years later Molloy Westmacott, a critic notorious for his displays of malice, patently had Planché in mind when he warned Madame Vestris against entrusting her affairs to 'a master-manager Mr Plank, . . . one of these *Wooden* translators or dramatic cobblers of French pieces' (*The Age*, 6 February 1831).

44 J. Hollingshead, *My Lifetime*, 2 vols. (London, 1895), I, 192.

45 W. D. Adams, *A Book of Burlesque* (London, 1891), p. 44.

46 'Extravaganza and Spectacle', p. 531. Cf. *Recollections and Reflections*, II, 153.

47 See, for instance, Adams, pp. 55, 76–7; Harley Granville-Barker, '*Exit* Planché – *Enter* Gilbert', in *The Eighteen-Sixties*, ed. J. Drinkwater (Cambridge, 1932), pp. 102–48; Ernest Reynolds, *Early Victorian Drama, 1830–70* (Cambridge, 1936), pp. 69, 71–2; St. Vincent Troubridge, in *Notes and Queries*, 179 (1940), 442–3; 180 (1941), 200–5; 181 (1941), 17–18; V. C. Clinton-Baddeley, *The Burlesque Tradition in the English Theatre after 1660* (London, 1952), pp. 115–16; George Rowell, *Theatre in the Age of Irving* (Oxford, 1981), pp. 135–6. It may also be noted that Gilbert was one of the subscribers to the testimonial edition of Planché's extravaganzas.

48 *Recollections and Reflections*, II, 223.

49 Granville-Barker, p. 127.

50 *Proceedings of the British Archaeological Association*, 36 (1880), 262; Yates, II, 155.

BIOGRAPHICAL RECORD

27 February 1796	James Robinson Planché born in Old Burlington Street, Piccadilly, London, to Jacques Planché, watchmaker, and his wife Catherine Emily, *née* Planché, first cousins and descendants of Huguenot refugees. Educated at home by his mother, speaking fluent French.
1804–8	Following his mother's death in 1804, attends the Reverend Mr Farrer's boarding school in Lawrence Street, Chelsea.
1809–10	Studies geometry and perspective with M. de Court, landscape painter.
1810	Articled to a bookseller. (Scurrilous journalistic report has it that he 'once kept a shop for pattens in Broad Street, Golden Square'.)
1816	Death of his father.
1818	Writes his first play, *Amoroso, King of Little Britain*, for performance at one of several private theatres where he acts in amateur productions.
21 April 1818	*Amoroso* successfully produced at Drury Lane, and JRP turns to playwriting as a career.
May 1818	Makes first of many visits to Paris in search of material to translate or adapt for the English stage.
1818–19	Writes a 'speaking harlequinade', *Rodolph the Wolf*, and an 'operatic drama' for Elliston at the Olympic; has melodramas and burlettas produced at Drury Lane, Sadler's Wells and the Adelphi.
9 August 1820	*The Vampire* well received at the Lyceum.
1820–1	Writes ten pieces, including adaptation of Scott's *Kenilworth*, for winter season at the Adelphi and others for Sadler's Wells, the Haymarket and the Lyceum.
26 April 1821	Marries Elizabeth (St) George and honeymoons in Paris, seeing *Riquet à la houppe*, a *comédie féerie* at the Porte Saint-Martin.
1821–2	Briefly employed as stock-author at the Adelphi and provides pieces for the Olympic and the Lyceum.
1822	JRP and his wife set up house in suburbia, at 20 Brompton Crescent (now Egerton Gardens, SW3), their home for more than 20 years. Joins Charles

	Kemble as stock-author for six years at Covent Garden, where his first full-scale opera, *Maid Marian*, is produced (3 December).
1823	Birth of daughter, Katherine Frances. JRP designs costumes and accessories for *King John*, first of several 'antiquarian' productions of Shakespeare plays superintended by him at Covent Garden. Publishes *Shere Afkun, a Legend of Hindoostan* and continues to write for the Lyceum and the Adelphi.
1823–5	Publishes costume designs, with explanatory notes, for Shakespeare productions.
14 October 1824	His adaptation of Weber's *Der Freischütz* produced at Covent Garden. Commissioned by Kemble to write libretto for *Oberon*, exchanging lengthy correspondence with the composer.
9 November 1824	His adaptation of Rowley's *A Woman Never Vext* produced at Covent Garden, first of several reworkings of seventeenth-century comedies.
29 May 1825	Attends coronation of Charles X at Rheims to make drawings for design of a pageant of the coronation (staged at Covent Garden 11 July).
23 November 1825	Birth of second daughter, Mathilda Anne.
12 December 1825	*Success* produced at the Adelphi, first of his *revues* in the French style.
12 April 1826	*Oberon* produced at Covent Garden.
1826	Spends summer as manager of Vauxhall Gardens, arranging concerts with Henry Bishop, and embarks on tour of Belgium, Germany and Holland, which provides inspiration for *Lays and Legends of the Rhine* (published 1827).
1827	Adapts *All's Right* from a French vaudeville for Laporte's début at the Haymarket (15 June) and again organises performances at Vauxhall Gardens during summer. Further tour of Germany and Austria, recorded in his *Descent of the Rhine from Ratisbon to Vienna* (published 1828).
1828	Joins Stephen Price as stock-author at Drury Lane.
1829	Following pirate performance of *Charles XII* in Edinburgh, JRP mobilises opinion in favour of copyright protection and persuades Hon. George Lamb to introduce (unsuccessful) Parliamentary Bill on Dramatic Writings in February 1830.
24 December 1829	Elected fellow of the Society of Antiquaries.

1830	Instrumental in gaining recognition by music publishers of librettist's copyright in opera. Engaged as 'acting manager' at the Adelphi.
3 January 1831	Production of *Olympic Revels*, first of his 'classical' extravaganzas, opens Madame Vestris's management of the Olympic and marks the beginning of their long and close collaboration.
1831	Becomes founder member of Garrick Club.
1831–4	His prolific output comprises 25 plays and operas in four years for the two patent houses, the Olympic, the Haymarket and the Adelphi.
10 July 1832	Gives evidence to Bulwer-Lytton's Select Committee on Dramatic Literature.
10 June 1833	Act amending laws relating to Dramatic Literary Property receives royal assent.
1833	Engaged by Samuel Arnold as 'acting manager' for summer season during the Lyceum company's occupation of the Adelphi.
1834	Publishes his *History of British Costume to the Close of the 18th Century*.
1835	Charles James Mathews joins the Olympic company.
1835–6	Contracted to Alfred Bunn as stock-author at Drury Lane and Covent Garden.
26 December 1836	*Riquet with the Tuft*, first of his 'fairy' extravaganzas, produced at the Olympic.
1837	Enters into successful litigation against John Braham for protection of copyright on his lyrics for *Oberon*.
1837–9	Works as stock-author at the Olympic while providing some pieces for Drury Lane.
1838	Commissioned by Messrs Chappell to write a libretto for Mendelssohn and begins long, abortive correspondence with the composer. Publishes his *Regal Records*. Following their marriage in July, Vestris and Mathews leave for American tour and JRP is manager of the Olympic from October to December.
1839	Vestris and Mathews become lessees of Covent Garden, appointing JRP as reader of plays and 'superintendent of the decorative department'; he designs costumes for opening production, *Love's Labour's Lost*.
1839–42	JRP writes exclusively for Covent Garden, including a masque in honour of Queen Victoria's marriage. Edits

	reissue of Joseph Strutt's *A Complete View of the Dress and Habits of the People of England* and *The Regal and Ecclesiastical Antiquities of England*.
1842	Advises members of the royal family on historical dress for the Queen's first *bal costumé* at Buckingham Palace on 12 May, publishing an illustrated *Souvenir* of the ball in 1843.
1842–3	Writes for Drury Lane under Macready, with whom Vestris and Mathews have taken an engagement.
1843	Theatre Regulation Act abolishes patent theatres' monopoly of 'legitimate' drama.
	Engaged by Benjamin Webster as stock-author at the Haymarket (where the company includes Vestris and Mathews) for 3½ years, undertaking to produce extravaganzas at Christmas and Easter.
	Becomes founder member of the British Archaeological Association.
1844	Moves to Michael's Grove Lodge, Brompton.
6 June 1845	The Queen holds a second *bal costumé*, JRP again advising on historical dress.
22 September 1846	Death of his wife, aged 50.
1847	Co-opted on to committee for the purchase and preservation of Shakespeare's 'birthplace' at Stratford.
	Vestris and Mathews take the Lyceum, with JRP supplying their Christmas and Easter productions and assuming overall control of stage decoration. His simultaneous exercise of a similar function at Drury Lane ends when lessee, Louis Jullien, goes bankrupt.
1847–52	After inaugural production, *The Pride of the Market*, JRP provides a further 16 plays in 5 years for the Lyceum.
1850	Meets Eugène Scribe on a visit to London.
1851	His services in demand for another royal *bal costumé*.
19 November 1851	Marriage of elder daughter.
1852	Terminates official connection with the Lyceum. *The Pursuivant of Arms* published.
21 December 1852	His younger daughter, already a successful authoress of children's books, is married and JRP leaves London to reside with her in Kent.
1852–6	Divides his writing between the Lyceum, the Haymarket and the Olympic, providing *revues* for the opening of J. B. Buckstone's management of the Haymarket and Alfred Wigan's of the Olympic.

1853	Publishes translation of *King Nut Cracker* by Hoffmann.
1854	Appointed Rouge Croix Pursuivant at the College of Arms and returns to live in Chelsea.
1855	Translation of the *Fairy Tales* of the Comtesse d'Aulnoy published. Madame Vestris retires from stage, dying in 1856.
1857–8	Writes nothing for the theatre, devoting himself to scholarly pursuits and heraldic duties.
1857	Arranges Meyrick collection of armour for exhibition in Manchester and writes official handbook. Tours Germany, Switzerland and France in summer.
1858	Publishes *Four and Twenty Fairy Tales* by Perrault and others and accompanies Garter mission to Lisbon to invest King Pedro V.
1859–62	Provides one comedy each for the Adelphi, the Princess's and the Haymarket, one opera for Covent Garden.
1864	*A Corner of Kent* published.
1865	Is attached to Garter mission to Lisbon to invest King Luis and visits Paris.
26 December 1865	Last extravaganza, *Orpheus in the Haymarket*, produced.
1866	Promoted to Somerset Herald and edits revised version of Hugh Clark's *An Introduction to Heraldry*.
1867	Member of Garter mission to Vienna to invest the emperor Franz Josef. Visits Paris and tours Scotland and Ireland.
1868	Arranges Meyrick collection for exhibition at South Kensington Museum. His younger daughter is widowed and returns with children to live with JRP.
1869	Invited to reorganise armoury at Tower of London.
1870	Engaged briefly as 'decorative and dress adviser' at the St James's.
21 June 1871	Granted a Civil List pension of £100.
1872	Writes songs for Boucicault's *Babil and Bijou* at Covent Garden, his last work for the stage. *Recollections and Reflections* published.
1873	*William with the Ring* published.
1874	*The Conqueror and his Companions* published.
1876–9	*A Cyclopaedia of Costume* published.
1878	Member of Garter mission to Rome to invest King Umberto I.

April 1879	Appears in benefit performance of *Money* at the Haymarket.
1879	*Suggestions for a National Theatre* and testimonial edition of the *Extravaganzas* published.
30 May 1880	Dies at 10 St Leonard's Terrace, Chelsea.
4 June 1880	Buried at Brompton Cemetery.
1881	*Songs and Poems, from 1819 to 1879* published, with preface by his younger daughter.

A NOTE ON THE TEXTS

In the case of all five extravaganzas the text used is substantially that of the collected edition, which was published as a testimonial to Planché in the year before his death and can be presumed to embody his final preferences. This has, however, been collated with the following first editions: *Beauty and the Beast* (London: S. G. Fairbrother, 1841); *Fortunio and his Seven Gifted Servants* (London: G. Berger, 1843); *The Golden Fleece* (London: S. G. Fairbrother and W. Strange, 1845); *The Camp at the Olympic* (London: Thomas Hayles Lacy, 1854), and with the manuscript licensing copy of *The Discreet Princess*, which remained unprinted until 1879. Collation has yielded few variations of note but has permitted the correction of some relatively minor textual corruptions. A handful of more significant variants is separately recorded in an appendix.

The text of the remaining two plays is that of the earliest published edition: by John Lowndes (London, 1820) for *The Vampire* and Thomas Hayles Lacy (London, 1855) for *The Garrick Fever*.

In all cases spelling has been modernised, but the original punctuation, which may be taken to correspond rather more to stage delivery than to literary style, has been largely preserved.

A NOTE ON SOURCES

The Vampire; or, the Bride of the Isles is adapted from a melodrama entitled simply *Le Vampire* by Pierre Carmouche, Charles Nodier and Achille de Jouffroy, with music by Alexandre Piccini, first performed at the Porte Saint-Martin theatre, Paris, on 13 June 1820. This piece was itself inspired by John Polidori's tale, *The Vampyre*, first published in 1819.

Of *The Garrick Fever* Planché's memoirs indicate that it was 'of Gallic origin, but fitted to an English subject, respecting which a similar story is told'; no further details about the source are given.

The first part of *The Golden Fleece* derives from the *Argonautica* of Apollonius Rhodius in Francis Fawkes's translation and borrows locution as well as incident from the original, but the second, while parodying Euripides' tragedy of *Medea* quite closely at times, makes a contrived departure from accepted myth. Bearing in mind, says a prefatory note, the historian Aelianus' claim that Medea's children were not killed by their mother but by the Corinthians, who 'paid five golden talents to Euripides to lay the guilt on Medea . . . the author of the present drama has, therefore, most generously expended the only talent he possessed in altering the catastrophe so as to redeem the character of the unfortunate heroine'.

All three fairy extravaganzas are based on French fairy-tales: *Beauty and the Beast* on Mme Leprince de Beaumont's 'La Belle et la bête', which appeared in her *Magasin des enfants* (London, 1756); *Fortunio and his Seven Gifted Servants* on the Comtesse d'Aulnoy's 'Belle-Belle, ou le chevalier fortuné', included in her *Contes des fées* (1698–1711); and *The Discreet Princess* on 'L'Adroite Princesse', at one time attributed – by Planché among others – to Charles Perrault, but in fact written by Mlle L'Héritier de Villandon and first published under the title of 'Les Aventures de Finette' in her *Oeuvres mêlées* (Paris, 1696).

THE VAMPIRE; OR, THE BRIDE OF THE ISLES

A Romantic Melodrama in two acts, preceded by an introductory vision.

First performed at the English Opera House (Lyceum), on Wednesday, 9 August 1820, with the following cast:

In the Vision

UNDA, *Spirit of the Flood*	Miss Love
ARIEL, *Spirit of the Air*	Miss Worgman
A VAMPIRE	Mr T. P. Cooke
LADY MARGARET	Mrs Chatterly

In the Melodrama

RUTHVEN, *Earl of Marsden*	Mr T. P. Cooke
RONALD, *Baron of the Isles*	Mr Bartley
ROBERT, *an English attendant on the Baron*	Mr Pearman
M'SWILL, *the Baron's henchman*	Mr Harley
ANDREW, *steward to Ruthven*	Mr Minton
FATHER FRANCIS	Mr Shaw
LADY MARGARET, *daughter to Ronald*	Mrs Chatterly
EFFIE, *daughter to Andrew*	Miss Carew
BRIDGET, *Lord Ronald's housekeeper*	Mrs Grove

RETAINERS, PEASANTS, BARGEMEN, etc., etc.

Overture by Mr Reeve; other music by Mr M. Moss and Mr Hart.
Scenery by Mr A. Thiselton, Mr Smith and assistants.

II *The Vampire*: introductory vision
ARIEL: Foul spirit, retire!
VAMPIRE: She is mine!
T. P. Cooke as the Vampire, Mrs Chatterly as Lady Margaret.

INTRODUCTORY VISION

The curtain rises to slow music and discovers the interior of the Basaltic Caverns of Staffa, at the extremity of which is a chasm opening to the air. The moonlight streams through it and partially reveals a number of rude sepulchres. On one of these LADY MARGARET *is seen, stretched in a heavy slumber. The Spirit of the Flood rises to the symphony of the following*

INCANTATION

Solo – UNDA
Spirit! Spirit of the Air!
Hear and heed my spell of power;
On the night breeze swift repair
Hither from thy starry bower.
CHORUS
Appear! Appear!
UNDA
By the sun that hath set
In the waves I love;
By the spheres that have met
In the heavens above.
By the latest dews
That fall to earth;
On the eve that renews
The fair moon's birth.
CHORUS
Appear! Appear!
QUARTETTO
By the charm of might and the word of fear,
Which must never be breath'd to mortal ear.
Spirit! Spirit of the Air,
Hither at my call repair!
(*Music – The Spirit of the Air descends through the chasm on a silvery cloud, which she leaves and advances.*)

ARIEL: Why, how now, sister! wherefore am I summoned?
What in the deep and fearful caves of Staffa
Demands our presence or protection? – Speak!
UNDA: Spirit of the Air! thy sister Unda claims
Thy powerful aid; – not idly from thy blue
And star-illumin'd mansion art thou call'd
To Fingal's rocky sepulchre – Look here. (*pointing to* LADY MARGARET)
ARIEL: A maiden, and asleep!
UNDA: Attend thee, Ariel!
Her name is Margaret, the only daughter
Of Ronald, the brave Baron of the Isles.
A richer, lovelier, more virtuous lady
This land of flood and mountains never boasted.

To-morrow Marsden's Earl will claim her hand,
Renown'd through Europe for his large possessions,
His clerkly knowledge, and his deeds of arms.
ARIEL: How came she in this den of death and horror?
UNDA: Chasing the red-deer with her father, Ronald,
A storm arose, and parted from her train,
She sought a shelter here – calmly she sleeps,
Nor dreams to-morrow's hymeneal rites
Will give her beauties to a Vampire's arms.
ARIEL: A Vampire, say'st thou! – Is then Marsden's Earl –
UNDA: Thou knowest, Ariel, that wicked souls
Are, for wise purposes, permitted oft
To enter the dead forms of other men;
Assume their speech, their habits, and their knowledge,
And thus roam o'er the earth. But subject still,
At stated periods to a dreadful tribute.
ARIEL: Aye, they must wed some fair and virtuous maiden,
Whom they do after kill, and from her veins
Drain eagerly the purple stream of life;
Which horrid draught alone hath pow'r to save them
From swift extermination.
UNDA: Yes; that state
Of nothingness – total annihilation!
The most tremendous punishment of heaven.
Their torture then being without resource,
They do enjoy all power in the present.
Death binds them not – from form to form they fleet,
And though the cheek be pale, and glaz'd the eye,
Such is their wond'rous art, the hapless victim
Blindly adores, and drops into their grasp,
Like birds when gaz'd on by the basilisk.
ARIEL: Say on. –
UNDA: Beneath this stone the relics lie
Of Cromal, called the bloody. Staffa still
The reign of fear remembered. For his crimes
His spirit roams, a Vampire, in the form
Of Marsden's Earl; – to count his victims o'er
Would be an endless task – suffice to say,
His race of terror will to-morrow end,
Unless he wins some virgin for his prey,
Ere sets the full-orb'd moon.
ARIEL: And with this view
He weds the Lady Margaret.
UNDA: Aye, Ariel;
Unless our blended art can save the maid.
ARIEL: What can be done? – our power is limited.
What can be done, my sister?
UNDA: We must warn

The maiden of her fate. Lend me thine aid,
To raise a vision to her sleeping sight.
ARIEL: Let us about it.
(*They perform magical ceremonies to the symphony of the following Charm.*)
Charm – ARIEL *and* UNDA
Phantom, from thy tomb so drear,
At our bidding swift arise;
Let thy Vampire-corpse appear,
To this sleeping maiden's eyes.
Come away! come away!
That the form she may know
That would work her woe;
And shun thee, till the setting ray
Of the morn shall bid thy pow'r decay;
Phantom, from thy tomb so drear,
At our bidding rise! – appear!
(*Thunder*)
Chorus – ARIEL *and* UNDA
Appear! Appear! Appear!
(*A Vampire succeeds from the Tomb of Cromal and springs towards Margaret.*)
VAMPIRE: Margaret!
ARIEL: Foul spirit, retire!
VAMPIRE: She is mine!
ARIEL: The hour is not yet come.
UNDA: Down, thou foul spirit; – extermination waits thee:
Down, I say!
(*Music – The Vampire sinks again, shuddering, and the Scene closes.*)
End of the introductory vision

ACT I

SCENE 1. *A Hall in the castle of* LORD RONALD. M'SWILL *and a group of retainers are seen seated round a table in hunting dresses, drinking. The sun is seen just rising behind the hills through the large Gothic window at the back of the scene.*

Chorus – *'Johnny Cope'*
Come fill, let the parting glass go round,
With a stirrup cup be our revelry crown'd,
See the sun that set to our bugles' sound
Is changing the night into morning.

As darkness shrinks from his rising ray,
So sorrow and care will we keep at bay,
By the bowl at night and the 'Hark away',
That awakes us, brave boys, in the morning.
(*Enter* BRIDGET *and* ROBERT. M'SWILL *gets under the table.*)

BRIDGET: Very pretty doings, upon my word! Here's our poor mistress, the Lady Margaret, been lost for nearly the whole night in the forest; and no sooner is she by good fortune found again and trying to get a little rest in her own apartments, but you make all this noise, as if on purpose to disturb her.

ROBERT: Nay, Mrs Bridget, don't be angry with them. They've been celebrating my lady's return.

BRIDGET: Return! Don't tell me. – They never want an excuse to get drunk – out of the castle directly – don't stand ducking and scraping there – go along directly, when I tell you. (*Exeunt retainers.*) Where is that rascal, M'Swill? he's at the bottom of all this; – but if I – (M'SWILL *attempts to steal off.*) Oh! oh! there you are, sir – come here, sir. (*Seizes him by the ear and brings him forward.*) Down on your knees directly, and ask my pardon.

M'SWILL: I do, Mrs Bridget.

BRIDGET: How came you under the table?

M'SWILL: What a question, when a man has been drinking all night.

BRIDGET: Will you never leave off taking your drops?

M'SWILL: I don't take *drops*, Mrs Bridget.

BRIDGET: Here has poor Robert been running through the forest all night, seeking my lady, and peeping in all the holes of the grotto, whilst you –

M'SWILL: The grotto, Mrs Bridget! Good guide us! Why, you didn't go into the grotto, did you?

BRIDGET: And why not, booby?

M'SWILL: O, dear! O, dear! the ignorance of some people – but you're an Englishman, and that accounts for it. Why, didn't you know that the grotto was haunted?

ROBERT: Ha! ha! ha!

M'SWILL: Aye! aye! laugh away, do – but I can tell you it's full of kelpies and evil spirits of all sorts; only ask Mrs Bridget.

BRIDGET: It's very true, Robert, and you shouldn't laugh, for they always owe a grudge to anybody that jests about them.

M'SWILL: Did you never hear the story of Lady Blanch?

BRIDGET: Hush! don't talk so loud.

M'SWILL: You know it, Mrs Bridget?

BRIDGET: No! but Lord Ronald is very angry with everybody who circulates stories of that description – so speak lower, if you are going to tell it.

M'SWILL: Well, then – once upon a time –

ROBERT: Ha! ha! ha! – Mother Bunch's fairy tales.

M'SWILL: Well, isn't that the proper way to begin a story?

BRIDGET: Go on.

Mother Bunch: a London ale-wife whose name was used in the title of many seventeenth-century collections of jests and anecdotes.

M'SWILL: Once upon a time –
ROBERT: You've said that once twice.
M'SWILL: Will you be quiet with your fun. I won't tell it at all.
ROBERT: Well, well, then – Once upon a time what happened?
M'SWILL: Once upon a time, there lived a lady named Blanch, in this very castle and she was betrothed to a rich Scotch nobleman; all the preparations for the wedding were finished, when, on the evening before it was to take place, the lovers strolled into the forest –
BRIDGET: Alone?
M'SWILL: No; together, to be sure.
BRIDGET: Well, sot, I mean that; and I think it was highly improper.
M'SWILL: Well, they were seen to enter the grotto, and –
ROBERT: And what?
M'SWILL: They never came out again.
ROBERT: Bravo! – an excellent story.
M'SWILL: But that isn't all. – The next morning the body of the lady was found covered with blood, and the marks of human teeth on her throat, but no trace of the nobleman could be discovered, and from that time to this he has never been heard of; and they do say, (I hope nobody hears us) they do say that the nobleman was a *Vampire*, for a friar afterwards confessed on his death bed, that he had privately married them in the morning by the nobleman's request, and that he fully believed it some fiend incarnate, for he could not say the responses without stuttering.
ROBERT: Better and better! and how came you by this precious legend?
M'SWILL: The great uncle of my grandfather had it from the great grandfather of the steward's cousin, by the mother's side, who lived with a branch of the family when the accident happened; and moreover, I've heard my great uncle say, that these horrible spirits, call'd Vampires, kill and suck the blood of beautiful young maidens, whom they are obliged to marry before they can destroy. – And they do say that such is the condition of their existence, that if, at stated periods, they should fail to obtain a virgin bride, whose life blood may sustain them, they would instantly perish. Oh, the beautiful young maidens! –
BRIDGET: Of beautiful young maidens – merciful powers! what an escape I've had. – I was in the cavern myself one day.
M'SWILL: Lord, Mrs Bridget, I'm sure there's no occasion for you to be frightened.
BRIDGET: Why, you saucy sot, I've a great mind to – (*A bell rings.*) I declare there's my lady's bell – no occasion indeed – an impudent fellow; but men, now-a-days, have no more manners than hogs. (*Bell rings. Exit* BRIDGET.)
M'SWILL: There's a she-devil for you. I don't think there's such another vixen in all Scotland. She's little and hot, like a pepper-corn. What a lug she gave me by the ear.
ROBERT: Nay, nay, you mustn't mind that; all old ladies have their odd ways.
M'SWILL: Curse such odd ways as that, tho'; I shall feel the pinch for a month. – Pray, Mr Robert, as you've been in London with Lord Ronald, do you know who this Earl is that the Lady Margaret is to be married to?
ROBERT: I only know that he is the Earl of Marsden, and master of the castle on the coast facing this island.

M'SWILL: What? where the pretty Effie, your intended, lives?
ROBERT: Exactly.
M'SWILL: He'll arrive just in time, then, to be present at the wedding.
ROBERT: I hope so.
M'SWILL: That will be glorious! Two weddings in one day – such dancing, such eating, such drinking –
BRIDGET: M'Swill!
M'SWILL: Ugh, choke you, you old warlock! What's in the wind now, I wonder?
BRIDGET: M'Swill, I say!
M'SWILL: Coming, Mrs Bridget. (*Exit.*)
ROBERT: Yes, as soon as the Earl arrives, I shall certainly take an opportunity to request him to honour the wedding with his presence – how pleased my dear Effie would be. Charming girl, I shall never forget the hour when first we met –

Song – ROBERT – '*The Lass of Patie's Mill*'

The hour when first we met, my dear,
The hour when first we met;
I never can forget, my dear,
I never can forget.
So sweet on me those eyes were turn'd,
That beam thy cheek above,
They look'd like lamps that only burn'd
To light the heart to love.
To light the heart to love, my dear,
To light the heart to love,
They look'd like lamps that only burn'd
To light the heart to love.

And while they shine on me, my dear,
And while they shine on me,
I'll ne'er be false to thee, my dear,
I'll ne'er be false to thee.
Oh never, never slight me, then,
Nor leave me, love, to say,
Like fires that glimmer o'er the fen
They beam but to betray.
They beam, &c. (*Exit.*)

SCENE 2. *An Apartment in the castle. Enter* LADY MARGARET *and* BRIDGET.
BRIDGET: Oh! my lady, you must not tell me; I'm sure the fright and the fatigue you have undergone has made you ill.
LADY M: Indeed, no – I feel quite recovered, I assure you, my good Bridget.
BRIDGET: But I know better, my lady; that smile is not like your usual ones – something ails you –
LADY M: Something certainly troubles me, but my health is not affected. I would confide the cause of my uneasiness to you, but fear you will laugh at me when I tell you. It is a dream I have had.

BRIDGET: A dream! For heaven's sake tell me, my lady.

LADY M: A horrible one, Bridget. Last night, as I was endeavouring to join the hunters, from whom, in the hurry of the chase, I had been separated, I wandered near the famous Basaltic Caverns, to which the vulgar attach so many strange traditions. The storm grew violent. By the strong flashes of lightning I discovered the opening of the grotto; I entered it for shelter, and overcome with fatigue, fell asleep upon one of the rocky tombs. On a sudden, a sepulchre opened, and a phantom approached me. I trembled. But an invisible hand seemed to prevent my flight. I could not even turn mine eyes from the apparition. To my surprise the countenance was that of a young and handsome man, but it was pale and woe-worn. His eyes, fix'd upon mine with the most touching expression, seemed to implore my pity. He uttered my name, and had nearly reach'd me, when a beautiful being stood between us, and check'd his progress. Then, oh horror! the features of the spectre grew frightfully distorted; its whole form assum'd the most terrific appearance, and it sunk into the tomb from which it had issued with a shriek that froze me.

BRIDGET: Mercy preserve us! I tremble all over.

LADY M: I awoke. The moon stream'd into the grotto, and I sprung into the open air. I heard the voices of those who sought me. I answered them as loudly as I was able. With shouts of joy they surrounded me, and bore me safely hither.

BRIDGET: I shall never sleep in peace again. Oh, my dear young lady!

RONALD: (*without*) My daughter risen, say you?

BRIDGET: But here comes your father – shall you tell him, my lady?

LADY M: Oh, no; he is such an enemy to what he calls superstition that I dare not expose myself to his ridicule.

(*Enter* LORD RONALD.)

RONALD: Well, my dear daughter. – What, up and dress'd again already. Come, this is a happy omen. Bridget, order my henchmen to ascend the turrets of the keep, and give notice of the Earl of Marsden's approach. (*Exit* BRIDGET.) This day, my dear Margaret, will be one of the happiest of my life. But what's the matter? You appear sorrowful.

LADY M: Ah! my dear father, the description we have had of Marsden has been such certainly as should prejudice us in his favour; yet, the nearer the moment approaches of his arrival, the more I feel uneasy. Oh, sir, my fate is (next to heaven) in your hands. – Do not – do not make your daughter miserable.

RONALD: Why this agitation, Margaret? I have never wished to force your inclination. I certainly desire this alliance most ardently; nevertheless, if you dislike him –

LADY M: I do not know that I shall. But you, sir, who wish me to accept him, do not know him personally.

RONALD: 'Tis true; but if he resembles his brother, you cannot fail to love him. – Alas! poor Ruthven.

LADY M: You never mention his name but with a sigh.

RONALD: Is it possible I can ever cease to lament so dear a friend?

LADY M: I have heard you say that he sav'd your life, and for that reason I revere his memory myself. But are you sure he no longer exists?

RONALD: Would that I could harbour a doubt on the subject; but, alas! the fatal scene of his death is ever present to my imagination. When called, as you know, by the sudden illness of my now lost son to Athens, I found Lord Ruthven, with whom he had contracted an intimacy, hanging over his sick couch, and bestowing on him the attentions of a brother. Such behaviour naturally endear'd him to me; and after my poor boy's death, his lordship being, like myself, an enthusiastic admirer of the beauties of nature and the works of art, became the constant companion of my excursions. The more I saw of him, the more I admired his extraordinary talents. In my eyes he appear'd something more than human, and seem'd destin'd to fill that place in my affections which had become void by my son's decease. I show'd him your miniature – Never shall I forget his emotion on beholding it. 'By heavens!' he exclaim'd, ''tis the precise image my fancy has created as the only being who could ever constitute my happiness.' We were on the point of returning to Scotland to learn your sentiments on the subject, when one evening – but why should I afflict you with a repetition of so dreadful a story?

LADY M: Pray proceed, sir. I sympathise in your affliction, and feel a melancholy gratification in contemplating the devotedness and heroism which preserved to me so dear a father.

RONALD: Returning to Athens, then – one evening, after a short excursion, we were attack'd by some banditti. I was disarm'd. Ruthven threw himself before me, and received the ruffian's sabre in his own breast. Our attendants, however, succeeded in overcoming the villains. I threw myself into the arms of my expiring friend – he press'd my hand – 'Lord Ronald', said he, 'I have sav'd your life – I die content – my only regret is that fate has prevented me from becoming your son.' Gallant, unfortunate Ruthven! what a destiny was thine to fall in a foreign land, in the flower of thy youth, deprived of sepulchre.

LADY M: How! deprived of sepulchre!

RONALD: An extraordinary circumstance prevented my fulfilling that last melancholy duty. In his dying agonies he conjur'd me to quit the spot, lest the assassins should return in number. The moon was rising in unclouded majesty. 'Place me', said he, 'on yonder mound, so that my fleeting spirit may be sooth'd by the soft and tranquil light of yon chaste luminary.' I did so – he expired. I left the body to collect our servants, who were in pursuit of the defeated villains, and ere we could return to the spot, it had disappeared.

LADY M: Remov'd for plunder, doubtless.

RONALD: I ne'er could ascertain. The stains of the grass sufficiently mark'd the spot where I had lain him; but all search was in vain. On quitting Greece I heard Lord Marsden was in Venice. To him I sent his brother's property, and amidst it he found your picture which, in my desire for his alliance, I had given Ruthven. The Earl proposed immediately to replace the loss we had sustained in his brother, and nothing, I am confident, remains to complete our happiness but his arrival.

LADY M: Why is not Ruthven living? Methinks I could have lov'd him for his preservation of you.

(*Bugle and response. Re-enter* BRIDGET.)

BRIDGET: The Earl has arrived, my lord.

RONALD: Come, Margaret, let us haste and receive him.

LADY M: My dear sir, I cannot see him yet; indeed I cannot.

RONALD: Retire, then, for awhile to your apartment. Bridget, attend your lady. (*Exeunt* LADY MARGARET *and* BRIDGET. *Enter servants*.) I'll fly to meet the Earl – Ha! he is here. (*Enter* LORD RUTHVEN.) My lord, the honour you have done me! – Heavens! what do I see?

RUTHVEN: Do I recall the memory of a friend, Lord Ronald?

RONALD: His voice too! – Ruthven!

RUTHVEN: Such was my name till the death of an elder brother put me in possession of my present title.

RONALD: Can I believe my senses! or does some vision mock my waking sight!

RUTHVEN: My dear friend, let this embrace banish your doubts.

RONALD: Ruthven, my friend! But by what miracle have you been preserved to me?

RUTHVEN: Unexpected, but powerful assistance recalled my fleeting spirit. When sufficiently recovered to join you, you had quitted Greece. The news of my brother's death reach'd me. I wrote to you under my new title, and, arriving in Scotland to take possession of my paternal estate, determined to give you this pleasurable surprise.

RONALD: Oh, happy hour! I once more embrace my friend. Be sure, Ruthven, that my daughter would only have become your brother's bride to acquit me of the debt I owe to you.

RUTHVEN: My generous friend, but think you I shall be fortunate enough to gain the lovely Margaret's affections?

RONALD: I cannot doubt it – she has pitied your misfortunes – she has wept over your fate. She comes. (*Exeunt attendants*.) What will be her astonishment – (*Re-enter* LADY MARGARET.) My dear, behold that generous friend, whose loss we have so long deplor'd. 'Tis Ruthven claims your hand.

LADY M: My lord, duty to a beloved parent will – (*Raises her eyes slowly to his countenance – starts and falls, with a shriek, into the arms of* LORD RONALD.)

RONALD: Margaret! O heavens! she is ill. Help there!

LADY M: (*shuddering and aside*) That countenance! The phantom of last night. (*Relapses into insensibility*.)

RUTHVEN: What can have occasioned this emotion?

RONALD: Alas! I know not. Margaret! my sweet child!

LADY M: (*reviving*) Pardon, my lord, this weakness – the effect of last night's adventure.

RUTHVEN: Last night!

RONALD: We hunted late yesterday. My daughter lost her way, and suffered much fatigue.

RUTHVEN: Beautiful Lady Margaret, how am I to interpret this emotion?

LADY M: The surprise of seeing one whose death we were even now deploring.

RUTHVEN: Is it possible that, without knowing me, the recital of my misfortunes alone could thus have interested you?

LADY M: I am the daughter of Lord Ronald, and my heart, touched with gratitude – (*aside*) I dare not look at him.

RUTHVEN: With gratitude? and what will be my gratitude, if you but deign to approve your father's generous designs? Tell me, oh, tell me you confirm them; or never, never will I rise from your feet. (*kneeling and seizing her hand*)

LADY M: (*aside*) Heavens! how strange a thrill runs through my frame.
RUTHVEN: (*aside*) Then she's mine.
LADY M: These transports, my lord –
RUTHVEN: Must not alarm you. It is in the presence of your father. It is at his desire I here vow my eternal fidelity. O, my friend, join your supplications to mine.
RONALD: My daughter is well aware of my wishes.
RUTHVEN: Speak, dearest lady, I conjure you.
LADY M: (*aside*) What spell is it that moves me thus? (*aloud*) My lord, my father has never yet found me disobedient to his will.
RUTHVEN: You consent, then?
LADY M: Spare my confusion, my lord. My dear sir, allow me to retire.
RUTHVEN: Lady, dear lady –
LADY M: Pardon me, my lord; a strange confusion, a wild emotion overpowers me; let me retire. (*Exit* LADY MARGARET.)
RONALD: Ruthven, the wish of my heart is gratified; you are my son.
RUTHVEN: Dearest sir, I have still a boon to ask. Let our marriage be celebrated without delay.
RONALD: It is my intention; and to-morrow –
RUTHVEN: To-night, my friend; business of the utmost importance recalls me to London. To-morrow's dawn must witness our departure.
RONALD: Impossible! Have you not to take possession of your estate?
RUTHVEN: It is but showing myself at the castle, from which I can return ere the sun sets this evening.
RONALD: Well, if my daughter makes no objection, I will go, plead your suit, and hear the reasons for haste afterwards. – I know not how you have infatuated me, Ruthven, but rest assured I feel for you all that a father's heart can feel. (*Exit*.)
RUTHVEN: (*Walks the stage agitated*.) Daemon, as I am, that walk the earth to slaughter and devour, the little that remains of heart within this wizard frame – sustained alone by human blood, shrinks from the appalling act of planting misery in the bosom of this veteran chieftain. Still must the fearful sacrifice be made! and suddenly; for the approaching night will find my wretched frame exhausted – and darkness – worse than death – annihilation is my lot! Margaret! unhappy maid! thou art my destined prey! thy blood must feed a Vampire's life, and prove the food of his disgusting banquet!

(*Enter* ROBERT *timidly*.)

ROBERT: My lord!
RUTHVEN: What would you?
ROBERT: I beg your lordship's pardon for my boldness – but I am a servant of Lord Ronald's, and would fain request your lordship's patronage.
RUTHVEN: In what respect?
ROBERT: I am betrothed, an please your lordship, to Effie, your steward's daughter; and as I hear it is your lordship's intention to visit your estate, I –
RUTHVEN: (*eagerly*) Betrothed, say you?
ROBERT: Yes, my lord.
RUTHVEN: And when is the marriage to take place?
ROBERT: This evening, my lord.

RUTHVEN: (*half aside*) I will be there.
ROBERT: Oh, my lord, I was afraid to ask you – but your lordship has made me so happy!
RUTHVEN: What distance are we from my castle?
ROBERT: The sea is calm, my lord – we may row there in a few minutes.
RUTHVEN: Order the barge instantly, then.
ROBERT: Yes, my lord. (*Exit.*)

(*Enter* RONALD.)

RONALD: All is arranged to your wishes.
RUTHVEN: (*with joy*) Your daughter consents?
RONALD: She does; and I have ordered the chapel to be prepared by our return.
RUTHVEN: You go to Marsden with me, then?
RONALD: Certainly; your stay is so short, I will not leave you for a moment.
RUTHVEN: My dear friend, this kindness –

(*Re-enter* ROBERT.)

ROBERT: The barge is ready, my lord.
RUTHVEN: Away! Away! (*Hurried music. Exeunt.*)

SCENE 3. *Garden of* LORD RUTHVEN*'s Castle; the sea in the background.*
ANDREW *and* EFFIE *discovered, surrounded by village lads and lasses, dressed as for a fête.*
EFFIE: What can be the reason Robert does not arrive?
ANDREW: Something has happened to detain him; he will be here soon.
EFFIE: I see nothing like a boat at present.
ANDREW: Why, what is that to the right, there?
EFFIE: Not a boat, I'm sure, father.
ANDREW: But I say it is a boat; and making for the castle, too.
EFFIE: Hark! father, hark!

(*A boat is seen at sea, which gradually approaches to the symphony of the following Boat Song, sung as if at some distance, and growing louder and louder as the boat nears the land.*)

Boat Song – 'Ye Banks and Braes'
Row on – Row on . . . across the main
So smoothly glides our bark to shore,
While to our boat song's measured strain
So truly dips the well tim'd oar.

Row on . . . Row on . . . in yonder isle
Impatient beauty chides our stay,
The head-land past . . . her sweetest smile
Our labour richly will repay.
Solo – EFFIE – *'There's nae luck about the house'*
'Tis he . . . 'tis he . . . his form I see,
Full soon he will be here,
Then neighbours haste, prepare the feast
The bonny lad to cheer.
For there's nae luck about the house,

There's nae luck at a',
There's little pleasure in the house
When my dear lad's awa'.
Chorus
There's nae luck about the house,
There's nae luck at a',
There's little pleasure in the house
When Robert's far awa'.

(*Shouts without. Enter* ROBERT.)

EFFIE: My dear Robert –

ROBERT: My sweet Effie!

EFFIE: What has kept you so long?

ROBERT: Oh, I've news for you. Lord Ronald has come with me, and who do you think beside, father-in-law?

ANDREW: Nay, I'm sure I can't guess.

ROBERT: Lord Ruthven.

ANDREW: Lord Ruthven! Why, he has been dead these twelve months.

ROBERT: Has he? – I believe you're mistaken, father-in-law. (*shouts*) Do you hear that?

ANDREW: Pho, poo, I tell you it must be some impostor. (*Enter* RUTHVEN, RONALD *and attendants*.) Merciful Providence, it is my young master!

RUTHVEN: Yes, my good Andrew; behold me restored to you.

ANDREW: Thank heaven! Thank heaven! But I could not believe that I should ever have the pleasure of seeing my dear master again.

RUTHVEN: I shall never forget your attachment to our family and your attentions to their interest. Let me not interrupt your felicity – you are about to celebrate a marriage, I think?

ANDREW: Yes, my lord. – Here's my daughter, Effie, whom your lordship remembers a little girl.

RONALD: She's very pretty.

EFFIE: Yes, my lord – that is, thank you, my lord.

RUTHVEN: You must allow me to give the bride her dowry and patronize the whole ceremony.

ANDREW: Oh, my lord, this is such an honour. Well, then, before the dance commences, neighbours, let us go and arrange the supper-table, where we will drink our good lord's happy return.

ROBERT: Away with you, then.

(*Exeunt* ANDREW *and peasants*.)

RONALD: I must leave you a moment, Ruthven, to give some directions to my bargemen. (*Exit, with attendants*.)

ROBERT: (*to* EFFIE) Come, Effie, let's follow our neighbours. (*going*)

RUTHVEN: (*detaining* EFFIE) Fair Effie, I would speak with you.

EFFIE: (*with hesitation*) If Robert has no objection, my lord –

ROBERT: How, you silly girl, when his lordship does you so much honour. – You'll find me with Andrew. (*Exit*.)

RUTHVEN: Come nearer, charming maid.

EFFIE: My lord, I – I dare not, my lord.

RUTHVEN: Fear nothing. (*aside*) Yet, she has cause to fear. – Should I surprise her heart, as by my gifted spell I may, the tribute that prolongs existence may be paid, and Margaret may (at least awhile) be spared. How delightful 'tis to gaze upon thee thus! – An atmosphere of joy is round about thee, which whosoever breathes becomes thy slave.

EFFIE: My lord, what mean you?

RUTHVEN: My heart ne'er throb'd but for one woman, and you have just her features. This morning the flame of love was extinguished in my soul; but now, now it burns with redoubled ardour.

EFFIE: But the lady whom you admir'd, my lord? –

RUTHVEN: She is dead!

EFFIE: Dead!

RUTHVEN: Yes, dead, Effie – but in you she lives again.

EFFIE: What do I hear!

RUTHVEN: Oh, Effie, can you not conceive the happiness of once more beholding the object we adore?

EFFIE: I shall never love anyone but Robert.

RUTHVEN: Happy Robert, and unfortunate Ruthven! Why did I ever behold thee, Effie?

EFFIE: See me no more, my lord, if that has occasioned your uneasiness. (*going*)

RUTHVEN: Stay! Effie, it is in your power to console me for all I have lost. Love me. – Nay, start not; mine you must and shall be.

EFFIE: My lord, I'll hear no more. If Robert –

RUTHVEN: Think not of him; the bridal preparations are complete; – my bride thou art – no power on earth shall tear thee from me: say, Effie, that you love me. (*taking her hand*)

EFFIE: (*starting*) Mercy on me! My lord, I – I know not what to say. My heart beats so that – Oh, pray leave me, my lord.

RUTHVEN: You weep: those tears are for me.

EFFIE: No, no: – indeed, my lord –

RUTHVEN: This instant let me bear thee to the priest.

EFFIE: My lord, for pity's sake –

RUTHVEN: You plead in vain: – Effie, thou art mine for ever. (*Bears her off.*)

(*Re-enter* ROBERT.)

ROBERT: How long she stays – not here! Why, (EFFIE *shrieks.*) Heav'ns! what do I see – borne off, and struggling – Villain, loose your hold! (*Draws a pistol and runs after them. Stage gradually darkens.*)

(*Enter* ANDREW *and* LORD RONALD.)

RONALD: Why, Andrew, said you not the Earl was here?

ANDREW: 'Twas here I left him but just now, my lord. (*A pistol is fired without and* EFFIE *shrieks*: O save me! Save me!) My daughter's voice!

(*Rushes out, as* LORD RUTHVEN *enters, wounded.*)

RONALD: Ruthven!

RUTHVEN: (*falling*) I die!

RONALD: What murderous hand –

(*The moon is seen descending.*)

RUTHVEN: Exclaim not. I have but a moment to live. – Ronald, swear by the host of heaven to obey my last commands.

RONALD: Young man, the word of Ronald needs no oath to bind it.

RUTHVEN: I die – delay not a moment – but swear to –

RONALD: I do, I do. – I swear by all that is most dear and sacred to honour and to man to fulfil your last desire.

RUTHVEN: Conceal my death from every human being, till yonder moon, which now sails in her meridian splendour, shall be set this night; and ere an hour shall elapse after I have expired, throw this ring into the waves that wash the tomb of Fingal.

RONALD: I will, I will, Ruthven! – Dear Ruthven.

RUTHVEN: Remember your oath. The lamp of night is descending the blue heavens; when I am dead, let its sweet light shine on me. – Farewell. Remember – Remember your oath. (*Dies.*)

(*Solemn music.* RONALD *lays the body of* RUTHVEN *on a bank in the garden and kneels mournfully beside it. The moon continues descending till the light falls full upon the corpse; and the curtain drops upon the picture.*)

ACT II

SCENE 1. *The Tomb of Fingal in the caverns of Staffa. The sea. Moonlight. A boat enters the cavern with* ANDREW, ROBERT *and* EFFIE. *They land. Music.*

ANDREW: Here, Robert, you may rest concealed till Lord Ronald's anger shall have subsided; or should he be deaf to explanation and refuse to believe Lord Ruthven's treachery, arrangements shall be made to convey you over to the main land. Here is sufficient provision for the short time I hope you will be forced to remain. And so now bid Effie good-bye for awhile; I'll look out in the mean time and see if the coast be clear for our return. (*Exit.*)

ROBERT: Come, cheer up, Effie, all will be well yet. It was in defence of innocence I fired, and therefore that act will never be a load on my conscience.

EFFIE: But if Lord Ronald should get you into his power!

ROBERT: I will put it to Lord Ronald's self to say whether a man should stand tamely by and see the wife of his bosom dragged to misery and dishonour. – Come, come, kiss me, Effie, and farewell till better times.

Duetto – EFFIE *and* ROBERT – *'Down the Burn, Davie'*

ROBERT: Tho' vanish'd be the visions fair,
By Fancy's pencil trac'd;
And blighted all the blossoms rare,
That Hope's gay chaplet grac'd;
Fear not my faith,
The pang of death
Alone can bid it flee.
Then fare thee well, my only love;
Fare thee well, my only love;
Fare thee well, my only love;
Thou'rt more than life to me.

BOTH: Fare thee well, &c.

EFFIE: Though clouded now the prospect seem;
Though grief usurp the hour;
A light may break, a ray may beam,
And joy resume its pow'r.
Fear not my faith,
The pang of death
Alone can bid it flee.
Then fare thee well, my only love;
Fare thee well, my only love;
Fare thee well, my only love;
Thou'rt more than life to me.

BOTH: Fare thee well, &c.

(*During the last verse* ANDREW *has returned; he places* EFFIE *in the boat and they exit.*)

ROBERT: And now to find some hole for a bed-chamber. Rather sorry accommodations, I fancy; but the superstitions of the peasantry will keep them from disturbing my repose; and as to other considerations, a man with a clear conscience may rest anywhere. (*looking*) Here's tolerable choice of apartments, as far as number goes: let me try what shelter this one will afford. (*Exit into cavern.*)

(*Music. A boat is seen at the entrance, with* LORD RONALD *and two attendants in it.* LORD RONALD *lands.*)

RONALD: Give me the torch and wait without the cave till you see me wave it thus. (*Exeunt attendants, with boat.*) How solemn is this scene. By heaven, my soul, that lately mock'd at superstition, is so subdued by circumstance that I could almost bring myself to give faith to every legend I have scorn'd as idle. Here is the ring – what am I about to do? – what horrible suspicion flashes across my brain? Ruthven, mysterious being, what mean these ceremonies? Before, when I supposed him dying, he bade me place his body in the light of the then rising moon; and now again. And wherefore make me swear to conceal his death till the moon be set? But let me not reflect or pause. Unhappy Ruthven! thy friend performs his promise. (*Throws the ring into the water; a peal of thunder is heard; after which the voice of* RUTHVEN: Remember your oath!) It is his spirit speaks. Ruthven! my friend, my preserver!

(*Re-enter* ROBERT.)

ROBERT: What voice was that? Lord Ronald!

RONALD: Ha! by heaven, justice hath given the murderer to my vengeance. (*Draws.*) Ruthven, this sacrifice I make to thee.

ROBERT: Hear me, my lord; Lord Ruthven would have wronged me.

RONALD: Would'st thou asperse the dead! – Down, villain, down. (*Attacks him.*)

ROBERT: Nay, in my own defence then –

(*They fight;* ROBERT *is disarmed.* RONALD *plunges him into the waves.* LORD RONALD *rushes to the entrance of the cavern and waves the torch. The boat approaches.*)

RONALD: Ruthven, thou art revenged! Away! Away!

(RONALD *leaps into the boat.* ROBERT *reaches and clings to the rocks; and the Scene closes.*)

SCENE 2. *An apartment in* LORD RONALD*'s castle. Enter* LADY MARGARET, *meeting* BRIDGET.

LADY M: Bridget, I was looking for you; I am so happy.

BRIDGET: Happy, my lady! and Lord Ruthven and your father not returned. I'm frightened out of my wits about them: 'tis ten o'clock, and they were to have been back again ere sunset.

LADY M: You may dispel your fears, then; Lord Ruthven has this moment announced to me my father's return.

BRIDGET: Lord Ruthven!

LADY M: On opening the casement just now that looks into the garden, I saw him by the moonlight crossing one of the walks. I call'd to him, and he will be here directly, that the ceremony may commence. We must depart for London ere day-break.

BRIDGET: So soon?

LADY M: Yes; he has explained the reason to me. The King of England wishes him to marry a lady of the court, and he has no other way of avoiding the match but by presenting me immediately as his wife.

BRIDGET: And here comes your father, I declare. Well, my lady, I'll away and see that everything is ready. (*Exit.*)

LADY M: I can hardly account for my sudden attachment to Lord Ruthven, especially after the shock his introduction gave me. (*Enter* LORD RONALD.) Well, sir, is Ruthven coming?

RONALD: Ruthven! alas!

LADY M: You sigh; what troubles you, my dear father?

RONALD: Nothing. (*aside*) What shall I say to her?

LADY M: Everything is prepared for the ceremony. Lord Ruthven has doubtless informed you of the pressing reason he has for our immediate departure: its suddenness at first alarmed me; but if you will accompany us, what a charming voyage – You do not listen to me – why, father, what's the matter?

RONALD: My dear Margaret, we must think no more of this union.

LADY M: Think no more of it! Have you not been yourself the cause, and do you now –

RONALD: Question me not; I cannot answer you.

LADY M: Good heavens! and Ruthven, who, not a moment ago, so warmly urged –

RONALD: (*starting*) Ruthven, not a moment ago – what mean you?

LADY M: You frighten me; but Ruthven will soon be here, and –

(*Enter* LORD RUTHVEN *behind.*)

RONALD: Ruthven is –

RUTHVEN: (*aside*) Remember your oath.

RONALD: (*starting*) Can the grave give up its dead! Spirit, what would'st thou?

RUTHVEN: Ronald, my friend, what means this wildness?

RONALD: My brain turns round; – I saw him fall – I heard his dying groan – Fiend! – Phantom – hence, I charge thee.

RUTHVEN: Alas, he raves!

LADY M: (*clinging to* RUTHVEN) My father! my poor father!

RONALD: Touch him not, Margaret! Fly the demon's grasp!

RUTHVEN: How dreadful is this wildness. – Ho! within there!

RONALD: I am not mad. Ruthven's dead! I saw –

RUTHVEN: (*aside*) Your oath! (*Enter two servants.*) Your master is not well, his brain is wandering; secure him and let aid be sent for instantly.

(*Servants take hold of* RONALD.)

RONALD: Stand off, slaves! 'tis a fiend in human shape. – I saw him perish; twice have I seen him perish; as I have life. Heaven saw and heard –

RUTHVEN: (*aside*) Your oath!

LADY M: (*to servants*) Oh, harm him not; but lead him gently in.

RONALD: That dreadful oath! (*Servants seize him.*) Stay but a moment. Margaret, promise me you will not marry till the moon shall set; then, fearful fiend, I am no longer pledged, and may preserve my child.

LADY M: Oh, my poor, poor father! (*Falls into the arms of* RUTHVEN, *fainting.*)

RUTHVEN: Remove him gently – suddenly, I say.

RONALD: No, I will not quit my child an instant; horror overwhelms me! I know not what thou art; but terrible conviction flashes on my mind, that thou art nothing human. A mist seems clearing from my sight; and I behold thee now – Oh, horror! horror! – a monster of the grave – a – a Vam –

(*Falls into his servants' arms, who bear off* LORD RONALD.)

RUTHVEN: Remember – She's mine! – my prey is in my clutch – the choicest, crowning victim. – Ha! revive, my bride.

LADY M: Where am I? Where, where is my father?

RUTHVEN: In safety, love, be sure; retired to his chamber.

LADY M: I know not what to think.

RUTHVEN: Alas! I have seen him often thus, during our travels together; his reason received a severe shock on the death of my young friend, your brother.

LADY M: Is't possible! I never knew him thus.

RUTHVEN: Rely upon the melancholy truth; but 'twill not last; so cheer thee, lovely Margaret.

LADY M: Alas! I need your consolation. How wild a fancy seized him that you were dead; and his request, too, not to marry till the moon had set. – Well, I will not.

RUTHVEN: (*aside*) Ha! (*aloud*) Sweet Margaret, you will not sure repent?

LADY M: Why, my good lord, so short a delay cannot be of consequence, and 'twill appease him probably – and such a slight request.

RUTHVEN: I reverence your motive; but if you love me, Margaret –

LADY M: You cannot doubt it.

RUTHVEN: Upon that love, then, my repose, my happiness, my life depends; swear to me, dearest Margaret, to forget these idle terrors, and to be mine – mine only – for ever.

LADY M: I do, by Him who reads all hearts, to be thine, and thine only, for ever.

RUTHVEN: Oh, happiness! Receive this ring, and let it be a sacred pledge between us. (*Places it on her finger.*)

LADY M: Ha!

RUTHVEN: (*smiling*) Her fate is seal'd, she cannot now retract. – You shudder; what ails my love?

LADY M: A strange sensation runs throughout my frame; tears fill my eyes, and my heart beats as though 'twould burst my bosom. – Methinks my father's voice still rings in mine ears, 'Wed not before the moon shall set.'

RUTHVEN: (*aside*) The hour approaches; no time is to be lost. (*aloud*) Think no more, I beseech thee, of these wanderings of the imagination, but let us hasten to consecrate the ties which unite us. Every arrangement must, by this time, have been made. Retire, my love, to your chamber; compose your spirits; and Ruthven then will lead thee to the altar.

(*Music. Exeunt* RUTHVEN *and* LADY MARGARET.)

SCENE 3. *Distant view of* LORD RONALD*'s Castle, by moonlight. Enter* ANDREW *and* EFFIE, *supporting* ROBERT.

ROBERT: Nay, nay, do not trouble yourselves; I have sustained no injury. – But what made you come back to me so soon?

EFFIE: We saw the boat pass with Lord Ronald in it, and we feared some mischief.

ANDREW: So we lay-to till he left the cavern, and returned just in time to render you assistance. Yonder is the castle; are you still determined to seek him?

ROBERT: Yes; he has been imposed upon; and ere now, I am sure, he regrets having drawn upon me. I will lay open Lord Ruthven's villainy to him; and I know his noble nature too well to fear a continuance of his anger. Here, therefore, we will part for a while; and when we meet again, I trust all obstacles to our happiness will be removed. – Be faithful.

Song – EFFIE – *'Of a' the Airts'*

Though many a wood and heath-clad hill
　　Should rise betwixt us twain;
And many an envious stream and rill
　　Run babbling to the main;
This fond and faithful heart believe,
　　Howe'er apart we be,
Though in my breast it seem to heave,
　　Will linger still with thee.

Thus when the silver lamp of night
　　Sails through the quiet sky,
And sheds its lustre pure and bright
　　Upon the traveller's eye;
Though o'er him still the fond orb seems
　　To glide where'er he'll roam;
Its faithful light as sweetly beams
　　Upon his distant home.

(*After* EFFIE*'s song*, M'SWILL *sings without.*)

ANDREW: Soft; who comes here?

ROBERT: By his gait it should be M'Swill, the baron's toping henchman.

(*Enter* M'SWILL.)

M'SWILL: My master's gone mad – there's a pretty job. If he had been going to be married, instead of the Earl, I shouldn't have wonder'd so much; but for an old man to go mad, who can sit and drink all day, without any one to snub him for it, is the most ridiculous thing that ever came under my observation. Old mother Bridget never lets me drink in quiet at home, so I carry a pocket pistol about with me. (*Pulls out a flask.*) Now this is what I call my 'Young Man's Best Companion'; it's a great consolation on a night excursion to one who has so respectful a belief in bogles and warlocks as I have. – Whisky's the only spirit I feel a wish to be intimately acquainted with.

ROBERT: (*slapping him on the shoulder*) M'Swill!

M'SWILL: (*dropping on his knees*) Oh, Lord, what's that!

ROBERT: Why, how now, booby; where have you been at this time of night?

M'SWILL: Eh! what, Robert, is it only you? I was just kneeling to – This stupid latchet, you see, is – (*pretending to fasten it*).

ROBERT: Oh, yes, I see; but where have you been, I ask you?

M'SWILL: Been! Oh, I've been for Father Francis; – my lord's gone crazy, and the Earl of Marsden sent me.

ROBERT:
EFFIE: } The Earl of Marsden!

M'SWILL: Whew! what's in the wind now?

ANDREW: The Earl of Marsden sent you?

M'SWILL: Yes, to be sure; he's in the castle there, and just going to be married to my Lady Margaret.

ROBERT: Fool! the Earl of Marsden is dead.

M'SWILL: Nay, now you're mad. My master's been telling the same story this half hour; but the Earl says it's no such thing; that he is not dead, and never was dead; that my master's out of his wits; – and off he sends me for Father Francis to come and talk to my master, and marry my mistress.

ROBERT: What mystery is this? There is some foul play towards – At any rate, the Lady Margaret must know her danger. Is the friar gone?

M'SWILL: Oh yes, he's there before now. The very name of a wedding made him chuckle and waddle off at a rate, which obliged me to stop so many times for refreshment that he has been out of sight these some minutes.

ROBERT: Let us haste, father; we may foil the villain yet.

(*Exeunt* ROBERT, ANDREW *and* EFFIE.)

M'SWILL: It appears there is something wrong, but I can't positively pretend to say what it is; and as my flask seems as much exhausted as my speculations, I'll make the best of my way home and ruminate how much whisky I shall drink at the wedding.

Song – M'SWILL – *'Fy, let us awa' to the Bridal'*

Faith, I'll awa' to the bridal,
For there will be tippling there;
For my lady's a going to be married,
To whom I don't know, and don't care.
But I know we shall all be as frisky
And tipsy as pipers, good lack;
And so that there's plenty of whisky,
She may marry the devil for Mac.
So faith I'll awa' to the bridal, &c.

I once left the bottle for Cupid,
And bade an adieu to my glass;

I simper'd, and sigh'd and look'd stupid,
And courted a cherry-cheek'd lass.
She turn'd out a jilt: – 'twere a lie should I
Say that it gave me no pain;
For sorrowing made me so dry that I
Took to my bottle again.
So faith I'll awa' to the bridal, &c.

They say there's five reasons for drinking,
But more I am sure may be got;
For I never could find out by thinking
A reason why people should not.
A sixth I'll not scruple at giving,
I'll name it while 'tis in my head;
'Tis if you don't drink while you're living,
You never will after you're dead.
So faith I'll awa' to the bridal, &c. (*Exit.*)

SCENE 4. *A Gothic Chamber. Enter* LADY MARGARET *and* BRIDGET.

LADY M: The approach of this ceremony strikes me with an unaccountable awe; I can scarcely breathe. A few moments will decide my fate! – but I shall be happy. Oh, yes, I feel I shall. But my father!

BRIDGET: (*aside*) What a fluster my lady's in! but it's quite natural, poor thing.

LADY M: Yes, yes; I cannot be otherwise than happy.

BRIDGET: (*aside*) I can't account for it, but the Earl Ruthven's face seems quite changed within this last hour; it looks as if – Well, it's very extraordinary, but I say nothing.

(LADY MARGARET *appears lost in thought*; BRIDGET *coughs to arouse her*.)

LADY M: Bridget! I had forgotten you were near me.

BRIDGET: I didn't like to speak to you, my lady, as I saw you were thinking; but pray tell me what is the matter with my lord, your father?

LADY M: Alas, I know not. They have forced him to his couch, where he remains, almost insensible; or only rousing to utter incoherent sentences.

BRIDGET: I'm frighten'd out of my wits. (*in a low tone of voice*) Do you know, my lady, I almost think he's possessed by a spirit!

LADY M: Ridiculous! Bridget, how can you be so weak as to indulge these fancies? His feelings have been too much excited by the recovery of a dear friend, so long thought dead: he will be calmer soon.

BRIDGET: I hope so, I am sure, my lady; but somehow I fear –

RUTHVEN: (*within*) Margaret!

BRIDGET: Oh, my lady, 'tis the Earl's voice.

LADY M: He calls me to the altar! How shall I support the ceremony, without my dear father's presence?

RUTHVEN: (*within*) Margaret!

LADY M: Again! It is too late for reflection – I yield to my fate!

(*Exeunt.*)

SCENE 5. *The Chapel. A large Gothic window, through which the moon is seen setting.* LORD RUTHVEN *discovered, with priest, vassals, &c., &c. Music.*

RUTHVEN: All is prepared; o'er the great fiend once more
I triumph! Ere yon orb shall kiss the wave,
The tributary victim shall be paid.
Bow, ye less subtle spirits – bow abashed
Before your master.
– Margaret!
'Tis Ruthven calls thee. Hasten, sweet, and crown
Thy lover's happiness. (*Music. Enter* LADY MARGARET *and* BRIDGET.)
Lady, to the altar.

LADY M: I follow you, my lord – and yet –

RUTHVEN: (*impatiently seizing her hand*) Come, Margaret, come!
(*Distant thunder. A loud gust of wind shakes the casement.*)

LADY M: What noise was that?

BRIDGET: 'Tis but the wind, my lady; we shall have another storm, I think, when the moon sets.

LADY M: When the moon sets! – Ah, my poor father! See, 'twill set soon, my Ruthven; let me again beseech you to delay, till then, the ceremony!

RUTHVEN: (*more impatiently*) Nay, this is folly, Margaret. – Father, commence the rites.

(*Enter* LORD RONALD, *preceded by* ROBERT *and followed by* ANDREW, EFFIE *and attendants.*)

ROBERT: Make way! make way, I say! Lord Ronald shall be heard!

RONALD: My daughter! my daughter!

RUTHVEN: (*aside*) Confusion! – Ronald!

RONALD: Where is she? – Give me my daughter.

LADY M: My dearest father, be calm. What would'st thou with me?

RONALD: Ha! Do I again embrace thee? Follow him not – he drags you to the tomb.

RUTHVEN: (*furiously*) Margaret, we are waited for.

RONALD: Barbarian! I forbid the ceremony. You have no right over her – I am her father.

LADY M: You are – you are my loving, tender father: – I will not wed against his will. (*throwing herself into his arms*)

RUTHVEN: I'll hear no more! She is my bride betrothed: this madman would deprive me of her.

LADY M: (*indignantly*) No. – Why this violence? Wait till the hour is past.

RUTHVEN: Will you listen to his ravings?

RONALD: I do not rave. (*Loud thunder. Another gust of wind blows open the casement.*) See! see! the moon already rests upon the wave! – One moment! – but one moment! – (*detaining* MARGARET)

RUTHVEN: Nay, then thus I seal thy lips, and seize my bride. (*Draws his poignard and rushes on* RONALD. LADY MARGARET *shrieks when* ROBERT *throws himself between* RUTHVEN *and* RONALD *and wrenches the dagger from his grasp.*)

LADY M: Hold! hold! – I am thine; – the moon has set.
RUTHVEN: And I am lost.

(*A terrific peal of thunder is heard*; UNDA *and* ARIEL *appear; a thunderbolt strikes* RUTHVEN *to the ground, who immediately vanishes. General picture, as the curtain falls*.)

THE GARRICK FEVER

A farce in one act

First performed at the Olympic Theatre, on Monday, 1 April 1839, with the following cast:

MAJOR DERRYDOWN, *of the Westmeath Militia*	Mr Brougham
MR HARDUP, *manager, Theatre Royal, Ballinaslough*	Mr T. Green
UNDERTONE, *prompter*	Mr Wyman
PUMPWELL	Mr Connell
DECIMUS GINGLE, *a strolling actor*	Mr Keeley
DRESSER	Mr Kerridge
CALL BOY	Master Ireland
HAIR DRESSER	Mr Ireland
LADY O'LEARY	Mrs Macnamara
MRS HARDUP	Miss Jackson
MISS POLLY HARDUP	Miss Agnes Taylor
KITTY	Miss Goward

SCENE. *A room in* MR HARDUP*'s house, connected with the theatre, to which a door opens in flat centre; doors right and left. Enter* HARDUP *and* UNDERTONE.

HARDUP: Well – well – any news? Any news?

UNDERTONE: None at all, sir. So, in this case, we can give the lie to the old proverb, for no news is anything but good news with us.

HARDUP: What is to be done, Mr Undertone?

UNDERTONE: We are to be done, sir – brown! The game's up, sir – it's all over with us!

HARDUP: What can it mean? There must have been some accident! There can be no mistake – the letters are clear enough! (*Takes two letters out of his pocket.*) Here is a copy of my own letter. (*Reads*). 'To Mr Garrick. Sir, – Understanding your engagement at the Theatre Royal, Dublin, will terminate on Saturday next, I beg to know whether it will answer your purpose to play six nights in this town, before your departure for England, commencing on Monday, with Hamlet. Share, above ten pounds. Clear Benefit, &c. &c.' And here's the answer. (*Reads.*) 'Dear Sir, – In reply to yours, just received, I have only to say, yes! – with great pleasure. I will be with you between four and five, on Monday, which will just give me time to dress. Yours, in great haste, David Garrick.' Addressed to 'Mr Hardup, Manager, Theatre Royal –'

UNDERTONE: If that's not plain, I don't know what is.

HARDUP: And here's five o'clock struck, and no tidings of him.

UNDERTONE: The whole street is filled with people – the pit and gallery will overflow with the first rush.

HARDUP: And every place taken in the boxes – and a guinea offered for a chair behind the scenes! It's a fortune within my grasp!

UNDERTONE: And to be obliged to make an apology – return the money –

HARDUP: I can't do it, Mr Undertone – it would break my heart! It's hard enough, in these times, to get money – to return it, is an impossibility! Why, I've gone to the expense of ten pounds in printing! Here's a bill! Here's an announcement! I flatter myself I've done it this time! (*Reads bill.*) 'Theatre Royal, Ballinaslough. Unparalleled Attraction! First Appearance of the Immortal Mr Garrick! The Greatest Actor that ever was or ever will be!!! The Nobility, Gentry, and Public in general are respectfully informed that on Monday next will be presented, with entirely new Scenery and Decorations, Shakespere's Tragedy of Hamlet, Prince of Denmark, or the Mad Son and the Murdered Father! The part of Hamlet, Prince of Denmark (the Mad Son), by that Inimitable Tragedian, Mr David Garrick, (from the Theatres Royal Drury Lane and Smock Alley,) who has been engaged for a limited number of nights. Nota Bene. – Mr Garrick's attraction at the Theatre Royal Dublin, on his last visit to Ireland, was so great, that the crowded state of the Theatre produced an epidemic which was called the Garrick Fever! And, to use the words of that sublime Poet, the late Mr Alexander Pope to my Lord Orrery – "We may safely declare that Mr Garrick never had his equal as an Actor, and will never have a Rival!"'. There's a

---

Smock Alley: Dublin's Theatre Royal, opened in 1662.
Pope: Pope is said to have made this remark to his friend Lord Orrery after seeing Garrick play Richard III at Goodman's Fields Theatre in 1741.

quotation for you! And from such an authority! (*handing bill to* UNDERTONE)

UNDERTONE: (*looking over bill*) But what does this mean, sir? (*reading*) 'The Ghost of Hamlet's Father, murdered by Mr Hardup.'

HARDUP: (*snatching bill*) Eh! What! – 'murdered by' – confound the printers! One of their cursed blunders! – 'The Ghost of Hamlet's murdered Father, by Mr Hardup' – not 'Father murdered'. (*noise of wheels without*) Hark! – there's a chaise! (*running to window*) Yes! it stops here! It must be he! The modern Roscius! The great Garrick!

UNDERTONE: I'm afraid not, sir. Mr Garrick is a young man, and, as well as I can see, the person in the chaise is an old woman!

HARDUP: Lady O'Leary, by all that's disappointing! And her shadow, Major Derrydown! The devil fly away with them both!

UNDERTONE: Have they got a box?

HARDUP: No – the major wrote too late – everything was gone. There'll be a famous scene with her ladyship. She comes forty miles, on purpose. Where's my daughter Polly? Polly! Polly Hardup!

(*Enter* POLLY.)

POLLY: Here I am, father.

HARDUP: Run down stairs, Polly! There's your grand god-mother, Lady O'Leary, at the door, in a post-chaise. She'll be in a fine passion when she learns there's no box for her. Tell her she shall have a chair in the orchestra – just behind the big drum.

POLLY: She's coming up stairs. (*Exit.*)

HARDUP: The deuce she is! Then I'll be off! Follow me, Undertone, into the theatre, and let's see all is ready before they open the doors.

UNDERTONE: You will open the doors, then?

HARDUP: At all hazards! He must come! He's sure to come, if he's alive! – if not – why, it's no fault of ours. And if they tear up the benches, and break the chandelier, the county must pay the damage. I stick to the old text – 'Vivant Rex and Regina! No money returned'!

(*Exeunt* HARDUP *and* UNDERTONE. POLLY *re-enters with* LADY O'LEARY *and* MAJOR DERRYDOWN.)

LADY O: No box! I shall expire! Why, major –

MAJOR: My angel! –

LADY O: Do you hear what my god-daughter, Miss Polly Hardup, says, sir? There is no box, and I must sit in the orchestra, behind the big drum!

MAJOR: Behind the big drum! I'll run the big drum through the body, before you shall submit to such an indignity – and the big drummer into the bargain.

POLLY: My father's very sorry, my lady. If he had but known your ladyship wanted a box –

LADY O: Had but known! Why, major –

MAJOR: My Venus!

LADY O: Do you hear that, sir? If he had but known! As if you had not written to him three days ago, at my especial request.

Roscius: Quintus Roscius Gallus (*c.* 120–62 BC), celebrated Roman actor.

MAJOR: It is as you say, exactly as if I had not written to him three days ago.

POLLY: Of course it must be, sir – because you did not.

LADY O: Did not! Why, major –

MAJOR: My darling!

LADY O: Do you hear my god-daughter, Miss Polly Hardup, assert that you did not write, as I desired you?

MAJOR: Indeed I do. And if she don't retract the assertion, she shall give me the satisfaction of a gentleman.

POLLY: I only know that the letter did not arrive till this morning. I took it in myself, and heard my father read it.

MAJOR: Oh, you only know that, don't you? Then why didn't you say what you only knew, at first – and not what you didn't know? Does the mere appearance of a postman prove that I didn't write it at the time specified?

LADY O: Where is Mr Hardup? Let me see him instantly.

MAJOR: Ay – where is Mr Hardup?

POLLY: I'll send for him, my lady. If your ladyship will condescend to wait here, and excuse me, as I shall hardly have time to dress for my part –

LADY O: Your part, my child! What do you play, then?

POLLY: Ophelia, madam! Only think, what an honour! To play Ophelia to Mr Garrick's Hamlet!

'The expectancy and rose of the fair state;
The glass of fashion, and the mould of form –
The observed of all observers!'

I'll send my father to you directly, madam.

'For bonny sweet Robin is all my joy.' (*Exit, singing*.)

LADY O: The girl's crazy, in downright earnest!

MAJOR: It's the Garrick fever they speak of. You've a touch of it yourself, my darling.

LADY O: Don't call me your darling! If I find that it is through your negligence –

MAJOR: It's the blundhering postman – bad luck to him! But if I don't give him such a double knock on his head as he never gave a street door, I'll give anybody leave to say I'm not Major Derrydown of the Loyal Westmeath Militia.

LADY O: If I do not see Garrick, I shall die.

MAJOR: You would not dream of it, would you? Die for the sake of a dirty little play-actor, when you've promised to live to be Mrs Major Derrydown.

LADY O: I have promised no such thing, sir. I have merely suffered you to hope. A dirty little play-actor! But what should a muddle-headed major of militia know of art or its professors? Mr Garrick, though a little man, is a great genius! – A man for whom duchesses are dying by the dozens, sir! Read the bill, sir! – Read what the great poet, Pope, says of him, sir – 'That he will never have a rival!'

MAJOR: That will depend entirely upon whether or not he makes love to a certain beautiful creature of my acquaintance. For, by the powers, if he play Romeo to Lady O'Leary's Juliet, he'll have Major Derrydown for a rival, in spite of Pope or Pretender, as the saying is.

LADY O: Don't talk nonsense, major! Where is Mr Hardup? It is nearly half-past five – the doors will be opened, and we shall get no seat.

MAJOR: This door leads to the theatre. Let's go in, and beat up his quarters. I'll teach him the respect due to a lady of quality, and a major of the Westmeath Militia. (*Exeunt.*)

(*Enter* GINGLE.)

GINGLE: (*looking about him*) 'Thus far into the bowels of the land have we march'd on without impediment.' They said the manager was in his room: 'There's no such thing!' Well, I must sit down, at all events, for I'm tired to death! Five and twenty miles have I walked this blessed day, and without eating since my breakfast. (*Takes out a play-bill.*) The sight of this bill, however, as I entered the town, gave me fresh spirits. Garrick is here! – the great unrivalled Garrick! If I could but get an engagement – were it only to carry a letter, or deliver a message; anything by which I might meet the eye of the great Roscius, and, perhaps, obtain his approbation and patronage – who knows what might happen? – He might take me with him to London – get me an appearance at Drury Lane – fancy our names in the same bill – 'Duke of Gloster, Mr Garrick. The Lord Mayor, Mr Gingle, from the Theatre Royal, Ballinaslough (being his first appearance in London.)' Oh, ambition! 'By that sin, fell the angels'! I can't help it. I feel, somehow, I shall be somebody, some day or another.

'Swift it mounts on eagles' wings;
Kings it makes gods, and meaner creatures kings.'

There must be a chance for me, here. (*looking at the bill*) They seem horribly off for members, and the whole family is pressed into the service. (*Reads.*) 'Ghost, Mr Hardup – Ophelia, Miss Polly Hardup – and Polonius and Osrick, doubled by Mr Terence Hardup.' They're all Hardup! If they'd let me play Osrick, now, I might make – 'a hit, my lord – a palpable hit'! Somebody comes – should it be the manager!

'Hold, hold, my heart –
And you, my sinews, grow not instant old,
But bear me stiffly up!' (*Retires.*)

(*Enter* HARDUP, *not seeing* GINGLE.)

HARDUP: The doors are open! The house is crammed to the ceiling, and no Garrick! – no tidings of him! What shall I do?

GINGLE: No Garrick! 'Angels and ministers of grace defend me!'

HARDUP: I must change the play, and make an apology. Return the money I will not.

GINGLE: (*aside*) 'Oh! my prophetic soul!' It is the manager.

HARDUP: And the splendid supper I ordered at the King's Arms for the great Roscius and a few select friends, after the play.

GINGLE: Splendid supper! And I who 'am as hungry as the sea, and could digest as much –'

HARDUP: I must send immediately, and countermand that.

GINGLE: (*aside*) 'Oh, cursed spite!' Countermand the supper! I've a great mind – if I could only be sure –

---

beat up his quarters: arouse him, visit him 'unceremoniously' (*OED*).

HARDUP: But what shall I say to the audience? Read them Mr Garrick's letter, in which he positively promises to be here, and say that as I am an utter stranger to that gentleman –

GINGLE: (*aside*) An utter stranger! Good!

HARDUP: I am at a loss to imagine the cause of his non-appearance, and that I throw myself upon the generosity of – &c., &c., &c.

GINGLE: I will – I'll run the risk – I'm up in the part. They can but pelt me, and I'm used to that.

HARDUP: Here goes, if I die for it!

GINGLE: And here goes, if I die for it! (*advancing and laying his hand on* HARDUP*'s as he is about to move*) 'Rest, rest, perturbed spirit!'

HARDUP: Hollo! Who are you?

GINGLE: 'Thine evermore, while this machine is to him, Hamlet!'

HARDUP: Hamlet! Is it possible? Can it be? (*aside*) It's about the height – the – age – the – (*aloud*) My dear sir, I'm on the rack. Speak – Your name?

GINGLE: D. G. (*aside*) That's no lie, at any rate.

HARDUP: Ah! you then are –

GINGLE: I am.

HARDUP: The great – the unrivalled –

GINGLE: Nay, my dear sir –

HARDUP: The immortal Mr Garrick!

GINGLE: You are too polite.

HARDUP: Oh, sir! permit me – (*offering to embrace him*)

GINGLE: With all my heart. (*They embrace.*)

HARDUP: You have snatched me from the very depth of despair.

GINGLE: You seemed rather down in the mouth, I confess.

HARDUP: (*aside*) Down in the mouth! How familiar! How void of all affectation! As if he had known me for years. There's the mark of your truly great man. (*aloud*) But, excuse me, you are covered with dust; you have walked –

GINGLE: You are right.

HARDUP: Some accident?

GINGLE: Right again.

HARDUP: As I suspected! Your carriage broke down?

GINGLE: Worse than that.

HARDUP: Worse! Gracious powers! You are not hurt?

GINGLE: No; but I've had a narrow escape.

HARDUP: The horses ran away?

GINGLE: No – I ran away.

HARDUP: You!

GINGLE: When I could fight no longer.

HARDUP: Fight! Preserve me! I feared as much! You were stopped on the road?

GINGLE: By a band of highwaymen armed to the teeth. Postillion severely wounded – horses killed – chaise ransacked – portmanteau, trunk, hat-box, sword-case – all gone!

HARDUP: Terrible! And your servant – you had a servant?

GINGLE: Don't mention him, cowardly dog! Left me to fight for myself.

HARDUP: In league with the villains, perhaps.

GINGLE: Shouldn't be at all surprised. But here I am, safe and sound; though how I got here, I hardly know. I knew you expected me between four and five, in time to dress. I walked the last five miles ready to drop.

HARDUP: Bless my soul! bless my soul! You shall have some refreshment instantly. One moment, my dear sir, only to set our friends at rest. Mrs Hardup – Mr Undertone – Mr Garrick's come! Mr Garrick has arrived! (*Runs out calling*.)

GINGLE: Well, I'm astonished at my impudence, and frightened into the bargain, now that I've done it. If anybody here should happen to know Mr Garrick, what would become of me? I shall never be able to keep it up. I've a great mind to run for it now. I will, too, while the coast is clear. (*going*)

(*Enter* POLLY, *dressed as Ophelia, carrying wine and cake on a small tray*.)

POLLY: If you please, sir, here's some wine and – gracious! what do I see? Mr Gingle!

GINGLE: My fair unknown! Powers of love! my long-lost –

POLLY: How on earth came you here? If my father should know –

GINGLE: Who is your father?

POLLY: The manager – Mr Hardup.

GINGLE: The devil he is!

POLLY: Yes; and if he finds you in this house –

GINGLE: He shan't – I'm off.

(*Re-enter* HARDUP.)

POLLY: It's too late! – he's here!

HARDUP: Mr Garrick! Mr Garrick! I've arranged everything.

POLLY: Mr Garrick!

GINGLE: (*aside*) There's nothing for it, but brazening it out. (*aloud*) Well, sir! (*Makes signs to* POLLY, *who stands in astonishment*.)

HARDUP: I've been forward, sir, just as I am, to the public, who were getting rather impatient, and begged their permission to perform the farce – a short, neat piece – first, in order to give you time to dress, and refresh yourself.

GINGLE: You are very kind, but I really feel so unwell, that I don't think I can act to-night at all.

HARDUP: Oh, sir! Mr Garrick! don't say so. Take some wine, sir. (*handing him wine*)

GINGLE: Yes, I'll take some wine, but I don't think it possible that I can play Hamlet.

POLLY: (*aside*) I'm sure he can't. Why, they hissed him as Bernardo.

HARDUP: My dear Mr Garrick, consider the consequences. It would be ruin to me. Take another glass, sir! You'll be better presently.

POLLY: (*aside*) He'll be tipsy presently – that will be the end of it.

GINGLE: Not bad sherry, by any means.

HARDUP: I'm delighted you fancy it. It's from the King's Arms, over the way – a capital house. I've taken the liberty of ordering a little supper there, after the play, and trust you will do me the honour –

GINGLE: You are very kind! Wouldn't there be time before the play – I'm rather peckish.

HARDUP: I'm afraid not before.

GINGLE: Well, 'After, be it, then', as Richard says.

HARDUP: But a wing of a fowl, perhaps, while you dress –

GINGLE: Dress! Ah! There! (*aside*) A capital excuse! (*aloud*) You see it's impossible I can play – I have no dress – those rascals have taken all.

HARDUP: Don't be uneasy, sir; I've thought of everything. As luck would have it, Doctor Killmany, who is just your size, was in the stage box, in a new black velvet suit. I told him your predicament, and, in the handsomest manner possible, he volunteered to go home, and change his dress, and send you the new suit in a twinkling.

GINGLE: How very polite! (*aside*) There's no backing out any way!

POLLY: (*aside*) He doesn't mean – surely, he never will have the impudence –

(*Enter* CALL BOY, *with a bundle*.)

BOY: Doctor Killmany's servant, sir, brought this bundle, with his master's compliments.

HARDUP: That's right – take it into that room. Mr Garrick will dress there. I'll see if all is ready, sir. (*Exit with* CALL BOY, *into room left*.)

POLLY: There – now! Run! Now!

GINGLE: What for?

POLLY: Why, to get off with a whole skin to be sure.

GINGLE: Pooh! pooh!

POLLY: Pooh! pooh! Are you mad? Or are you tipsy already?

GINGLE: Tipsy? No! 'That which hath made them drunk, hath made me bold!' 'There is a tide in the affairs of men, which, if taken at the flood, leads on to fortune.' I've got a chance at last, and I won't fling it away.

POLLY: You'll stay?

GINGLE: I'll stay.

POLLY: And play Hamlet?

GINGLE: And play Hamlet.

POLLY: As Mr Garrick?

GINGLE: Perhaps not exactly as Mr Garrick. I don't presume –

POLLY: I mean in his name?

GINGLE: Decidedly! I'm perfect in the part – studied it long ago.

POLLY: There'll be murder!

GINGLE: Don't be rude, Miss Hardup.

POLLY: Dear Mr Gingle! for my sake –

GINGLE: It is for your sake! When you played at Cork, under the name of Hopkins, you told me your father would never give his consent, unless I became 'somebody' in my profession. This is the first chance I've had – and I tell you I won't fling it away!

POLLY: But how came you to be mistaken for Mr Garrick?

GINGLE: 'Be innocent of the knowledge, dearest chuck, till *they* applaud the deed!'

POLLY: Applaud! They'll fling the benches at you!

GINGLE: I don't care! I'm desperate! 'My fate cries out, and makes each petty artery in this body as hardy as the Nemean lion's nerve.'

(*Enter* HARDUP *from room right; and* LADY O'LEARY *and* MAJOR DERRYDOWN *from door centre*.)

HARDUP: }
LADY O: } Bravo! Bravo! (*They applaud*.)

HARDUP: Beautiful!
LADY O: Sublime!
MAJOR: As a puddle in a storm!
GINGLE: (*to* POLLY) There! – you hear?
LADY O: Mr Hardup, present me, I entreat, to your illustrious friend!
HARDUP: Mr Garrick, allow me to introduce Lady O'Leary, relict of Sir Phelim O'Leary, late member for the county. (*aside to him*) A widow with two thousand a year.
GINGLE: (*aside*) Two thousand! (*aloud*) Madam, I – Ahem! 'If I profane, with my unworthy hands, this holy shrine – the gentle fine is this' – (*kissing her hand*)
LADY O: Oh! Mr Garrick! this is the proudest moment of my life!
GINGLE: 'Gad, if it wasn't for – (*looking at* POLLY)
HARDUP: Major Derrydown, of the Westmeath Militia (*presenting* MAJOR DERRYDOWN, *who bows stiffly*)
GINGLE: Major, I'm yours – to the ground. (*bowing to the ground*)
MAJOR: Faith, and you may soon be there, without breaking your neck, my honey – for it's a small way you are above it, at any time.
HARDUP: I believe I did introduce my daughter, Miss Polly Hardup, who will have the honour to play –
GINGLE: 'My soul's idol, the most beautiful Ophelia!' 'Nymph, in thy orisons, be all my sins remembered.'
LADY O: How apt! How delicate! Why, major –
MAJOR: My beauty!
LADY O: You don't seem struck by him!
MAJOR: By the powers! I wish I was – for I'm in a mighty good humour to strike him again.
LADY O: Strike Garrick! What profanity!
CALL BOY: (*within*) Farce over, ladies and gentlemen!
HARDUP: There! The Farce over, I declare, and you have not begun to dress yet! My dear sir, you'll find everything in that room! I have to play the Ghost – but I shan't be five minutes – all the rest are ready. Mr Undertone!

(*Enter* UNDERTONE.)

UNDERTONE: Sir!
HARDUP: Send Mr Garrick's dresser to him directly, with my best sword and the ribbon.
UNDERTONE: Yes, sir. Shall I ring in the overture?
HARDUP: Not yet! not yet! Give us all the time you can! (*Exit* UNDERTONE.) Now, my dear sir –
GINGLE: But you said something about the wing of a fowl.
HARDUP: It will be here directly. (*Enter* DRESSER.) Here's your dresser! Quick, Dennis, and show Mr Garrick every attention! I must fly! (*Exit.*)
GINGLE: (*aside*) Another glass – just to – 'Screw my courage to the sticking place!' (*taking wine*)
POLLY: You'll be tipsy!
GINGLE: 'Not a jot! not a jot!' (*Drinks and sings.*)

''Tis wine inspires us, and fires us
With courage, love, and joy!' (*Exit.*)

LADY O: Delightful! What a voice! What expression! His genius is unrivalled.

MAJOR: He sings – as he looks – like a crow in a gutter!

POLLY: Major! You're jealous!

MAJOR: May be I am.

LADY O: Major! You're a fool.

MAJOR: I'm not such a fool as he looks – any way!

LADY O: Mr Garrick look a fool! Major!

MAJOR: My jewel!

LADY O: Don't speak to me again this night!

MAJOR: I'm as dumb as a fish! But I'll speak to little Davy there, and pretty plainly, I warrant me!

POLLY: Little Davy! Mr Garrick is six feet high when he's in a passion, sir!

MAJOR: Then I'll make him a foot taller before he's an hour older – take my word for it!

LADY O: What! Would you pick a quarrel with him? Why don't you answer me, major?

MAJOR: Because you told me not to speak to you again to-night.

LADY O: You shall never speak to me again, if you do not instantly promise to drop all idea of so monstrous a proceeding. Swear to me that you will not hurt a hair of –

(DRESSER *runs out of room left.*)

DRESSER: Mr Garrick's wig! Mr Garrick's wig! (*Enter* HAIR DRESSER, *with wig, and runs against him.*) Ugh! You stupid fellow! Can't you see! (*Exit with wig.*)

MAJOR: There! I've hurt it by deputy!

LADY O: No evasion, sir! Swear!

HARDUP: (*underneath stage*) Swear!

LADY O: Mercy upon me!

MAJOR: What the devil's that?

POLLY: It's only papa! He's dressing for the Ghost, in the room below, and heard his cue.

LADY O: I declare he frightened me out of my wits! But, come, major! I insist, on pain of my lasting displeasure –

MAJOR: Well, there then! I bind myself over to keep the peace, upon one condition –

LADY O: And what may that be?

MAJOR: That you'll fix the day, my darling – the happy day!

LADY O: Major! how can you? Before that young person! Another time when we are by ourselves!

MAJOR: By and by, then – in the orchestra – behind the big drum.

(*Enter* CALL BOY.)

BOY: Here's a letter for the master, if you please miss.

POLLY: (*aside, looking at it*) The Dublin post-mark, and D. G. in the corner! It must be from Mr Garrick, to explain his absence. What's to be done? If I give it to my

---

''*Tis wine inspires us* . . .': air from Act II of John Gay's *The Beggar's Opera*, produced at Lincoln's Inn Fields Theatre in 1728.

father, poor Gingle is ruined! He must not see it yet! (*aloud*) Very well – it's post-paid, I see – you needn't wait. I'll give it to him. (*Exit* CALL BOY.) When the play's over, perhaps! (*Puts it in her pocket.*)

CALL BOY: (*within*) Overture on, ladies! Overture on, gentlemen!

POLLY: (*to* LADY O'LEARY) There's the overture begun, my lady! Won't your ladyship go down to your seat?

LADY O: Not yet – not yet! Do you go down, major, and keep it for me.

MAJOR: (*aside*) Faith, it's bothered enough that I will be to keep my own seat. This divarting vagabond has made the ould girl so skittish, she'll fling me, to a certainty.

LADY O: Well – ain't you gone, major?

MAJOR: To be sure I am, my darling! Don't you see I'm gone! (*aside*) This is the last stage of the Garrick Fever, and she may be carried off by it! I'll get the big drummer to be my deputy, and steal up again, to watch the proceedings. (*Exit.*)

POLLY: Here come papa and mamma, in their new dresses, ready for the tragedy.

(*Enter* HARDUP, *dressed as* GHOST, *with his face floured*; MRS HARDUP, *as* QUEEN; MR PUMPWELL, *as* CLAUDIUS; *and other performers as* POLONIUS, LAERTES, &c. &c.)

HARDUP: Well! well! Is Mr Garrick dressed? I want to run through our first scene, before we ring up. (*knocking at door of room left*)

GINGLE: (*within*) Where's that wing of a fowl you promised me?

HARDUP: Bless my soul! haven't they sent it? (*calling off*) Kitty! run to the King's Arms, and ask why they have not sent the fowl I ordered for Mr Garrick. 'Murder most foul as in the best it is! But this, most foul, strange, and unnatural.'

(*Enter* GINGLE *from room left, dressed as* HAMLET.)

GINGLE: 'Haste me to know it, that I, with wings as swift as meditation, or the thoughts of love, may sweep to my revenge.'

LADY O: Exquisite!

HARDUP: What fire!

LADY O: What pathos! Nobody but Garrick could speak like that!

POLLY: (*aside*) And yet, Shakespeare says, 'What's in a name?'

LADY O: What an eye he has! It penetrates the soul!

GINGLE: Like a cobbler's awl! eh, my lady? Sharp's the word, and quick's the motion. I hate your dull, drawling fellows, who dole out speeches at a line a minute by a stop-watch. I'm for getting over the ground – flustering an audience – taking 'em by storm. Eh, Mr Thingemmy?

HARDUP: Undoubtedly, sir! Listen! listen! gentlemen, to the great master of your art.

POLLY: (*aside*) He's taken too much sherry! – I knew he would!

HARDUP: Shall we run through your first scene as we've had no rehearsal? I think there's just time.

GINGLE: As you please, my dear fellow; anything to be agreeable.

LADY O: How condescending!

HARDUP: Mrs Hardup, you hear Mr Garrick! Mr Pumpwell, you'll give the cue, if you please.

PUMPWELL: 'And now, my cousin Hamlet, and my son – '

GINGLE: 'A little more than kin, and less than kind – '
PUMPWELL: 'How is it that the clouds still hang on you?'
GINGLE: 'Not so, my lord! I am too much i' the sun.'
POLLY: (*aside*) He has been too much in the sun, as the saying is.
MRS HARDUP: 'Good Hamlet, cast thy nighted colour off, and let thine eye look like a friend on Denmark – '

(*Enter* CALL BOY *with chicken, &c., on tray*.)

GINGLE: I beg your pardon again, but here's my chicken, and – 'I have that within which passeth show.' Never mind me – 'Go on! I'll follow thee!' You see I'm at the wing!
HARDUP: Ha! ha! excellent! At the wing! A professional joke, my lady!
LADY O: What wit! What playful fancy!
CALL BOY: (*to* HARDUP) And please, sir, there's a gentleman below, as comed in by the Dublin Mail, and wishes to know if you've ever got a letter from Mr Garrick?
POLLY: Oh, mercy!
GINGLE: (*aside*) A letter from me!
HARDUP: A letter from Mr Garrick? Why, to be sure I have – had it a week ago. What does the man mean?
LADY O: He wants the autograph, no doubt. But don't let him have it. If you part with it at all, let it be to me. I'll give you ten guineas for it.
GINGLE: Nonsense, my lady! I'll write you as many as you please. (*aside*) Love letters!
LADY O: Oh, Mr Garrick! Fascinating creature!
CALL BOY: (*to* HARDUP) If you please, sir, what am I to say to the gentleman?
HARDUP: Tell him I'm just going on the stage with Mr Garrick, and I can't be troubled now. He must call to-morrow morning if he wants to see me.
CALL BOY: Very well, sir. (*Exit*.)
POLLY: (*aside*) It's all over with us – there *is* a letter – it came this evening – I've got it in my pocket!
GINGLE: The devil!
HARDUP: What does she say about a pocket?
GINGLE: Nothing! Only prompting me – 'That from a shelf the precious diadem stole, and put it in his pocket.' Come, ladies and gentlemen, it must be near the time; let us go down upon the stage. Mind, I give you all notice, though I say it that shouldn't say it, you are going to see such a piece of tragic acting as you never saw before in all your lives!
OMNES: We have no doubt of it! (*Exeunt all through door centre, but* POLLY *and* LADY O'LEARY.)
POLLY: (*detaining* LADY O'LEARY) One word if you please, my lady.
LADY O: What, now, my dear child! Impossible! I shall miss his entrée – his reception!
POLLY: Oh, but indeed, my lady, you must hear me! It's of the greatest consequence! I shall be ruined if you don't.
LADY O: Mercy on the child! Speak quickly, then! What is the matter?
POLLY: It must be found out, and then my father will kill us both, if you don't interfere.

LADY O: Both? What, you and me, child?

POLLY: No, my lady – me and Gingle.

LADY O: Gingle! Who's Gingle?

POLLY: Mr Decimus Gingle; the young man who is playing Hamlet.

LADY O: The poor girl has lost her senses, surely! Hamlet! You don't mean Hamlet, child! Mr Garrick is playing Hamlet.

POLLY: That is not Mr Garrick, my lady.

LADY O: Not Mr Garrick, Miss Polly Hardup! Are you really mad, or do you mean to insult me?

POLLY: No, indeed, my lady. Mr Garrick has not arrived. Here's a letter from him, most likely to explain – you heard what the boy said, just now, about the gentleman, my lady?

LADY O: I shall go crazy myself. Is it possible that anyone can have dared to assume –

POLLY: It was for my sake, my lady. Mr Gingle thought if he succeeded, father would give his consent.

LADY O: And I had nearly quarrelled with the major about this impostor!

POLLY: Oh, dear, my lady!

LADY O: Have been trapped into praising, admiring a trumpery strolling player – a fellow without fame, figure, voice, or any single recommendation for his profession.

POLLY: Oh, my lady!

LADY O: A stamping, storming, ranting, vulgar, horrid, little wretch!

POLLY: Indeed and indeed, my lady, he may not be a very good actor, but he's a very nice young man.

CALL BOY: (*looking in at door centre*) Stage is waiting, miss!

POLLY: The stage waiting for me! Oh, dear! what shall I do? – what shall I do? (*Exit.*)

LADY O: I'm ready to sink with shame! – I, who have been considered an oracle on such matters. The more I think of it, the more astonished I am that I could be deceived for a moment. He, Hamlet! He's no more like Hamlet –

(*Enter* MAJOR DERRYDOWN.)

MAJOR: (*entering*) Exactly my opinion, Lady O'Leary; and I'm delighted to find you've come round to it at last, where'er you have been to get it. But the public, you see, are not of the same way of thinking.

LADY O: The public!

MAJOR: Did you ever hear such acclamations – such a hububoo of applause, in your born days?

LADY O: At his entrance, of course.

MAJOR: At his exit – at the end of his ghost scene, and all through it as well. Devil a word in twenty could you hear for the shouting. They've got the Garrick Fever, my lady, badly, and a noisy disorder it is.

LADY O: You don't say so?

MAJOR: Why, where could your ladyship be not to hear it yourself?

LADY O: (*aside*) If it should be Garrick after all. The Major is no judge of acting, and the girl herself may be mistaken. There certainly was a sort of a kind of a – I have not seen the performance. I was detained by particular business; but I will hasten, and pronounce at once upon his merits.

(*Enter* HARDUP, MRS HARDUP, POLLY, *and* ACTORS, *hastily, the latter bearing* GINGLE *in a chair.*)

HARDUP: This way! This way! Take care! Quietly!

MAJOR: / LADY O: } What's the matter?

HARDUP: / MRS HARDUP: } Mr Garrick has fainted! Mr Garrick is very ill!

HARDUP: Have you such a thing as a smelling bottle, my lady?

LADY O: Here! here! Bless my soul!

HARDUP: How unfortunate! In the midst of such a magnificent effort, with the house in a tumult of applause.

POLLY: (*aside*) It's the wine! – I knew it would be so! – He's not used to it!

MRS HARDUP: He opens his eyes! He moves!

HARDUP: Do you feel a little better, sir?

GINGLE: 'Speak the speech, I pray you, as I pronounced it to you – (*Hiccups.*) trippingly on the tongue.'

MAJOR: Ill! Why, the man's drunk!

GINGLE: (*staggering up*) 'To be, or not to be, that's the question.'

HARDUP: Mr Garrick drunk! Impossible!

GINGLE: 'My custom always in the afternoon.'

LADY O: How very disgraceful. (*aside*) It cannot be Mr Garrick.

MRS HARDUP: I'm all astonishment!

GINGLE: 'Oh, wonderful son, that can so astonish a mother!'

HARDUP: Was there ever anything so provoking? I must make an apology, after all, or dismiss the audience.

GINGLE: 'Alas, poor ghost!' – 'Lady, shall I lie in your lap?' (*to* LADY O'LEARY)

LADY O: Major, protect me!

MAJOR: Keep off, fellow! or I'll make a tragedy actor of you in earnest.

GINGLE: You! You make a tragedy actor of me! I defy you! I scorn your words, sir! I can draw, sir, as well as you, sir. (*Draws. The* WOMEN *scream.*)

HARDUP: Here'll be bloodshed! Major! Mr Garrick!

GINGLE: (*trying to pass at the* MAJOR) 'A rat! a rat! a rat! Dead for a ducat! – dead!'

POLLY: Gingle! My dear Gingle! (*pulling his coat*)

ALL (*but* LADY O'LEARY): Gingle!

HARDUP: Gingle! What does the wench mean by Gingle?

LADY O: That you have been imposed upon, as this letter may, perhaps, explain. (*Gives letter to* HARDUP.)

HARDUP: To me! (*Breaking letter open hastily – reads.*) 'Dear sir, I have just discovered, to my great concern, that I have misdirected two letters, and sent you the answer to a dinner invitation from a friend a few miles out of Dublin. I enclose, in all haste, the note intended for you, declining, with many thanks, your liberal proposal, and trust it will arrive in time to prevent any disappointment to the public. Your obedient servant, D. G.' D. G.! Confusion! Then who the devil are you?

GINGLE: Your obedient servant, D. G.

HARDUP: D. G.! What D. G.? How D. G.?

GINGLE: Decimus Gingle!

HARDUP: The fellow who made love to my daughter at Cork?
GINGLE: 'The same, my lord, and your poor servant ever.'
MAJOR: (*laughing*) Ha! ha! my lady! 'You don't seem struck by him! What a voice! What expression! His genius is universal!'
LADY O: Laughed at by him, too! I shall die with vexation!
POLLY: (*aside*) Say you knew it all the while, my lady, and kept the secret to serve me. Nobody can laugh at you then.
LADY O: An excellent idea!
HARDUP: You drunken rascal! You shall suffer for this!
GINGLE: That I shall! I've a horrid head-ache to begin with.
HARDUP: You've ruined me!

(POLLY *goes to* LADY O'LEARY, *and entreats her to interfere*.)

GINGLE: Don't say so, sir! I hoped to make your fortune, and my own, too. It's all the fault of the sherry – upon an empty stomach.
HARDUP: I wish it had been poison, with all my heart.

(*Enter* UNDERTONE, *centre*.)

UNDERTONE: Mr Hardup. There's a terrible noise in front, sir. They're calling for the manager.
HARDUP: I can't face 'em! Do you go, Mr Undertone. Tell 'em –
GINGLE: No – stop! I'll go! I don't mind an apple or two – and I'm getting sober fast.
HARDUP: Go to the devil! They'll want their money again!
LADY O: (*advancing*) And if they do, I'll make it up to you!
HARDUP: You, my lady! Why, it's a hundred and twenty pounds!
LADY O: I have promised my god-daughter, Miss Polly Hardup, to arrange matters between you, and I shall keep my word. The young man, I am assured, is not an habitual drunkard, and he may have talent in another line.
MAJOR: To judge from his figure he'd be better in Low Comedy, than High Tragedy.
POLLY: Nay! you must own, father, that you said he was magnificent, even in Hamlet, as far as he went.
HARDUP: Yes – because I thought he was Mr Garrick – and of course –
POLLY: And because he is not Mr Garrick, you will say he has no merit at all.
HARDUP: If he can get me out of this scrape with the audience, I'll say whatever you please.
GINGLE: Done! It's a bargain! I'll go forward to them, and I'll say – 'Ladies and Gentlemen, I throw myself on the generosity of an enlightened Public! I candidly confess to you that I am not the immortal Mr Garrick! But don't be angry! I assumed his name in the humble hope of affording you some entertainment. This is my first appearance in Hamlet. I took the part at a very short notice, and respectfully solicit the usual indulgence.'

Finale

PUMPWELL

MRS HARDUP MR UNDERTONE

POLLY

LADY O'LEARY GINGLE

MAJOR HARDUP

Curtain

BEAUTY AND THE BEAST

A grand, comic, romantic, operatic, melodramatic fairy extravaganza in two acts.

First performed at the Theatre Royal, Covent Garden, on Monday, 12 April 1841, with the following cast:

BEAUTY	Madame Vestris
THE BEAST, *alias* PRINCE AZOR	Mr W. Harrison
SIR ALDGATE PUMP, *knight, alderman and merchant adventurer, in difficulties – Beauty's father*	Mr J. Bland
JOHN QUILL, *his ex-clerk and present humble servant, a livery-man out of livery*	Mr Harley
DRESSALINDA, } *Beauty's sisters*	Miss Rainforth
MARRYGOLDA, } *Beauty's sisters*	Miss Grant
QUEEN OF THE ROSES	Miss Lee
MEMBERS OF THE PARLIAMENT OF ROSES	Mesdames Cross, Jackson, A. Jackson, Lane, Collett, Goward, Garrick, Kerridge, Charlton
ZEPHYRS, *in waiting*	Mesdames Payne, Ryals, Miller, Kendall, A. Kendall, Taylor, Fitzjames, Gardiner, Platt, Hatton, Travers, L. Payne
DRIVER OF FAIRY OMNIBUS	Miss Kendall
CAD	Master Marshall
NOBLES AND LADIES OF THE COURT OF PRINCE AZOR	Messrs Collett, Green, S. Smith, Gledhill, Butler, Kerridge, Connell, Davis, Healey, Hodges, Mesdames Rushton, Edgar, Scott, Marsano, Bishop, Granby, Franklin, Osborne

Scenery by Mr Grieve, Mr T. Grieve and Mr W. Grieve
Decorations and appointments by Mr W. Bradwell
Dresses by Mesdames Glover and Rayner
Machinery by Mr H. Sloman
Overture and music composed and arranged by Mr J. H. Tully
Action and dances by Mr Oscar Byrne

III *Beauty and the Beast*: Act II. Madame Vestris as Beauty singing 'Oh, get along, get along, do.'

ACT I

SCENE 1. *A Bower of Roses, not by Bendemeer's stream.* ZEPHYRS *discovered sleeping. Enter a* ZEPHYR *to the 'Gavotte de Vestris'.*

ZEPH: How's this? what still asleep, my rosy posies?
Come ope your eyes and blow your little noses.
Not a leaf stirring yet – why gracious powers,
Are you aware the time of day, my flowers?
Have you forgotten that your Queen proposes
This day to ope the Parliament of roses?

Chorus – ZEPHYRS – *'Der Freischütz'* – 'Bridesmaids' Chorus'

Sweet Zephyr, don't make such a breeze,
We're rather late this morning,
But don't be angry, if you please,
We shan't be long adorning;
Sleep, you know, will sometimes thus enthral us,
You should earlier call us.

(*Music.* THE QUEEN OF THE ROSES *appears.*)

ZEPH: Behold your sovereign! Silence, all and each,
To hear her Majesty's most flow'ry speech.

QUEEN: My Buds and Blossoms, I rejoice to say,
That I continue to receive each day
Assurances from all the foreign flowers
Of their good will towards these happy bowers.
I have concluded, on the best foundations,
A treaty with the King of the Carnations,
And trust ere long to lay the leaves before you.
I'm sorry now to be obliged to bore you
On an old subject, but, for your digestion
At Easter, we must have an Easter question –
And on my faithful Roses I depend
To bring the matter to a happy end.
The facts are these – a youth of royal race,
Of noble mind and matchless shape and face,
Has been transformed by a malicious fairy
Into an ugly monster, huge and hairy
And must remain a downright beast outside,
'Till some fair maid consents to be his bride.

Bendemeer's stream: Persian river, with a bower of roses, mentioned in 'The Veiled Prophet of Khorassan', one of four long poems recited by the minstrel Feramorz in Thomas Moore's oriental romance, *Lalla Rookh* (1817).

Der Freischütz: opera by Weber, performed (in English) at the Lyceum in 1824.

Easter question: doubtless an allusion to the perennial Eastern question, a succession of international problems arising from the weakness of Turkey and the disintegration of the Turkish empire which exposed it to foreign encroachment and obliged Britain to seek ways of safeguarding her interests in the Mediterranean and the overland routes to India through Syria and Egypt; the years 1840–1 witnessed a great deal of diplomatic activity.

My Buds and Blossoms, you will take that measure,
Of course, which best may work your sovereign's pleasure –
Which is, that through a Rose's mediation
The Prince may be restored to form and station.
Ere nightfall, I expect you'll break the spell,
And so, my Buds and Blossoms, fare ye well.
CHORUS – *'Coal Black Rose'*
Queen of Roses, we'll take care
To lay before this honourable house the affair;
If we can get two acts pass'd, without its being nettled,
The beast will be re-formed, and the Easter question settled!
No rose here that blows,
Will vote against a measure, ma'am, that you propose.
(*Tableau and the scene closes*.)

SCENE 2. *Interior of 'Pump's Folly'. Enter* MARRYGOLDA *and* DRESSALINDA.
MAR: Oh, sister! sister! times have altered sadly,
To think we should live poorly –
DRES: And dress badly!
MAR: We who have banqueted in fair Guildhall,
DRES: We who have opened Easter Monday's ball –
MAR: The daughters of Sir Aldgate Pump, Lord Mayor
Of London once –
DRES: And now, though past the chair,
A knight and alderman, who might again
Wear o'er the velvet gown the golden chain,
Had not malicious Fortune, at one blow,
Ruined the famous firm of Pump and Co.
MAR: Out on the jade! could she none else have fix'd on
To banish from Threadneedle Street to Brixton?
Sad change from merriment to melancholy,
From lordly Mansion House to poor 'Pump's Folly'.
DRES: It makes me mad to hear our sister Beauty
Say we should be content, and prate of duty,
And resignation, and that sort of stuff –
She thinks a grogram gown is fine enough.
MAR: And so it is for her to scrub the floor in,
To cook the dinner, or to ope the door in.
That's all she's fit for – with her wax doll's face,
What matters what she thinks in any case?

---

two acts: a pun on agreements between the European allies which stabilised Turco-Egyptian relations and effectively restrained domination of the Near East by the Russian *beast*.
Threadneedle Street: location of the London Stock Exchange and the Bank of England in the heart of the City of London.
Brixton: in 1841, a residential suburb of London favoured by city businessmen and their families.
Mansion House: official residence of the Lord Mayor of London.

We are her elders, and her betters too,
And need more ornament than she can do.
DRES: Here comes papa – and in a mighty hurry!
(*Enter* SIR ALDGATE PUMP *hastily, in great agitation, with an open letter in his hand.*)
SIR A: Oh, Gog and Magog!
MAR: Bless me, what a flurry
You seem in, sir! Is anything amiss?
Or have you heard good news?
SIR A: Girls, come and kiss
Your happy father. Pumps are up! Behold
This precious letter. List, whilst I unfold
The glorious tidings. Fortune, in her sport,
Has brought the good ship 'Polly' into port.
DRES: The bark you thought was lost on some vile rock –
SIR A: Is safe in Plymouth Sound.
MAR: You're sure, sir.
SIR A: Cock!
DRES: Why, she was thought the richest of your fleet.
SIR A: Her cargo's worth would buy all Lombard Street.
MAR: Then we again in gilded coach shall ride.
DRES: And wear the richest clothes in all Cheapside.
SIR A: Again a roaring trade on 'Change I'll drive!
But I must hence with speed, so look alive –
Where is my youngest hope, my Beauty fair?
MAR: I'm sure, pa, I don't know.
DRES: And I don't care!
BEAU: (*Sings without.*) 'Gondolier, row, row.'
SIR A: Hark! that's her voice! as any bell 'tis clear.
MAR: I'm sick of that eternal 'Gondolier.'
(*Enter* BEAUTY, *singing.*)
AIR – BEAUTY – *'Gondolier Row'*
Gondolier, row, row,
Gondolier, row, row;
'Tis a pretty air,
I do declare.
But it haunts a body so,
Gondolier, row, row,
Gondolier, row, row;
At work or play,
By night or day,
I sing it where'er I go.

Gog and Magog: fourteen-foot wooden statues at the Guildhall, commemorating two giants captured and brought to London by Brutus, legendary first king of Britain.
Lombard Street, Cheapside: business streets in the City.
'Change: the Stock Exchange.

BEAU: Good morning, sir.
SIR A: Rejoice, my child, for know,
The 'Polly's safe in port.
BEAU: You don't say so?
SIR A: Read! you can read?
BEAU: Both print and written hand.
SIR A: Accomplished creature! And can understand
What you do read?
BEAU: Affirm that quite I wouldn't,
Because, at times, e'en those who write it couldn't.
SIR A: Where's my ex-clerk and faithful drudge, John Quill?
(*Enter* JOHN QUILL.)
JOHN: Here, master. I am your remainder still.
SIR A: Run to the 'Goat in Boots'.
JOHN: Yes, master – Dot
And carry one – (*going*)
SIR A: Stop! you've not heard for what.
Order a chaise and four – and mind, John, you
Must travel with me –
JOHN: Dot and carry two. (*Exit*.)
SIR A: Rot your arithmetic, and stir your stumps –
This is a glorious day, girl, for the Pumps!
BEAU: Where go you, father?
SIR A: To the ship, my dear.
To land her cargo, and the Customs clear.
DRES: You'll bring some present home, I hope, for me.
SIR A: With all my heart, my love – what shall it be?
DRES: Oh, any trifle that falls in your way –
A hundred guinea shawl suppose we say.
SIR A: A hundred – humph – but then your sisters too.
MAR: Oh, sir, I wouldn't think of asking you
To buy a shawl for me – that were too rash –
I'll take a hundred guineas, sir, in cash.
SIR A: Considerate child! But first, love, I must net 'em;
In the meanwhile, I'll wish that you may get 'em.
But what says Beauty? Is my pet so happy
That she's no boon to ask of her own pappy?
You've heard the choice of your two sisters here,
One's for mere cash, the other for Cashmere.
What says my duck?
BEAU: (*aside*) If nothing, I suppose
They'll call me proud. (*aloud*) Well, bring me, sir, a rose.
SIR A: A rose!

---

remainder: sole remaining assistant, an obsolete usage characteristic of Quill's arithmetical turn of phrase.

BEAU: Yes – in our little garden here
There is not one at this time of the year.
And I'm so fond of roses.
DRES: }
MAR: } Well, if ever!
SIR A: Only a flower! Nonsense, child; endeavour
To think of something else.
BEAU: No, sir; 'twill be
Enough to prove that you have thought of me
When far away.
DRES: }
MAR: } (*sneeringly*) Sweet sentimental soul!
SIR A: I'll bring one though I search from pole to pole
To find it.

(*Re-enter* JOHN QUILL.)

JOHN: Sir, they've brought over the shay.
SIR A: Brought over! brought it to the door you'd say.
JOHN: Yes, sir.
SIR A: Are all my things well packed behind?
JOHN: I've added up, sir, all that I can find,
And here is the grand total. (*showing a small parcel*)
SIR A: A small stock, it
Won't take much room up – put it in your pocket.
And now, farewell, my darlings! Behave pretty,
I'll come back and astonish all the city!

Quintette – 'The Fox jumped over' – 'Guy Mannering'

JOHN: I've just looked over the garden gate,
And sorry am to observe it snows!
SIR A: O-ho! does it so, John? I'll wrap up my pate;
One last embrace, and away we goes.
BEAU: Wrap, father, wrap this round your chest;
The day's caught cold, I do protest.
For, ah! you hear, – it blows, it snows.
SIR A: One last embrace, and away we goes.
DRES: Beaux will swarm –
JOHN: Multiplication –
MAR: Cash be plenty –
JOHN: Sweet addition –
SIR A: Now, without more conversation,
Here at once we part –
JOHN: Division.

(*Exeunt* SIR ALDGATE, JOHN QUILL, DRESSALINDA, *and* MARRYGOLDA.)

Guy Mannering: melodrama by Daniel Terry from Scott's novel, with music by Henry Bishop, produced at Covent Garden in 1816.

BEAU: More snow! He'll have sharp weather, there's no doubt;
But pa was always fond of 'cold without'.
Song – Air – 'Susannah don't you cry' – Nigger Melody
I had a dream the other night,
When everything was still,
I dreamt I saw my father,
Half seas over with John Quill

The cold within was nearly out,
A drop was in his eye;
He says to bolt I am about,
So, Beauty, don't you cry.
Oh, my Beauty, don't you cry for me,
I'm going to California to dig gold upon my knee.

And when I to the diggings get,
I'll dig up all the ground,
Until I find a lump of gold,
That weighs ten thousand pound.
Then in the good ship Polly
Home I'll bring it presently,
Then we'll all again be jolly,
So, Beauty, don't you cry for me.
Oh, my Beauty, etc. (*Exit.*)

SCENE 3. *A Forest. Snow storm. Crash without.*
SIR A: (*without*) Holloa! confusion! help! holloa! John Quill!
(JOHN QUILL *enters with* SIR ALDGATE.)
JOHN: Here, master!
SIR A: Mercy on us, what a spill!
The leaders shied at that confounded drover.
JOHN: Fours in a ditch, go once, sir, and two over.
SIR A: 'Go once', indeed – a very pretty go –
And fancy too, a heavy fall in snow!
As the Scotch gentleman says in the play,
'What wood is this before us?'
JOHN: I can't say.
SIR A: It isn't Birnam, that's as clear as light.
JOHN: Why, no, it's more like Freez'em, to my sight.
SIR A: John, we are in a pretty situation!
JOHN: I'm out completely in my calculation.
SIR A: Fate seems determined, John, to use me queerly,
The chaise is broken all to shivers nearly.
JOHN: I shouldn't mind the shivering of the shay,
If we could keep from shivering here all day.

---

cold without: 'spirits mixed with cold water without sugar' (Partridge).

SIR A: Is there no friendly power to shield or spare
A knight and alderman who's been Lord Mayor.
Protecting Genius, to my rescue fly.
JOHN: Law! you've no more a genius, sir, than I.
SIR A: The deuce I haven't. See, my prayer is heard
By some kind spirit – never mind the word.
(*Scene gradually changes, the snow melting from the trees, and the forest opening and showing a beautiful garden with a magnificent castle in the background.*)
The sky is clearing, it has left off snowing –
The wood is 'all a growing, all a blowing';
And yonder I behold a castle fair,
Such as I've built too often in the air.
JOHN: Oh, Bonnycastle! Sir, I ask your pardon,
Your genius has cast up a lovely garden,
With beds of roses, and with bowers of myrtle,
Where the fond turtle –
SIR A: Oh, don't mention turtle!
I'm famished, and would give I know not what,
For a good quart from Birch's, smoking hot.
(*A table rises, with a basin of soup on it.*)
Amazement! at my wish a basin see!
JOHN: Oh, master, wish again a pint for me!
(*A smaller basin appears on the table.*)
SIR A: 'Tis there!
JOHN: Now was't because I wished, or you?
Perhaps I've got a little genius, too;
I'll try – a nice French roll, sir, if you please;
(*A basket with bread rises.*)
Now that I call getting one's bread with ease,
And that's what geniuses don't often do.
SIR A: This is the best bred one I ever knew.
Delicious soup!
JOHN: I say, good master mine,
Suppose we both wish for a little wine.
SIR A: With all my heart.
JOHN: What shall it be? Champagne?
SIR A: Stop! punch with turtle – punch à la Romaine.
(*The punch rises; they drink.*)
Perfect!
JOHN: I should say quite. Some more to eat?

Bonnycastle: punning reference to John Bonnycastle (1750?–1821), teacher and author of books on elementary mathematics.
Birch's: a grocery shop in St John Street, Clerkenwell, patronised by city gentlemen.
punch à la Romaine: a cold punch made with champagne or dry white wine, sugar, orange and lemon juice, egg whites and rum.

SIR A: A slice of venison now would be a treat.

(*The soup is replaced by a silver dish, with a lamp under it, and filled with hashed venison.*)

A better hash ne'er smoked upon a table.

JOHN: If this were told they'd count it a mere fable.

SIR A: Now if you'd fancy some superior sherry?

JOHN: Bless you, I do.

(*A decanter replaces the punch*; SIR ALDGATE *drinks.*)

Is it superior?

SIR A: (*setting down his glass*) Very! (*Rises.*)

John, I feel all the better for my lunch.

JOHN: My head is none the better for that punch.

SIR A: Come, let us try if we can find our way.

JOHN: D'ye think, sir, there is anything to pay?

SIR A: I don't know, but I won't wish for the bill.

JOHN: No, don't; the gentleman might take it ill.

Which is the way out? I can't tell, can you?

My eyes are multiplying all by two.

SIR A: I say, John, Beauty asked me for a rose;

I'll take her one of these.

JOHN: Yes, do.

SIR A: Here goes.

Duet – SIR ALDGATE *and* JOHN – *'I know a bank'*

I see a bank whereon a fine one blows;
It can't be wrong to pluck it, I suppose;
When 'tis by Beauty seen, if we get home tonight,
So fond of flowers, she'll dance, sir, with delight.

(SIR ALDGATE *gathers a rose; thunder, lightning, etc.*)

(*Enter the* BEAST *with an enormous club.*)

Air and Chorus – 'Garde à vous' – 'La Fiancée'

BEAST: Tremble you! tremble you!
Who dare to pluck my roses,
I'll tear ye limb from limb, and with your bones the churchyard strew.
Tremble you! tremble you! tremble you!
On turtle soup and punch, rogues,
You've made a hearty lunch, rogues,
Now I will lunch on you, lunch on you, lunch on you.

CHORUS: (*behind the scenes*) On turtle soup, etc.

BEAST: Is this your gratitude for lunching gratis?
Trespass on my preserves! *Ohe jam satis*!
But I will have your bones ground into dust,
And make a pie of you with your own crust.

SIR A: Mercy, great king of clubs! one moment pause.

La Fiancée: Auber's opera performed (with a libretto by Planché, as *The National Guard*) at Drury Lane in 1830.

Ohe jam satis!: Is that not enough?

BEAST: Well, take a rule, then, rascals, to show cause,
Why I should not beat with this oaken plant,
The brains of both out –
JOHN: Brains from one you can't.
SIR A: Pity the sorrows of a poor old Pump,
Whose trembling knees against each other thump,
And listen, with a kind attentive ear,
While he explains what now seems rather queer.

Air – SIR ALDGATE – *'Under the Rose'* – *'Love in a Village'*

Great sir, don't fly out, for a trifle like this,
What harm have I done, sir? one rose you can't miss.
Don't make, if you please, sir, so fierce a grimace,
You'd have done the same thing, had you been in my place.
I'm a family man, sir; fair daughters I've three.
There's one they call Beauty, because she's like me;
Her pleading resistless what heart could oppose, –
'Papa', said the pretty girl, 'bring me a rose.'

BEAST: I don't believe a word of this affair.
SIR A: As I'm an alderman, and have been Mayor,
You may depend on the account, I give.
JOHN: As I'm a liveryman, who hopes to live,
If you examine his account, you'll find it
Correct.
BEAST: Your promise, then, and oath to bind it,
That you will bring that daughter here to die
Instead of you –
SIR A: To die! Oh, my!
JOHN: Oh, cry!
BEAST: Come, make your mind up quickly, you or she?
Decide! It's immaterial quite to me.
SIR A: My lord! –
BEAST: I'm not a lord, sir; I'm a beast.
SIR A: You wouldn't have us call you one, at least?
BEAST: I would – I like the truth – I'm a plain creature.
JOHN: The plainest that I ever saw, in feature.
BEAST: Is it a bargain? Speak, I wait to strike it.
SIR A: I'll go and ask my daughter if she'd like it.
BEAST: Of course, man, that's exactly what I meant;
I wouldn't eat her without her consent.
SIR A: If *I* object, then, sir, you won't eat me?
BEAST: Oh! that's another matter quite, you see!
Come, swear you will return in either case.
SIR A: I do!

Love in a Village: opera by Thomas Arne and others, with text by Isaac Bickerstaffe, performed at Covent Garden in 1762.

BEAST: By what?
SIR A: The city sword and mace!
BEAST: 'Tis well; away! I shall expect you back
In half-an-hour –
SIR A: In half-an-hour! Good lack!
How far are we from home?
BEAST: Four leagues and more,
But here's an omnibus goes past your door,
And only stops to take up and set down.
(*A car on which is written 'Time flies, No stoppages', with a* ZEPHYR *for a driver, and another for a* CAD, *appears at the back of the stage.*)
CAD: Now, sir, Bank! City! Bank! Going up to town?
SIR A: (*getting in, followed by* JOHN) Pump's Folly, Brixton.
BEAST: With the speed of light!
(*to* CAD)
In half-an-hour? (*to* SIR ALDGATE)
SIR A: Certainly!
CAD: All right!
(*They fly off. Exit* BEAST.)

SCENE 4. *Interior of Cottage (as before). Enter* DRESSALINDA, MARRYGOLDA *and* BEAUTY.

Air – MARRYGOLDA – *''Tis really very strange'*
'Tis really very strange.
But people say, on 'Change,
That some ill-natured folks
Have dared papa to hoax,
And that in Plymouth Sound
No 'Polly's to be found.
'Tis really very strange,
But that's the news on 'Change.
They also say, on 'Change,
What's even still more strange,
That Beauty's above par;
And we at discount are!
Now if this should be true,
Oh dear, what shall we do?
'Tis really very strange,
But that's the news on 'Change.

DRES: Hark! there's the gate bell! why, who can it be?
MAR: Beauty! how now? why don't you run and see?
BEAU: I'm going, sister. (*Exit*.)
DRES: Going! – stir, then, stir!
She really wants a maid to wait on her.

CAD: 'omnibus conductor' (*OED*).

MAR: What has she done today?
DRES: Her work – no more.
MAR: The lazy hussy!
(*Re-enter* BEAUTY.)
DRES: Well, who's at the door?
BEAU: My father! in his habit as he started.
MAR: Can it be possible?
DRES: The dear departed!
(*Enter* SIR ALDGATE *and* JOHN QUILL.)
MAR: Returned so soon!
JOHN: Returned, like a bad penny.
DRES: You've got my shawl?
SIR A: No, for I've not seen any.
MAR: The money, sir, for me, at least, you've brought.
SIR A: I've seen no money –
JOHN: Dot and carry nought.
DRES: No shawl!
MAR: No money! what a horrid bore.
SIR A: I've brought a rose for Beauty – nothing more.
BEAU: Oh, thanks! I hope it has not cost you dear?
SIR A: Only my life, my love.
BEAU: What's this I hear?
SIR A: 'Forlorn, deserted, melancholy, slow',
(For we'd been overturned, love, in the snow)
We wandered, like two large babes in the wood,
Except that no cock robins brought us food,
When, lo, a splendid mansion rose to sight,
Which, talk of Robins, George alone could write
A true description of – Meand'ring streams,
Perennial bowers that mocked the poets' dreams;
Surpassing all that e'er that great magician
'Submitted' yet 'to public competition!'
Nor was the eye alone allowed to feed,
Turtle and punch were furnished us with speed.
Nothing to pay – Turtle without a bill,
And Punch that made a Judy of John Quill.
John, tell the rest, for out I cannot bring it.
JOHN: I haven't heart to say it, sir.
BEAU: Then sing it.
JOHN: I'll try – perhaps the air may do you good.
BEAU: I shouldn't wonder really if it would.
Air – JOHN QUILL – *'I have plucked the fairest flower'*
He thought of Beauty's flower,
And he popp'd into a bower,

Robins, George: an auctioneer of Covent Garden, notorious for grandiloquent descriptions of the properties he *submitted to public competition*.

And he pluck'd the fairest rose
That he found beneath his nose;
But scarce had he done so,
When a monster, black as crow,
Like an arrow from a bow,
Flew out and cried, 'Holloa!
Here's a very pretty go, a very pretty go,
You rascals, Oh!
You have spoiled my flower-show,
And to pot you both shall go
In a squab pie, oh!'

Then we fell upon our knees,
And we said, 'Sir, if you please,
We did *not* mean to offend,
'Twas to please a lady friend.'
On which he answered 'Oh!
If indeed the truth be so,
You'll be good enough to go,
And just let that lady know
She must pay for Pump and Co.,
Pay for Pump and Co.'
'Twas a horrid blow,
And it made us very low,
And we've come to let you know,
With a sad heigho!

BEAU: The horrid brute!
MAR: How could you be so silly?
DRES: What was he like?
JOHN: The Black Bear, Piccadilly.
SIR A: (*to* BEAUTY) To cut my story short, or you, or I
Must for the brute be made into squab pie.
BEAU: Oh horror! make a squab pie of my father!
I'd rather – oh, I don't know what I'd rather.
MAR: I hope, Miss Beauty, you are satisfied.
DRES: Your rose has proved a nice thorn in your side.
MAR: Our father's death will lie, miss, at your door.
BEAU: Never! I'll die a hundred deaths before.
SIR A: My noble child!
JOHN: The very Queen of Trumps!
SIR A: Oh fate! come to the succour of the Pumps!
Let not the flower of our ancient race
Be made into a pie before my face.

Black Bear: an inn sign which stood near the Albany in Piccadilly.

JOHN: 'Time flies!' – you told the omnibus to call
As it went back.
DRES: This time *do* get my shawl.
MAR: And if you can but bring me fifty pounds,
Or only five-and-twenty, sir –
SIR A: Odd zounds!
Is this a time about such trash to tease,
When your poor sister –
(*Enter* CAD.)
CAD: Now, sir, if you please.
BEAU: Farewell, dear sisters, I forgive you both.
Go, father.
SIR A: And fare worse – oh, cruel oath!
JOHN: Don't cast up hope, dear master, fate may save her
And strike a balance yet, sir, in our favour.
Quintette – 'Mild as the Moonbeams' – 'Artaxerxes'
To death, per omnibus, poor Beauty goes,
And all because her pa just plucked a rose.
Mild as the moon, when a cream-cheese she resembles,
And sweet as sugar-plums, Birch's best.

SCENE 5. *Saloon in the Palace of the* BEAST. *A banquet set out. Enter* BEAST.
BEAST: Gallop apace, ye fiery-footed steeds.
Oh, if this little scheme of mine succeeds,
The smile of Beauty will the spell destroy,
And I shall jump out of my skin with joy!
Air – 'My love is like a red, red rose'
I sent my love a red, red rose,
And hoped she would come soon.
She can't be long now, I suppose,
For, by my watch, 'tis noon.
Oh, haste and try, my bonny lass,
In love with me to fall,
And you may find 'twill come to pass,
I'm not a beast at all, my dear,
I'm not a beast at all.

I know I look a fright, my dear,
But yet my hopes are high;
There's many a girl has loved, my dear,
A greater brute than I.
Say but you'll wed me, sweet Miss Pump,
And to my own fair isle,

Artaxerxes: opera by Arne, performed at Covent Garden in 1762.

Out of my skin, for joy I'll jump,
At least ten thousand mile, my dear,
At least ten thousand mile.

She comes! be still, my heart – yes, she is there,
And something like a beauty, I declare.
Let me retire, nor shock, at first, her sight;
But minister, unseen, to her delight. (*Retires.*)
(*Enter* SIR ALDGATE, BEAUTY *and* JOHN QUILL.)
SIR A: Well, here we are.
BEAU: It is a lovely place
To live in.
JOHN: Yes, but that's another case –
You've come to die.
BEAU: That makes it rather duller.
SIR A: A horse, my dear, of quite another colour.
JOHN: There's dinner ready; take a mouthful, will you?
SIR A: They'd fatten you, it seems, before they kill you.
BEAU: The thought quite takes my appetite away.
JOHN: Master, you'll pick a morsel? do, sir, pray.
SIR A: I couldn't touch a bit, 'twould make me ill;
There isn't any turtle, is there, Quill?
JOHN: Plenty, both calipash and calipee.
SIR A: Indeed! Well, if I must, I must.
BEAU: Ah me!
I'm getting nervous. (*noise within*) Ugh! what's that?
JOHN: The Beast –
The – the – that is – the founder of the feast.
(*Enter* BEAST.)
BEAST: Madam, you're welcome; won't you take a seat?
BEAU: I come, sir, to be eaten, not to eat.
BEAST: And come you, madam, of your own accord?
Answer me truly.
BEAU: Yes, indeed, my lord.
BEAST: Don't call me lord, I beg. I told your father
My title is 'The Beast'.
BEAU: Well, if you'd rather –
BEAST: But now to business. I'm o'erjoyed to know
You came here willingly. Pump, you may go!
Concerted Piece – 'Begone, dull Care'
BEAST: Begone, old Pump,
I prithee begone from me;
Begone, old Pump,
Thy face let me no more see;
Thy daughter who is tarrying here,

---

calipash and calipee: parts of the turtle esteemed as delicacies.

Instead of thee I'll kill;
So begone, old Pump,
And take with thee young John Quill.
SIR A: When Lord Mayor,
Had anyone dared to say
Half that, there
Would have been the deuce to pay;
But, alas, they snap their fingers now
At Sir Aldgate Pump and say,
Ex-Lord Mayor,
Like a dog, you've had your day.
(*Exeunt* SIR ALDGATE *and* JOHN QUILL.)
BEAST: Now, madam, we're alone, dismiss your fear,
I trust to make you very happy here;
Although I feel that I could eat you up,
I'd rather *with* you breakfast, dine and sup,
If you'll permit me, but I won't intrude;
You'll find, I hope, my outside only rude;
I beg you'll make yourself at home completely.
BEAU: I never thought a beast could speak so sweetly!
BEAST: You find me very hideous, I'm afraid.
BEAU: Why, I –
BEAST: Oh, speak out, call a spade a spade!
I like to hear the truth, whate'er it be.
BEAU: Indeed! Oh there, then, we shall both agree!
BEAST: Did you e'er see aught like me?
BEAU: Yes, the what-d'ye-call
They once had at the Surrey Zoological.
BEAST: The what-d'ye-call! and *was* that like me?
BEAU: Very.
A great baboon – they called him 'Happy Jerry!'
BEAST: Were I *your* 'Jerry', I *should* 'happy' be.
Oh! could I fancy you could fancy me.
BEAU: *My* Jerry! nay, in that light, truth to speak,
There's more of 'Bruin' in your looks than 'Sneak'.
BEAST: This candour's quite enchanting! Matchless fair,
'Your eyes are loadstars, and your tongue's sweet air
More tuneable than lark to shepherd's ear';
Allow me to take wine with you.
BEAU: Oh dear!

Surrey Zoological: zoological gardens in south London, established by Edward Gross in 1831 and renowned for flower shows, firework displays and spectacular entertainments, as well as an exotic menagerie.
Bruin: the bear in *Reynard the Fox* and the conventional representation in Western Europe for Russia.
Sneak: Jerry Sneak, the henpecked husband in Samuel Foote's farce, *The Mayor of Garratt*, produced at the Haymarket in 1763.

Air – BEAST – *'Drink to me only'*
Drink to me only with your eyes,
If you object to wine;
But if you'll taste this claret cup,
I think you'll own 'tis fine.
But drink to me only with your eyes,
If you object to wine.

BEAST: 'Tis late, and you need rest – I will retire;
Pray call for anything you may desire!
Behold your room.

(*Over the door of a room appear, in letters of gold, the words 'Beauty's Apartment'.*)

You'll find a wardrobe there,
With every sort of dress you'd like to wear.
Costumes from every land, North, South, West, East.

BEAU: Delightful!

BEAST: Good-night, Beauty!

BEAU: Good-night, Beast!

(*Exit* BEAST.)

Well, I declare! a very civil brute!
If manners make the man, beyond dispute
He must be one, though he don't look the part.
He seems a perfect gentleman at heart,
And one that, cruelly, no girl would e'er cut,
If he'd just shave his beard, and have his hair cut;
Come, downy sleep, a balm from thee I'll borrow,
And look at all these fine affairs tomorrow.

(BEAUTY *flings herself on the couch and falls asleep; the Hall is immediately filled with* SPIRITS OF THE ROSE *and* ZEPHYRS, *the* QUEEN OF THE ROSES *in the midst.*)

QUEEN: Beauty, you've been a good girl, and I'll see
That you're rewarded as you ought to be;
Dance round her couch, ye flowers and spirits bright,
And give her pleasant dreams and slumbers light.

(*Dance. Tableau.*)

ACT II

SCENE 1. BEAUTY*'s Boudoir in the Palace of the* BEAST. *Enter* BEAUTY, *richly attired, with a rose in her hand.*

Air – BEAUTY – *'Jim along Josey'*
Oh, Rose, as in yon garden you happened to grow,
P'rhaps, my pretty Rosey, its master you know?
He looks like a brute, but he acts like a king,
And – bless me! I scarcely know what 'tis I sing.
Oh, get along, get along, Rosey;
Oh, get along, get along, do.

Poor old papa he kindly let go,
And he hasn't ate me yet – as far as I know;
And if he should really offer, instead,
To marry me – pshaw! what put that in my head?
Go, get along, get along, Rosey,
Go, get along, get along, do.

(*Enter* BEAST.)

BEAST: Good morning, fairest Beauty; how d'ye do?
BEAU: I'm pretty well, I thank you; how are you?
BEAST: Dying for love; I couldn't sleep all night
For thinking of you.
BEAU: Oh! you're too polite.
I've had a nice nap, and such pleasant dreams;
I've got a fairy friend at court, it seems;
With loves and graces, all in flowers and wings,
She came last night, and said such pretty things.
BEAST: You feel quite happy then?
BEAU: Oh, no, not quite!
BEAST: Say, what can make you so?
BEAU: Dear Beast, a sight
Of my poor father; I'm afraid he's ill.
Will you oblige me?
BEAST: Certainly I will;
Look in that glass, my charming fair – 'Veluti
In Speculum!' – Behold him there, my Beauty.

(*Music. The glass expands, and shows the inside of the cottage, with SIR ALDGATE PUMP, JOHN QUILL, DRESSALINDA, and* MARRYGOLDA, *in a tableau vivant.*)

BEAU: Oh, dear! he's looking very sad and poorly;
Could you just let me hear his voice, sir?
BEAST: Surely.

(*Music. Waves his hand.*)

(SIR ALDGATE PUMP *sings without.*)

Oh! where, and oh! where, is my darling Beauty gone?
She's gone to fight the French, for King George upon his throne!
And it's oh! in my heart, I wish she was safe at home.

(*Tableau closes.*)

BEAU: His mind seems wand'ring!
BEAST: What he calls his mind.
BEAU: Well, if not very wise, he's very kind,
And loves me dearly. Let me go, I pray,
And comfort him –
BEAST: How?
BEAU: Just to spend the day;
I will return ere Sol sinks in the deep.
BEAST: I dare say. Catch a weasel fast asleep.

'*Veluti in Speculum*': as if into a mirror.
Catch a weasel: you can't deceive me.

BEAU: You doubt my word! I thought you more gallant.
BEAST: Ask for aught else; but that I cannot grant.
BEAU: Then you don't love me, as you say you do.
BEAST: Not love you! Oh, my wig and whiskers! who
E'er loved so well as I –
BEAU: There's no believing
You brutes of men, – you're always so deceiving.
BEAST: (*aside*) I *am* a beast indeed, to make her cry;
Who pipes so sweet should never pipe her eye.
BEAU: My pa will die, and you will be the cause;
My fate is in your hands.
BEAST: Ah!
(*He looks at her and remains silent.*)
BEAU: (*looking at his hands*) Awful pause!
BEAST: You won't come back again – I know you won't.
BEAU: I wish I may be shot, then, if I don't.
BEAST: You'll be the death of me, mind, if you stay
One moment after sunset –
BEAU: Trust me, pray!
BEAST: Upon your mercy, then, myself I fling,
And so, to prove my love, behold this ring!
Don't start – it's not a wedding one –
BEAU: I vow
You make me feel – I – really – don't know how.
BEAST: The moment that this ring your finger's fixed on,
Hey, presto, pass, you'll find yourself at Brixton!
And vice versa – pull it off – you'll be
As quick as thought – at home, love, to a tea.
BEAU: Oh, give it me – I long its power to try.
BEAST: One chaste embrace before you say good-bye!
Duet – 'Tancredi'
BEAU: Embrace you? oh dear no!
BEAST: Ah, say, aren't you content to pare, here, my heart, pray, to the core?
Remember, I do this to please you, all else is naught to me now.
BEAU: Well, to appease you, though 'tis strange, I'll not say no.
(*He embraces her.*)
BEAST: Oh! say you'll marry me, I
Can't bear it any more;
Say 'yes', and all men shall see I
Can, for you, the world throw o'er.
BEAU: I'll tell you some other day,
When I come back, not before;
Don't press me now, dear sir, I pray,
I tremble, oh! dear me, all o'er.

---

pipe her eye: weep (Partridge).
'Tancredi': opera by Rossini, performed in London in 1820.

No, no, not now, I tremble, oh dear me, all o'er,
Let me go now, sir – to Brixton, to Brixton.
BEAST: To Brixton, to Brixton.
BOTH: { The ring but once fixed on } You find yourself there. / I find myself there.
BEAST: Go, then, away, now, to see thy father.
BOTH: Spite o' the distance { you'll / I'll } soon trip it o'er,
The ring will { lead her / lead me } to Brixton { speed her, / speed me,
And in a jiffy { she'll / I'll } be at the door.
(BEAUTY *puts on the ring. Exit* BEAST.)

SCENE 2. *Sudden change to the Cottage (as before).*
BEAU: This beats the railroad out and out, I vow.
This *is* a way to ring the changes now.
Here come my sisters – how surprised they'll be.
(*Enter* DRESSALINDA, MARRYGOLDA, *and* JOHN QUILL.)
ALL: (*scream*) Oh!
DRES: Mercy on us!
MAR: What is this we see?
BEAU: Dear sisters, don't you know me?
ALL: Oh! a ghost!
BEAU: No, no! No spirit from the Stygian coast –
I am your real flesh and blood relation –
So pray subdue this needless consternation!
DRES: / MAR: } Beauty alive!
JOHN: Fate up again has cast her,
And made all right. Here, master! master! master! (*Runs out.*)
MAR: I'm all amazement! how did this befall?
Hasn't the Beast, then, ate you after all?
DRES: Has he consented back his prey to render?
Were you too tough, or has he been too tender?
BEAU: Where is my father? let me calm his fears,
And then I'll tell you all about it, dears.
MAR: He was half crazy – now he'll be quite wild.
(*Enter* SIR ALDGATE *and* JOHN QUILL.)
SIR A: Where is my poppet – where's my precious child?
JOHN: There she is, 'all alive, oh!' like the eels!
SIR A: Oh, who can tell what a fond father feels,
When –

---

like the eels: eels, a favourite fish of Londoners, were sold in the streets by costermongers with cries of 'all alive, oh!'

DRES: La, papa, pray don't be so pathetic,
To me such stuff is worse than an emetic.
SIR A: Well, anything, child, for a quiet life.
MAR: Come, tell us all – are you the monster's wife?
Or is he dead, and left you his sole heiress?
DRES: You're drest as fine as any Lady Mayoress!
BEAU: I am not married – and he isn't dead.
SIR A: But from the monster have you naught to dread?
BEAU: If he kills me, 'twill be with kindness merely –
He's all attention – vows he loves me dearly –
Would marry me tomorrow, if I chose,
And gives me everything you can suppose.
MAR: He's rich?
BEAU: As Croesus.
SIR A: Croesus? Oh! I know,
He was Lord Mayor of Greece, some time ago.
DRES: And wears fine robes?
BEAU: A bear skin –
DRES: }
MAR: } How improper!
JOHN: A B,E,A,R, – Bear-skin – a rough wrapper –
A sort of pilot-coat.
BEAU: Just so – but here
I've brought you what you wished for, sisters dear;
There is your shawl, and there your hundred guineas.
BOTH: Oh, thank you!
DRES: (*aside*) Sister, we've been two great ninnies!
If you or I had volunteered to go,
We should have had all this good luck, you know.
MAR: (*aside*) To mar her triumph let us yet endeavour,
I hate the odious creature worse than ever.
SIR A: The fellow lives in fine style, I must say –
Turtle for dinner, no doubt, every day.
Gad, if I thought he'd hold his horrid jaw,
I shouldn't much mind being papa-in-law –
That's if you'd have him, child, not else, I vow.
BEAU: But as your ship's come home, you're wealthy now.
SIR A: Oh, no! 'twas all a hoax about the 'Polly.'
No matter, you're alive, so let's be jolly!
You are *my* treasure, as my Lady Crackeye
Said once –
BEAU: You mean the mother of the Gracchi.

---

pilot-coat: 'stout, short overcoat' (*OED*).
mother of the Gracchi: Cornelia, mother of the Roman tribunes Tiberius and Gaius Gracchus. Legend has it that, when asked one day to display her jewels, she summoned her two sons.

SIR A: Crackeye or Grackeye, it's all one. Let's see
What *we've* for dinner –
BEAU: I go back to tea,
Remember that!
SIR A: Go back?
JOHN: Not come to stay?
BEAU: Oh, no, I only come to spend the day:
I must return ere sunset, or the Beast
Will ne'er forgive me.
DRES: (*aside to* MARRYGOLDA) There's one chance, at least.
We'll try and make her overstay the hour.
And then the Beast will surely her devour!
SIR A: Come all, then, let's be merry while we can.
JOHN: If you're for fun, you know, sir, I'm your man.

Glee – SIR ALDGATE, JOHN QUILL, BEAUTY, DRESSALINDA, *and* MARRYGOLDA – *'Come stain your cheeks'*.

Come o'er a glass of good brown sherry,
Let's while we can be very merry.
LADIES: Pray don't get tipsy.
SIR A: }
JOHN: } Only merry.

(*Exeunt* SIR ALDGATE, JOHN QUILL, *and* BEAUTY.)

DRES: Press her to take some negus – then you brew it,
And pop a little poppy juice into it.
MAR: I take your hint – I'll dose her, never doubt it. (*Exit.*)
DRES: What fun! She'll make a precious fuss about it.

Air – *'On the Banks of Allan Water'*

By a glass of wine and water,
Made quite soporifical,
Soon our father's fine pet daughter,
Fast asleep shall fall;
And the Beast, who had besought her,
To return in time for tea,
When re-appearing, thus has caught her,
Breakfast will on she.

(*Re-enter* MARRYGOLDA.)

MAR: I've done the deed, and hither comes the gipsy.
DRES: Where's father?
MAR: He and John have got quite tipsy.
DRES: The sun is setting now – as red as brick.
MAR: Don't let her see it! Draw the curtains quick!

(*Re-enter* BEAUTY.)

BEAU: Sister, I feel so sleepy, you can't think.
MAR: (*aside*) It works! it works! (*Exit.*)
DRES: (*aside*) 'The drink, Hamlet, the drink!'
BEAU: How goes the time?
DRES: Oh, it's quite early yet;

We'll tell you when the sun's about to set,
So if you'd like to take a nap –
BEAU: Methinks
I'd give the world for only forty winks.
DRES: Then why not take them in that easy chair?
BEAU: If I was sure you'd wake me –
DRES: We'll take care.
BEAU: No, no, I'll drive this drowsiness away.
DRES: At any rate, sit down, dear, while you stay.
BEAU: I'm sure 'tis time – I must be going – going – (*Falls asleep.*)
DRES: You're gone, my dear, and see, the west is glowing
With the last rays of sunset – sleep, sleep sound;
I'd not disturb you for a hundred pound! (*Exit.*)

(*The scene opens at the back and the* BEAST *appears.*)

Air – BEAST – *'All is lost now' – 'Sonnambula'*

All is lost now – Oh, for me the sun is set for ever –
This poor heart in future never
One hope of bliss can see.
Go, ungrateful.
Counted on your word I had, miss,
Your behaviour's very bad, miss,
It has made me nearly mad, miss,
Quite unhappy, as you may see.
With all confidence appealing,
To any man of feeling,
I'd ask, is this fair dealing?
No! you've used me, madam, really very ill.
Though my looks might fail to charm you,
Though they rather might alarm you,
Yet I promis'd not to harm you;
Yes, false one, yes; and I'll keep my promise still.

(*The scene closes*; BEAUTY *seems exceedingly disturbed in her sleep. Enter* JOHN *and* SIR ALDGATE, *both tipsy*, JOHN *carrying a candle.*)

SIR A: John, take care how you go; you'll drop that candle.
JOHN: Never you mind, old Pump! here, where's your handle?
SIR A: John, is this language to a late Lord Mayor?
Where is my Beauty?
JOHN: (*Holds the candle to him.*) You may well ask 'where?'.
Not in your face, – it's ugly as a nigger's;
Nor in your form, if I'm a judge of figures!
SIR A: John! I discharge you.
JOHN: What! subtract your brains?
Take me from you, and, prithee, what remains?
A dry old pump!

Sonnambula: opera by Bellini, performed at His Majesty's in 1831.

SIR A: Well, well, you'll change this tone!
JOHN: 'Well –' Pump, be quiet, and let well alone;
If you don't know when you've got a good man,
I know when I've got a good master!
(*Music, con sordini.* BEAUTY *rises in her sleep, and stands up in the chair.*)
SIR A: (*starting*) Can
I trust my sight – back, John, at distance keep,
Here's Beauty, bolt upright, and in her sleep!
JOHN: Perhaps she's dead, and that's her ghost that's walking!
SIR A: Horrible thought! No! hush! I hear her talking!
(BEAUTY *descends from the chair in imitation of* AMINA *in the 'Sonnambula'. The* TWO SISTERS *enter, and are stopped by a sign from* SIR ALDGATE.)
Concerted Piece – 'Sonnambula'
ALL: Bless us, and save us, where is she going now?
(BEAUTY *steps from the chair upon the table.*)
Over the table. (*She kicks a book off.*) Oh, criky!
She'll tumble, by jingo!
(BEAUTY *steps off to another chair, and then to a stool, and then to the ground.*)
No, no; she's all right.
(BEAUTY *approaches the front of the stage.*)
BEAU: Don't cry, Beast; I'll come back.
SIR A: D'ye hear that, John?
BEAU: 'Tis tea time; Molly, put the kettle on.
ALL: Hear her! how she's dreaming, – speaking of tea.
BEAU: Yes, I have lost him; and yet I am not guilty.
ALL: Oh, listen!
BEAU: The ring he gave me, alas! he'll now take from me.
He'll never let me come out to tea more.
ALL: She wakes!
BEAU: Where am I? Arn't it very late?
I've overslept myself, as sure as fate.
It's dark as pitch! Oh, dear! what's to be done?
There's nothing left me but to cut and run.
SIR A: Dear daughter –
BEAU: Don't detain me, sir, good-bye
To all – off goes my ring, and off go I!
(*She pulls her ring from her finger.* SIR ALDGATE, JOHN, DRESSALINDA, *and* MARRYGOLDA, *sink through the stage as the scene changes and leaves* BEAUTY *in the centre of –*)

SCENE 3. *A Grotto in the Gardens of the* BEAST*'s Palace. Moonlight.*
BEAU: Bless me, I don't know where on earth I've got to.
Oh, yonder is the palace, this the grotto.
But where's its master, good as he is grim?

Oh, I've forgotten to remember him,
He'll say – Where are you, Beast, come out to play,
The moon is shining here as bright as day;
Come with a hoop, if you won't with a call!
(*The* LEADER *plays a note or two on his violin.*)
'That strain again, it had a dying fall',
And mocked his voice, sweet as a special pleader's.
(LEADER *taps on his desk.*)
Was that his tap? No, it was but the Leader's;
Oh, Mr Hughes! can you my doubts dispel,
And tell me he is safe, – and that all's well?

Duet – BEAUTY *and the* LEADER – *'All's Well'*
Deserted by his Beauty bright,
Who promised to be back by night,
The Beast who saw his hope a wreck,
Has broke his heart, or else his neck.
And though a voice salutes { her / my } ear
'Tis not the one { she / I } used (Hughes'd) to hear.

BEAU: Where is he? Leader, quickly tell;
Above –
LEAD: Below –
BEAU: All right? –
BOTH: All's well.
BEAU: It's very kind of you my heart to cheer,
But till I find him all's not well, I fear! (*Ascends the stage and sees the* BEAST *lying motionless on a piece of rock in the Grotto.*)
O Gemini! what's here! Who's this I see,
Stretched in a state of funeral bier! 'Tis he!
Alas! though I broke mine, he's kept his word,
His must have been the dying fall I heard!
He gave me up – perhaps drank poisoned tea!
And perished – all along of love for me!
Oh, now, indeed, I feel, as 'tis my duty,
That I have been the Beast, and he the Beauty!
Oh, were he but alive again – to pop
The question, I would have him in a –
(*The* QUEEN OF THE ROSES *appears.*)
QUEEN: Stop!
Is it a bargain? Would you really wed
The Beast, if I could prove he wasn't dead?
BEAU: The lady that I saw once in my sleep?

Mr Hughes: leader of the Covent Garden orchestra in 1841, who possessed a good baritone voice.

QUEEN: Precisely. Beauty, will you this time keep
Your word, and wed the poor Beast that lies by me,
If I revive him?
BEAU: Will I? just you try me.
QUEEN: Enough! Behold him in his native land,
A prince – and yet your servant to command!

(*The* BEAST *disappears as the scene changes, and discovers* PRINCE AZOR *upon his throne, surrounded by a brilliant Court, Guards, Banners, etc. The* PRINCE *descends and kneels to* BEAUTY.)

BEAU: What! can this be the Beast?
QUEEN: Why this surprise?
'Tis love hath so improved him in your eyes!
Where the mind's noble, and the heart sincere,
Defects of person quickly disappear;
While vice, to those who have been taught to hate her,
Would make, as soon, Hyperion seem a Satyr.

Finale – Chorus – 'Cinderella'

In light tripping measure,
Surrounded by pleasure,
We now to our own rosy bowers will fly,
Which care and sorrow dare not come nigh.

Tableau – Curtain.

Cinderella: presumably Rossini's opera *La Cenerentola*, performed at His Majesty's in 1820.

FORTUNIO AND HIS SEVEN GIFTED SERVANTS

A fairy extravaganza in two acts

First performed at the Theatre Royal, Drury Lane, on Monday, 17 April 1843, with the following cast:

BARON DUNOVER, *a nobleman in difficulties*	Mr Morris Barnett
HON. MISS PERTINA, *his eldest daughter*	Mrs Newcombe
HON. MISS FLIRTINA, *his second daughter*	Miss Ellis
HON. MISS MYRTINA, *his youngest daughter, assuming the name and arms of* FORTUNIO *by Royal Fairy Licence*	Miss P. Horton
HERALD	Mr S. Jones
THE FAIRY FAVOURABLE, *Elfin Queen and Lady Patroness*	Mrs Serle
MONS. BUMBLE, *a Wood Bee Colinet, conductor of the band*	Master Buzby
COMRADE, *a learned horse*	A real Arabian
STRONGBACK	Mr Howell
LIGHTFOOT	Mr C. J. Smith
MARKSMAN	Mr Bender
FINE-EAR	Mr Hance
BOISTERER	Mr Mellon
GORMAND	Mr T. Matthews
TIPPLE	Mr Yarnold
KING ALFOURITE, *surnamed 'The Amiable', a perfect specimen of the 'suaviter in modo'*	Mr Hudson
PRINCESS VINDICTA, *his half-sister, 'a little more than kin – and much less than kind'*	Mrs C. Jones
PRIME MINISTER	Mr Waldron
LORD IN WAITING	Mr Gilbeigh
FLORIDA, *lady-in-waiting on the Princess*	Mrs A. Wigan
PAGE	Mr Harcourt
THE DRAGON	Mr Stilt
CITIZEN	Mr Ellis
THE EMPEROR MATAPA, *surnamed 'The Merciless', 'Cousin to the Great Bear', etc., etc., a terrible sample of the 'fortiter in re'*	Mr Selby
THE PRINCESS VOLANTE, *his daughter, a high mettled racer*	Miss Clara Webster
GRAND CHAMBERLAIN	Mr Roberts
CAPTAIN OF THE GUARD	Mr Stanton

NOBLES, GUARDS, LADIES OF THE COURT, PURSUIVANTS, TOWNSPEOPLE, FAIRIES, etc.

---

suaviter in modo . . . fortiter in re: urbanely in manner, resolutely in action.

ACT I

SCENE 1. *A Market Cross. The House and Garden of* BARON DUNOVER. HERALDS, POPULACE, BARON DUNOVER *and his three* DAUGHTERS *discovered. Grand flourish.*

HERALD: King Alfourite thus maketh proclamation –
Whereas, without the slightest provocation,
The Emperor Matapa, in two battles,
Has drubb'd our troops and stole our goods and chattels
It is decreed that forthwith every man
Who has got arms shall bear them if he can:
And if he can't, he must produce the stumpy,
And not by no manner of means look grumpy.
Turn out, or fork out – fight or pay you must!
Up with your banners, or down with your dust.
Before the throne your purse or person fling,
Within three days – unless you wish to swing!
A special edict – so 'Long live the King!'

Chorus – 'Norma'

PEOPLE: Well! if this isn't a precious go,
We should be glad what *is* to know;
Fight or be fined, unless you've a mind
Just to be hang'd for treason!
Pray, sir, excuse the liberty,
But is not this some joke?

HERALD: No!
Soon you will find it's Hobson's choice,
Brave Volunteers – you *must* enroll!
Or pay your duty to the King –
So settle which you please on.

PEOPLE: Well, I'd as soon be hang'd as fall
Fighting for *any* reason!
So to secure his capital,
We must reduce our own.

(*Exeunt* HERALD *and* POPULACE.)

BARON: What's to be done? Alas! the heavy day!
Too old to fight and much too poor to pay.
Bear arms I can't – indeed, opposed to strife,
I never could bear arms in all my life!
A tender youth, the task of drilling bored me –
A carpet knight, the least exertion floored me!

---

stumpy: money (*OED*).
dust: money, cash.
Norma: opera by Bellini, performed at His Majesty's in 1833 and (with a libretto by Planché) at Drury Lane in 1837.
carpet knight: 'stay-at-home soldier' (*OED*).

A cripple now, to Court I can't stump down,
And to stump up, I haven't half-a-crown.
I have no son my substitute to be –
My family consists of daughters three,
All grown-up girls, whose fortunes are their charms;
So I haven't e'en a child in arms!
How to 'scape hanging – hang me if I know!
MYR: My dearest father, pray don't take on so;
Meet like a man your fortune, good or ill!
Or if you can't, why then your daughter will!
PER: What! like a *man*?
MYR: Aye, sister, like a man;
The only way that help him now I can.
A coat and waistcoat I intend to sport,
And be my father's deputy at Court.
PER: You?
FLIR: You?
BARON: With gratitude I'm almost mute!
What, daughter! you become my substitute?
PER: But should they make you fight?
MYR: To fight I'm willing.
I've oft been told that I *look very* killing.
FLIR: You storm a fortress?
PER: Or besiege a town?
MYR: Before one I can easily sit down.
BARON: You mount a breach?
MYR: Oh, sir, experience teaches, –
I mean at once to mount a pair of breeches!
PER: (*aside*) So, so, – but two can play, miss, at this game.
Why should this forward chit have all the fame?
I'm quite as bold as she is, I'll be bound,
And will show legs with her for twenty pound!
FLIR: (*aside*) In male attire should I not cut a figure?
I'm taller than Myrtina – aye, and bigger!
I don't much fancy handling sword or dagger,
But I'd engage as like a man to swagger!
PER: (*aside*) To get a suit I'll pawn the table spoons! (*Exit into house*.)
FLIR: (*aside*) I'll spout the tea-pot and buy pantaloons. (*Exit into house*.)
BARON: (*to* MYRTINA) Fortune your filial piety will bless,
But what, my darling, will you do for dress?
MYR: Why, there's your old Court suit, papa, you know;
All the gold lace was stripp'd off long ago,
But still the cloth's not much the worse for wear,

---

stump up: pay up.
spout: pawn (*OED*).

And there's enough of it, and some to spare!
Grant me that suit.
BARON: Your suit *is* granted. You
Shall have my sword – that's quite as good as new,
For I have never drawn it since I bought it!
Yes – once by chance – when 'twixt my legs I caught it.
MYR: Talking of legs – you'll add your boots, of course?
BARON: Yes, and my spurs – would I could add my horse.
MYR: So of your wardrobe give me quick the key.

(BARON *gives key, and* MYRTINA *enters house and returns with the suit, which the* BARON *examines during his solo*.)

BARON: How dull without her this old house will be.

Duet – Air – 'Row gently here, my Gondolier'

BARON: When you, my dear,
Are gone, dull here
The days will seem to glide;
But let us hear,
By post, my dear,
Whate'er may you betide.
My doublet take – (*aside*) 'Tis quite as well –
The skirts are gone, I see:
For now no tails it has to tell
Of where it went with me!
MYR: Now rest thee here,
My father dear,
Hush! hush! for up I go,
To put a light
Silk pair of tight
Etcaeteras on below.
Oh, if I look, in male attire,
But half as well as he
I saw one night dance on the wire,
What an angel I shall be!

(*Exeunt into house*.)

SCENE 2. *The Fairies' Haunt. A Picturesque Glen.* FAIRIES *discovered dancing 'Le Danois Quadrille'.* A FAIRY BAND, *à la Colinet, seated on a bank, and the* QUEEN OF THE FAIRIES *attended*.

Chorus to the Quadrille, 'Le Danois'

Here in our human shape,
We pass the summer day quadrilling
Like mortals, whom we ape,
Into the fashion falling.
No more in 'Fairy Ring'
Would well-bred Fay to dance be willing;

à la Colinet: in the conventional shepherdess costume of stage pastoral.

'Grande Ronde' is now the thing –
When such a figure calling.
Here 'tis 'Pastorale',
'La Trenise', 'Finale',
All 'L'Eté',
'Tis 'Balancez',
Or 'Promenade', till Pistolet
Pops off – and off pop we –
To music thrilling,
Led by the humming bee,
Our Elfin Colinet!

FAIRY: Break off! – my fairy nose a mortal smells!
Creep into acorn-cups and cowslip-bells!
Make yourselves scarce!

(*Music.* FAIRIES *disperse and vanish into flowers, etc; one sticks fast.*)

How now, you clumsy lout!
Is that the way you pull a flower about?
A pretty fairy 'pon my word. Pray who
D'ye think's to sleep in that rose after you?
Crumpling the leaves in this untidy way! (*putting them to rights*)
Now, get you in, you naughty, naughty fay! (*beating him*)
And here – whose wing is this? Pray hold it up!
You can't be cramp'd for room sure in that cup!
I'm quite ashamed of you, I do declare!
You're not a morsel like the elves you were,
But that your dress from common habits varies,
No soul on earth could fancy you were fairies!
As I'm your Queen, by my stop watch, I've reckon'd,
You've ta'en to vanish more than half a second!
Who is't that comes? – a girl in male attire!
She needs my aid – does she deserve't? – I'll try her.

(*Music.* FAIRY QUEEN *retires behind trees. Enter* PERTINA, *in boy's clothes.*)

PER: Of Miss Myrtina I have got the start –
I feel convinced that I can play my part!
In dress and manner I am quite the beau,
No one would take me for a girl, I know!

(*Music. Trees open and discover* FAIRY QUEEN *dressed as an old Shepherdess, bending over some broken ground.*)

FAIRY: Oh, dear! oh, dear! – what shall I do? – oh dear!
PER: Heyday! – why what old beldame have we here?
FAIRY: (*Advances.*) Oh, noble sir, – for you can be no less,
Help an old woman who's in great distress.
My lamb has fallen into this ditch, and I
Can't get it out, – help me, or it will die!
PER: I help to pull a sheep out of a ditch?
D'ye take me for a butcher, you old witch!
FAIRY: I take you for a pert, hard-hearted *girl*!

Oh, you need not your false moustaches twirl!
You feign to be a man, – why, who with eyes
Could fail to see through such a poor disguise?
PER: Discover'd! – Shame! – I'll try to bluster. Zoons!
FAIRY: Oh, come – no airs – who pawned her father's spoons?
(PERTINA *shrieks and runs out.*)
Ha, ha, ha, ha! I think that was a twister!
Another step – aye – this must be a sister.
(*Music. Enter* FLIRTINA.)
FLIR: I've stolen out by the back door – what sport!
In this dress I shall cut out all the Court.
FAIRY: Alack-a-day! alack-a-day!
FLIR: How now?
What do you mean by making such a row?
FAIRY: Oh sir, my lamb has fallen into this pool,
And will be drowned!
FLIR: Well, serve you right, old fool!
Why don't you take more care?
FAIRY: (*Advances.*) Alack, good youth,
Lend me a helping hand.
FLIR: Who, *I*, forsooth?
Do I look like a clown for such work fit? (*Looks at her legs.*)
FAIRY: You look like what you are – a vain young chit,
A silly girl, as any one can see.
FLIR: (*aside*) Provoking! – can they really? It can't be!
(*aloud*) Harkey, old hag –
FAIRY: Take care what you're about.
Who put her father's tea-pot up the spout?
(FLIRTINA *shrieks and runs out.*)
Ha, ha, ha, ha! So much for t'other! – stay –
Here comes a third – let's hear what she will say.
(*Music. Enter* MYRTINA, *as* FORTUNIO.)
MYR: This is the road, I think – I hope to get
Clear of this wood before the sun shall set,
Or wicked wags will sneer, and say delighted
A would-be knight was in a wood benighted;
So let me speed.
FAIRY: O dear, what shall I do?
MYR: Hey-day, some poor old soul, in trouble too!
I can't pass on and leave her sobbing so;
What is the matter, Goody, may I know?
FAIRY: Bless thy kind heart, young man; my pretty sheep
Has fallen into the water.
MYR: Well, don't weep.
'Tis still alive; and I have little doubt,
By hook or crook, that we can get it out.
Here, lend a hand. (*a chord*)

FAIRY: (*appearing in her own shape*) I will, but it shall be
To help you, charming girl, as you would me.
Be not alarmed, I am your friend, sweet maid;
Although discovered, you are not betrayed.
I know your errand, and its motive pure,
And will assist your fortune to secure.
Of many things I see you stand in need:
A better wardrobe, and a gallant steed.
(*Stamps. Music. A leather trunk rises.*)
Lo! in this Turkey leather trunk you'll find
Cash, jewels, arms, and dresses to your mind;
You've but to stamp, wherever you may be,
And at your feet this trunk you're sure to see.
Now for a horse.
(*Waves her wand. Music. Part of the wood opens, and discovers a horse, richly caparisoned.*)
Behold one in a trice!
Perfect in all his paces, free from vice,
And warranted to carry a lady; never
In fairy land was known a horse so clever.
He knows all things, past, present, and to come,
And eats but once a week!
MYR: The poor dear dumb –
FAIRY: Dumb! – he can speak; whole sentences can say,
While common steeds can only utter 'Nay.'
Taught elocution by a necromancer,
No horse your purpose half so well could answer.
MYR: Well, I have oft heard mention of a stalking-horse,
But never till this hour of a talking horse.
Pray, may I ask what name he answers to?
FAIRY: Comrade.
MYR: Dear Comrade, tell me how d'ye do.
HORSE: I'm pretty well, I thank ye; how are you?
MYR: Charming! delightful! what articulation!
Without the slightest lisp or hesitation!
I should have thought a horse had spoken hoarser.
FAIRY: His language is not coarse, though he's a courser.
And, apropos of names, your own should be
Fortunio, since you've a friend in me.
FOR: Of proper names 'twould be the one most proper;
But who is that man yonder, with a chopper?
FAIRY: A woodman, who cuts down five hundred trees
And carries them upon his back with ease.
You'd better hire him.
FOR: Surely, if I can.

Turkey leather: leather tawed with oil.

(*Music. Enter* STRONGBACK.)

Harkye, d'ye want a porter's place, young man?
STRONG: I don't much mind. What wages, sir, give you?
FOR: Whate'er you please.
STRONG: Well, I think – that will do.
FOR: To carry messages you won't refuse?
STRONG: I'll carry anything on earth you choose.
FOR: Your name is –
STRONG: Strongback.
FOR: Strongback, you're my man.
STRONG: Your carrier pigeon or your Pickford's van.
FAIRY: Here comes another gifted fellow.
FOR: Pray,
Why has he tied his legs in that queer way?
FAIRY: Because his speed is swifter than the wind,
And when he hunts he leaves the game behind,
Unless with ribbons he his legs can fetter.
FOR: Shall I engage him?
FAIRY: Yes – you can't do better.

(*Music. Enter* LIGHTFOOT, *his legs tied with ribbons*.)

FOR: Young man, I want a running footman; say –
Will you take service?
LIGHT: Yes, and bless the day,
For I'm in great distress.
FOR: How came you so?
LIGHT: (*whispering*) Outran the constable; lived fast, you know!
FOR: Well, you shall have a quarter in advance.
LIGHT: Oh, sir, to serve you I'd run any chance.
FAIRY: Yonder's a man who may be useful, too.
FOR: Why does he bind his eyes?
FAIRY: The less to view.
His name is Marksman, and whene'er he fires,
He kills more game than any one requires;
For objects full five leagues off he can see.
FOR: Oh dear, but that may very awkward be;
I'm bound for Court, you know, and who can tell
What mischief he may make who sees so well?
FAIRY: Oh, but he never talks of what he sees;
He's *too* sharp-sighted.
FOR: Then my mind's at ease.

(*Music. Enter* MARKSMAN, *his eyes bandaged*.)

An archer blindfold – why, you must be Cupid!
MARKS: Indeed, sir, I'm not anything so stupid.
FOR: (*aside to* FAIRY) '*Sir*!' He can't see that I'm a girl, that's clear.

Pickford's: long-established firm of carriers and removers.

FAIRY: (*aside*) He can; but sees you wouldn't one appear.
FOR: Well, as your sight's so good, pray can you see
Any objection, friend, to serving me?
MARKS: (*taking bandage from eyes*) None in the least.
FOR: Then we're agreed. And now,
(*to* FAIRY) Madam, I'll make you my most grateful bow.
FAIRY: Stay! you have but three servants!
FOR: Need I more?
FAIRY: You must have seven; here come the other four,
The first, who on the ground himself is throwing,
Has ears so fine he hears what grass is growing.
FOR: He's still more dangerous, unless discreeter;
So good a watch may make a bad repeater.
FAIRY: Oh, you may trust him. There's the second, blowing
To set yon mills, full six miles off, a-going.
FOR: A famous fellow he, the wind to raise,
So often done by puffing, now-a-days.
(*Music. Enter* FINE-EAR *and* BOISTERER.)
FAIRY: The other two will make your suite complete;
One any given quantity can eat,
The other drink the sea dry, if you please.
FOR: Mercy! and ought I to engage both these?
FAIRY: You'll want them.
FOR: Well, they'll be expensive pages;
I think I'd better put them on board wages.
(*Music. Enter* GORMAND *and* TIPPLER, *and are engaged by* FORTUNIO.)
FAIRY: For each you'll find a sumptuous livery
Within this trunk.
FOR: Indeed; but where's the key?
FAIRY: In Comrade's ear you'll see a ribbon green.
FOR: (*finding it*) I've got it!
(*Opens trunk. The* SERVANTS *take out liveries and a rich dress for* FORTUNIO, *sword, jewels, etc., during chorus.*)
FAIRY: Now to Court – see and be seen!
(*Music.* FAIRIES *re-appear in all directions.*)
Chorus – 'Oberon'
Speed, mortal, speed! Seven soon will chime,
You'll just arrive in pudding time!
(*A bank on one side changes to a car, in which the* FAIRY QUEEN *ascends, and as* FORTUNIO *puts his foot in the stirrup to mount the horse, the scene closes on the tableau.*)

---

board wages: allowance made to servants to keep themselves in food (*OED*).
Oberon: opera by Weber, with original libretto by Planché, produced at Covent Garden in 1826.

SCENE 3. *Chamber in the Palace of* KING ALFOURITE. *Enter* KING, *leading the* PRINCESS, *attended by his* MINISTER, *a* LORD-IN-WAITING, *and* FLORIDA, *lady's maid to the* PRINCESS.

KING: Hang out our banners on the outward walls!
The cry is still they come.
PRIN: Yet no one calls,
Even to say they can't come.
MIN: Not a soul
Has yet appeared who will his name enroll,
Nor who will pay his money; all hang back.
PRIN: They should all hang together, in a crack.
KING: Hang all my subjects! that would be too cruel.
We must have patience.
PRIN: Yes, and water gruel,
For that 'twill come to. Neither men nor money
To carry on the war! A mighty funny
Figure you'll cut! Oh, Minister of State,
How long d'ye think a monarch ought to wait
Before he puts himself into a passion,
When he's fobbed off in this rebellious fashion?
MIN: Madam, I think his gracious Majesty
Is far too patient.
PRIN: So do I –
LORD: And I.
FLOR: And I. If I were you, my royal liege,
The very lives out of the rogues I'd squeege!
KING: That would be screwing them a deal too tight.
No, no; you're all four wrong, I'm Alfourite!
PRIN: Aye, joke, that's right, whilst ruin's o'er you hovering;
You'll change your note, sir, when they change their sovereign.
KING: Let's change the subject, if not your opinions.
PRIN: I'd hang the rebels up in strings.
FLOR: Like inions!
KING: My people are my children.
PRIN: Yes, and purely
You'll spoil them.
KING: Better than despoil them, surely.
In short, the proclamation was too strong.
PRIN: Too weak, in short, as you will find ere long.
KING: Patience, I say. Still hope I fondly nourish.
PRIN: Nothing within your realm will ever flourish. (*Trumpet without*)
KING: D'ye call that nothing? Sure, that flourished bravely.
(*Enter a* PAGE.)
Good news, or bad, that thou com'st in so gravely?

---

in a crack: instantaneously (Partridge).
Like inions!: a play on 'inion', the rear part of the head, and 'onion'.

PAGE: Fortunio, a young and noble knight,
Craves audience of the great King Alfourite.
KING: Desire the gentleman to walk upstairs.
PRIN: 'Walk up!' – such jargon showmen use at fairs.
(*to* PAGE) Let him approach.
(*Exit* PAGE.)
Consider, sir, your state.
KING: I do, and think it very bad of late.
PRIN: You're so undignified! I blush for you.
KING: Sister, you've dignity enough for two.
(*Enter* FORTUNIO, *richly attired*.)
FLOR: (*aside*) Oh, Gemini! Oh, *what* a nice young man!
(*to* PRINCESS) Look, madam.
PRIN: I am, looking through my fan.
FOR: (*kneeling*) Sire, for my father 'tis my humble wish, a
Substitute, to serve in your militia.
KING: (*raising him*) Most sensible of your polite attention.
Do you take snuff? (*offering pinch*)
FOR: (*aside*) Amazing condescension!
KING: Fine weather –
FOR: (*bowing*) Very.
KING: Have you seen the comet?
FOR: No, sire. (*aside*) But feel as if I'd just dropp'd from it.
PRIN: Oh, Florida, I'm captivated quite!
In all my days I *ne'er* saw such a knight.
FLOR: (*aside*) The finest knight that ever I did see.
If she's in love with him, good night to me.
FOR: (*aside*) I've lost my heart, as sure as anything!
I never saw a king so good-looking.
KING: (*aside*) No age could ever boast a youth so pretty;
That he is not a girl 'tis quite a pity.
If I could find a fair one half so fair,
I'd marry her tomorrow, I declare.
PRIN: Brother, I'm sure you couldn't have the heart
To see this stripling to the wars depart.
He's much too young and handsome. (*to* FORTUNIO) You shall be
Groom of the Bedchamber, Sir Knight, to me.
KING: Nay, he shall office in *my* household take,
Fortunio Lord Treasurer we make.
FOR: Lord Treasurer! for such an office, sure –
MIN: (*aside to him*) Fear not, at present 'tis a sinecure.
FOR: Ah! then indeed, if there is nought to do,
I may be quite as capable as you.
KING: Your duty you will learn in half a minute;
'Tis but to hold a purse – there's nothing in it.

---

the comet: Faye's comet of 1843 was one of particular splendour.

PRIN: You'll eat your mutton with us, sir, today,
KING: And crack a bottle in a friendly way.
FOR: I crack a bottle! Sire, I'd venture, but
I fear I couldn't without being cut;
And now-a-days, save at some public spread,
Wine's never suffered to get in one's head.
KING: No, times are changed; I think it quite provoking
That in my reign there is so little soaking!

Song – KING – *Air* – *'The days that we went gipsying'*
Oh, the days that we got tipsy in – a long time ago,
Were certainly the jolliest a man could ever know!
We drank champagne from glasses long, and hock from goblets green,
And nothing like a cup of tea was ever to be seen.
All night we passed the wine, nor dreamed of hyson or pekoe
In the days that we got tipsy in – a long time ago.

Oh, those were days of bumper toasts, or salt-and-water fine,
Broil'd bones and devil'd biscuits, three-times-three and nine-times-nine!
When underneath the table you were bound your guest to land,
And no man rose to go – till he was sure he couldn't stand!
Tea-totallers we'd none to preach 'gainst brandy or bordeaux,
In the days that we got tipsy in – a long time ago.
How changed, alas! the fashion now – to booze you've scarce begun,
When clattering comes the coffee-tray and all your drinking's done;
Or John informs the gentlemen 'he's taken up the tea';
And 'twould be voted vulgar quite if drunk a man should be.
A plague upon such sober times – I often sigh 'Heigho!'
For the days that we got tipsy in – a long time ago.

(*Exit* KING, *attended by* MINISTER *and* LORD-IN-WAITING.
PRINCESS *dismisses* FLORIDA, *and detains* FORTUNIO.)

PRIN: Stay, gentle youth, and hear a Princess own
A secret – for her breast too mighty grown!
For ten long tedious minutes have I striven
To quell the pangs by which my heart is riven;
But such prodigious efforts fail at length –
The constant struggle is beyond my strength.
I love! nor care though all the world should know it;
And, in the words of our immortal poet,
Exclaim, 'If you love me as I love you,
No knife shall cut our love in two!'
FOR: (*aside*) Pooh – pooh!
(*aloud*) Madam, respectfully I must decline.

---

soaking: heavy drinking.
hyson or pekoe: types of China tea.
'If you love me . . .': Planché seems to have taken these two lines from 'Giles Scroggins', a song popular in the early 19th century, though the rhyme was an old one, with a number of variants.

PRIN: D'ye mean to say, then, that you won't be mine?
FOR: I am too much beneath your Royal Highness.
PRIN: Madness! Despair! Yet this may be but shyness.

Duo – Air – 'Au clair de la Lune'

PRIN: Sir, you can't refuse me,
Treason it would be!
FOR: Madam, pray excuse me,
There we don't agree.
Honour you I can, but
Wed you – there's the rub!
I am not a marrying man, but
I'll name it at the club.
PRIN: (*aside*) Yield, O Love, thy crown up,
And thy hearted throne!
In this virgin bosom
Hate now reigns alone!
If all your hairs were lives,
Young Mr What-you-call,
You'll find my great revenge
Has stomach for them all!
FOR: (*aside*) If she don't grow more tender,
I 'Police' must call;
That I'm a nice young *woman*
She don't think at all.

(*together*)

(*Exeunt* PRINCESS *and* FORTUNIO.)

SCENE 4. *Court-yard of the Palace. In the centre a large basin of water with jet d'eau; the Royal Stables; the Royal Gardens. At back, terrace, with balustrade, beyond which is seen the open country; sunset. Dinner bell rings. Enter* FORTUNIO.

FOR: There's the first dinner-bell, as I'm a sinner;
I scarcely shall have time to dress for dinner.

(*Enter* CITIZENS *and* PEASANTRY, *male and female*.)

Chorus – Air – 'The Campbells are coming'

The dragon is coming! oh! oh! oh! oh!
The dragon is coming! oh! oh! oh! oh!
The dragon is coming – we really aren't humming,
The dragon is coming! oh! oh! oh! oh!
His mouth is wider than any church door,
And three miles off you may hear him roar!
The terrible glutton eats men like mutton,
And hasn't a notion when he should give o'er!
The dragon is coming! oh! oh! oh! oh!

FOR: A dragon coming! Mercy on us! When?
CIT: Most likely, sir, a little after ten;
That is about the time he likes to sup.
FOR: How pleasant! Has he eaten many up?

CIT: Whole parishes, and lick'd them clean as plates;
And all the toll-men at the turnpike gates.
His monstrous appetite's beyond belief,
Sir, he has eaten even Tariff beef.
If you have any doubts, you've but to stay!
He'll clear them all up if he comes this way.
(*Enter* KING *and* PRINCESS, *attended*.)
KING: One woe doth tread upon another's heel,
Uncommon woe distracts the public weal.
War of my subjects has destroyed the best,
And now a dragon will devour the rest!
PRIN: (*aside*) Oh, vengeance! Now's my time! (*aloud*)
No, brother, no;
Fortunio has volunteered to go
And slay this monster –
FOR: I! Well; did you ever?
Upon my word, I never, no I never!
PRIN: He is so modest, it is quite distressing;
Indeed, he only wants a little pressing.
KING: If you would be so kind, upon the nation
You would confer the greatest obligation;
And if, by any chance, I could return –
FOR: Sir, that's exactly what *I* wish to learn.
If I saw any chance of my returning,
I shouldn't so much mind –
PRIN: (*aside to* KING) For fame he's burning.
(*aloud*) We'll go to dinner whilst you do the job,
And keep some hot for you upon the hob.
KING: Thou'lt not say 'No', – thy Sovereign supplicates thee;
Go, be our champion! 'Go where glory waits thee!'
(*Music. Exeunt all but* FORTUNIO.)
FOR: Fine words, I grant, and easy ones to utter,
But such, the proverb says, 'No parsnips butter.'
Now this is all that wicked woman's doing,
Because I wouldn't listen to her wooing.
What's to be done? Why, the first thing, of course,
Take an opinion of my learned horse.
Comrade, my friend, just look out of your stable,
And answer me one question, if you're able.
(*The horse,* COMRADE, *puts his head out of the stable-door*.)
HORSE: Is it the Corn Question? Because I'm gifted
To speak on one I've seen so often sifted.

Tariff beef: foreign produce imported under the unpopular terms of Sir Robert Peel's budget of 1842.
Corn Question: the Corn Laws of 1815, a subject of much agitation in 1843, were to be repealed three years later.

FOR: No.
HORSE: I but joked, for may I draw a wagon,
If you have not been asked to kill the dragon.
FOR: You're right.
HORSE: Well, you must do it.
FOR: Cool, I vow.
Will you be kind enough to tell me *how*?
HORSE: Call Fine-Ear.
FOR: Fi –
(*Enter* FINE-EAR.)
FINE: There is no need to bawl,
I heard, sir, you were just about to call.
What can I do to serve you?
HORSE: Say how near
The dragon is.
FINE: (*listening*) As well as I can hear,
About seven leagues, and, it may be, a quarter.
HORSE: Let Tippler, then, drink up that pond of water,
And Strongback bring as much wine as will fill it,
And when the dragon's dead drunk you can kill it.
FOR: Sagacious creature! Tippler, Strongback, speed!
(*Enter* TIPPLER *and* STRONGBACK.)
BOTH: Here, master.
FOR: Your assistance much I need.
(*to* TIPPLER) Drink this pond dry.
TIP: Is that all – in a minute!
(*Goes to pond and begins to drink.*)
FOR: (*to* STRONGBACK) Bring as much wine here as you can put in it.
STRONG: Yes, sir. (*going*)
FOR: You'll want a cart.
STRONG: A cart – for what?
For such a job I'd scorn to use a knot. (*Exit.*)
TIP: There, sir – I've mopp'd that up without a wink.
FOR: What shall I give you?
TIP: What you please to drink.
(*Music. Re-enter* STRONGBACK *laden with hogsheads of wine.*)
STRONG: I think I've brought enough to fill the pond;
At all events there's no more wine in bond. (*roar without*)
FOR: Make haste, make haste, for surely by that roar,
The dragon's nearer by some leagues.
FINE: Yes – Four.
FOR: Then to our posts – he'll do the other three
In a hop, step, and jump, immediately.

---

knot: porter's knot, 'a kind of double shoulder pad, with a loop passing round the forehead', used by London market-porters (*OED*).
in bond: stored in bonded warehouses.

Quartette – FORTUNIO, STRONGBACK, TIPPLER *and* COMRADE – *Air* – *'Master Poll', 'Midas'*

FOR: Master Drag,
In spite of his brag,
We'll buffet away from the plain, sir!
STRONG: And I will fight
With all my might,
HORSE: And I with all my mane, sir!
TIP: And I'll have a rap,
Though he may snap,
And kick up a wounded racket!
FOR: I'll hack!
STRONG: I'll whack!
TIP: I'll crack!
ALL: Good lack!
How we'll pepper his scaly old jacket!
FOR: In spite of his teeth,
Above and beneath,
I'll make him his jaw to hold, sir!
And teach him to dance
At the end of my lance,
As St. George did the dragon of old, sir!
As soon as he's dead,
I'll cut off his head!
TIP: Before 'twould be rather rash, sir!
FOR: I'll dare!
TIP: I'll tear!
STRONG: I'll bear!
ALL: Oh, rare!
And I warrant we'll settle his hash, sir!

(*Melo-dramatic music. It has become night, and moonlight.* FORTUNIO *and* SERVANTS *conceal themselves. Enter the* DRAGON; *he sniffs the wine and commences drinking immediately, shows symptoms of intoxication, staggers, reels and falls.*)

HORSE: Now, master, now!

(*Enter* FORTUNIO *and his* SERVANTS *armed.*)

FOR: (*stabbing the* DRAGON) 'Dead for a ducat, dead.'

TIP: I'll tell the tale – whilst you cut off the head!

(*Exit.* FORTUNIO *cuts off the* DRAGON's *head, and sticks it on the top of his spear.*)

STRONG: (*taking up the body*) I'll bear his body – it's no load to brag on.

FOR: Mind – it's down hill.

STRONG: No fear – I've got the drag on.

Midas: burletta by Kane O'Hara, produced at the Crow Street Theatre, Dublin, in 1762 and at Covent Garden in 1764.
settle his hash: make an end of him.

(*Shouts without. Re-enter* TIPPLER, *with the rest of* FORTUNIO*'s suite*; CITIZENS, PEASANTRY, *etc., the* KING, *the* PRINCESS, NOBLES, *etc., forming a procession à la 'Masaniello'.*)

Chorus – 'Masaniello'

Come, fill to the brim every flagon,
And dance while a leg's left to wag on!
E'en Warwick's old Guy
But a coward seems nigh,
To the hero who conquer'd the dragon.

(*They pass round the stage, and* FORTUNIO *comes to a halt before the* KING.)

PRIN: (*aside*) Confusion! – conqueror! the dragon slain!
FOR: (*showing the head to the* KING) 'Thus perish all that gives Alonzo pain.'
KING: We can't find words to speak our thanks.
FOR: Then don't.
PRIN: (*aside*) I cannot bear this triumph – and I won't.
KING: Money I've none; and so may truly say,
'More is thy due than more than all can pay.'
But kings, you know, of honour are the fount,
And therfore freely honours you shall count –
Aye, though you're nine at whist! Yon monster, there,
In your own arms we give you leave to bear;
And, to prove all the gratitude we feel,
We'll pass a patent under our great seal,
Declaring, henceforth, 'tis our royal will,
That none but you shall dare a dragon kill!
PRIN: That is, indeed, a privilege most gracious!
But, brother, on a deed much more audacious
This youth is bent.
KING: Indeed – what – which – when – how?
PRIN: You'll never guess.
FOR: (*aside*) What is she after now?
PRIN: His great ambition, brother, is to go
Ambassador to our most deadly foe;
He vows, without an army or a navy,
He'll force the Emperor to cry 'Peccavi!'

Masaniello: opera by Auber, performed (in English) at Drury Lane in 1829.
Warwick's old Guy: Guy of Warwick, hero of a fourteenth-century verse romance, who among many deeds of knightly prowess at home and abroad slays a ravaging winged dragon in Northumberland and rescues King Athelstan from the Danes. The tale remained popular until the nineteenth century in chapbook and other condensed versions, and had been the subject of a Covent Garden pantomime in 1841.
'*Thus perish all . . .*': a line from Edward Young's tragedy *The Revenge* (III.i), produced at Drury Lane in 1721.
nine at whist: nine (later ten) points, with honours counting, constituted a winning score in the earliest form of the game, now known as 'long whist'.

FOR: (*aside*) Good gracious me! I go their deadly foe to!
Where does that wicked woman think *she'll* go to?
KING: Since I can give him nothing, 'tis but just
I should refuse him nothing – go he must.
FOR: But, sire –
KING: No thanks, we still shall be your debtor.
PRIN: And so the sooner you set off the better!
Finale – 'Cruda Sorte'
FOR: Is she determined to make me a martyr?
Does she suppose me Van Amburgh or Carter?
First fight a dragon, then go catch a Tartar,
Is out of the frying-pan into the fire.
KING: If to his courage he don't fall a martyr,
He may depend on the first vacant Garter!
Fight with a dragon, then go catch a Tartar!
'Tis really much more than he ought to desire.
FLOR: O Etiquette! to your laws he's a martyr,
He daren't contradict, though he knows what she's arter,
First fight a dragon, then go catch a Tartar,
Is out of the frying-pan into the fire!
CHORUS: Never was hero more handsome or smarter,
Braver he is than Van Amburgh or Carter,
First fight a dragon, then go catch a Tartar!
He certainly next will the Thames set on fire!
Tableau. End of Act I.

ACT II

SCENE 1. *Hall of Audience in the Palace of the* EMPEROR MATAPA. *Large gates. The* EMPEROR *discovered seated on his Throne, attended by his* COURT, CHAMBERLAIN, OFFICERS *and* GUARD; *the* PRINCESS VOLANTE *and her attendant* LADIES.

EMP: Daughter, we're dull– we've got the devils blue!
Dance and amuse us, as you ought to do!
(VOLANTE *dances*.)
Enough, we're sleepy – sing, and let your numbers
Wrap our imperial soul in gentle slumbers!
Chorus – 'Away with Melancholy' (only a few bars), sung discordantly, which are interrupted by EMPEROR.
EMP: Silence – odds bobs, unless you'll all be swinging.
CHAM: Great sir – you bade us sing –
EMP: D'ye call that singing?
It may be for the million! – hurly-burling!
I wouldn't hear it for a million sterling!

Cruda Sorte: aria from Rossini's *L'Italiana in Algeri*, performed at His Majesty's in 1819.
Van Amburgh or Carter: famous lion-tamers and showmen.

So peace! or by the hangman's shears bereft
You shall not have an ear for music left.
CHAM: Great sir, your servants tremble and obey.
EMP: They'd better. (*Enter* OFFICER.)
Well, what have you got to say?
OFF: Most mighty Emperor – King Alfourite –
EMP: Ha! what of him? Does he again show fight?
OFF: An envoy from his court has just arrived,
Who craves an audience.
EMP: Is the fool nine-lived,
That thus he ventures into our dominions?
CHAM: Perhaps –
EMP: Perhaps! – who asked for your opinions?
Go, hang the fellow instantly – (OFFICER *going*)
No – stay! (OFFICER *returns*.)
We fain would hear what he has got to say,
Which, if we hang him first, he cannot tell.
Let him approach! – after will do as well.
(*Music. Enter* FORTUNIO *with his seven* SERVANTS.)
Now speak, young shaver – what's the news with thee?
FOR: Thus, after greeting, speaks my King by me –
To you, who've borrow'd all his treasure –
EMP: Borrow'd!
CHAM: A strange beginning!
EMP: Don't you be so forrard!
Go on, young gentleman, you shall be heard.
Borrow'd, I think you said.
FOR: That was my word.
I thought it not polite to use a stronger.
His Majesty can't do without it longer,
And therefore sends me, in a civil way,
To tell you he must have it back today!
EMP: What follows if we disallow of this?
FOR: His Majesty will take it much amiss.
EMP: On this fool's errand have you come alone?
FOR: I've seven servants with me, of my own.
(*All the* SERVANTS *bow*.)
EMP: You are a pleasant man for a small party!
Our wrath is smothered by our laughter hearty.
(*General laugh*. EMPEROR *checks them; laughs. They again echo him*.)
My Lord Ambassador, you've had your jest,
'Tis now our turn – we grant your *small* request,
On one condition – find, within this hour,
A man who, for his breakfast, shall devour
All the new bread baked in this town today.
FOR: Agreed. (*aside*) Here's luck!

EMP: Do you know what you say?
FOR: Most perfectly.
EMP: Oh, very well, we'll see.
Take heed; if but a crumb uneaten be,
Into a red-hot oven I will thrust ye,
And bake ye all, alive!
FOR: How very crusty!
EMP: (*to* OFFICER) Go, pile the bread up in the Palace-court;
Here, from our throne, we will behold the sport.
(*Exit* OFFICER *with some* GUARDS. *The* EMPEROR *retires up, with his suite.*)
FOR: Well, I am pretty easy on this head.
Gormand (GORMAND *advances.*), I hope you haven't breakfasted.
GOR: Why, sir, I ate a round of beef at ten,
But haven't made a meal I don't know when.
FOR: Can you eat all the new bread in this city?
GOR: Lord! If I couldn't, sir, 'twould be a pity –
And all the stale besides, just to complete it.
The job's to get one's bread, sir, not to eat it.
FOR: You're sure?
GOR: Don't be alarmed, sir, it's all right;
A round of beef just whets my appetite.
FOR: I joy to hear you say so. I declare
Bread's rising very fast in yonder square.
GOR: 'Twill fall much faster, sir, when I fall on it.
FOR: I hope so, for our lives depend upon it.
(*looking out*) They're bringing rolls and twists – all smoking hot.
GOR: They can't bring such a twist as I have got.
(*The* CHAMBERLAIN *advances.*)

The celebrated Duet, 'Tell me where is Fancy Bread'. Arranged for Three voices, by an Irish Composer.

FORTUNIO, CHAMBERLAIN, *and* GORMAND.

CHAM: } Tell me, tell me,
FOR: } Tell me, tell me,
New, d'ye fancy bread?
Smoking hot, from oven red –
Or prefer you *stale* instead?
Reply, reply, reply.
GOR: 'Tis all the same, sir, in my eye –
On both I've fed, and fancy size
In the loaf is all I prize.

CHAM: }
FOR: } 'Tis all the same, sir, in his eye, etc.

---

twist: 'hearty appetite' (*OED*).

ALL: { Let them bring all the stale as well,
{ I'll / He'll } go at it, ding, dong, bell!

(*The gates at the back are opened, and several enormous piles of loaves are seen in the court-yard, on a large table or platform.*)

EMP: There is the bread – now where's your man?
FOR: He's here.
EMP: Why, fellow, can you all that table clear?
GOR: I'll do my best your Majesty to please,
But if you would just add –
EMP: Ha!
GOR: A little cheese.
EMP: Dost mock us, villain? Eat all that, or die!
GOR: Oh, sir, it's quite a pleasure to comply.

(*Music.* GORMAND *devours the bread.*)

Chorus – EMPEROR *and* COURTIERS

What a gulp! oh, goodness, gracious!
Never wolf was so voracious!
Quartern loaves like pills to swallow!
Here's a chap beats Dando hollow!
Only see,
Goodness, gracious!
How capacious
Must his bread-room be!

FORTUNIO *and* SERVANTS

Down he crams 'em, smoking hot,
What a famous twist he's got!

(*During this chorus* GORMAND *demolishes all the heaps of bread.*)

OFF: There's not a crumb left! will you please examine?
EMP: Confound the cormorant, he'd breed a famine.
FOR: Bravo, dear Gormand, well may it be said
That you have proved yourself a thorough-bred!
GOR: I should have had the cheese, sir, I declare;
The last batch was light-weight – and that's not fair.
FOR: Now, great Matapa, I your promise claim –
Restore the treasure –
EMP: No!
FOR *and* SERVANTS: Oh fie, for shame!
A monarch pledge his word – and not stick to it?
EMP: Why, who the deuce had dreamed that he could do it!
FOR: Yet you'd have baked us had he chanced to fail;
Oh, sir, your Justice bears a sliding scale!

Dando: defined in the 1879 edition as a 'notorious oyster eater' and by Partridge as a 'seedy swell so named' given to eating heavily and bilking at restaurants.

EMP: I was but joking –
FOR: Sir, a bet's a bet,
I'll ask the Jockey Club –
EMP: One moment yet –
Find me a man can drink up all the water,
And one who in a race can beat my daughter;
And to restore your royal master's treasure,
We'll make a point – of full imperial measure!
We swear!
FOR: By what?
EMP: The Great Bear – whose relation
We have the honour to be.
FOR: A declaration
No one can doubt who knows your Majesty;
You are as like a great bear as can be!
EMP: By our celestial brother, Ursa Major,
We swear this time that if we lose our wager,
We'll pay!
FOR: Be witness all, then; 'tis a bet!
Tippler! – (TIPPLER *advances*.) – Your whistle if you'd like to wet,
There's a canal, five fountains, and a tank
To drain –
TIP: With pleasure, sir; but when I've drank
The water, I shall finish with the wine.
EMP: (*aside*) Eh, zounds! if that's the case, he'll finish mine!
My choice old port! – my fine Duff Gordon sherry!
An awkward customer this fellow – very! (TIPPLER *going*)
(*aloud*) Hold! this condition we will not exact.
We had forgotten an important fact!
Our doctors here, despising drug and pill,
Cure by cold water every mortal ill!
And should this man possess such powers of suction,
His faculty would doom ours to destruction!
Therefore, my Lord Ambassador, we think
We'd better drop this question of the drink;
And 'stead of losing all the running water,
Just stand to win upon our running daughter!
FOR: Content – will't please you name the time and place.
EMP: The Orange Walk – in half-an-hour –
FOR: The race –
P.P.?

Jockey Club: supreme authority for the control of horse-racing and breeding, established at Newmarket in the 1750s.
a point: a play on the standard British measure of a pint.
Duff Gordon: a firm of sherry exporters founded in Cadiz in 1768.
P.P.: play or pay, a racing term indicating that a bet must be paid whether the horse runs or not (Partridge).

EMP: Of course, P.P.
FOR: Sweepstakes – off-sweeping
All the King's plates and gold cups in your keeping.
(*Flourish and march. Exeunt* EMPEROR *and* FORTUNIO, *with their trains.*)

SCENE 2. *Another apartment in the Palace. Enter* FORTUNIO *and his seven* SERVANTS.

FOR: Lightfoot, I need not tell you 'tis your part
To beat the Princess.
LIGHT: Give me a fair start –
I'll beat the arrow from friend Marksman's bow.
FOR: You'll want a proper dress to run in though.
(*Stamps. The trunk rises. Giving him the key*)
Look in the trunk, – you'll find one, I dare say.
LIGHT: The very thing. (*pulling out a scarlet jacket and hose*)
Your lordship's colours, pray –
FOR: Go hence and dress, for you've no time to waste.
LIGHT: Sir, if I can make anything, 'tis haste. (*Exit.*)
FINE: Sir, may we crave a word?
FOR: I'm all attention.
BOIST: Lightfoot has hit upon a rare invention.
FOR: What is't?
FINE: A flying steam coach!
FOR: Ha! – indeed!
STRONG: Built on a principle that must succeed.
MARKS: Just like a bird – with body, wings, and tail.
TIP: Or like a fish –
FOR: Aye – very like a whale.
MARKS: You think we're joking, sir.
FOR: In truth I do.
GOR: Sir, it's in print –
FOR: Oh – then it *must* be true.
Or else I should have said, with all humility,
'Twas flying in the face of probability.
STRONG: We've formed a joint-stock company.
FOR: So, so.
STRONG: Boisterer can puff off anything, you know.
BOIST: And Strongback carries on the whole affair,
And all the onus will with pleasure bear.
FINE: Marksman will see the way clear through the sky.
MARKS: And Fine-ear tell folks when the coach is nigh.
FOR: Gormand and Tippler?
STRONG: Why, sir, we all think,
As they can nothing do but eat and drink,
They ought to be directors, and together
Meet upon board days, and discuss the weather.

FOR: I fear your scheme will end in smoke.
FINE: Aye, so
I heard them say of gas some years ago.
FOR: Faith, you're right there, and who on earth shall say
We may not one day skim the milky way?
Still, in these times of quackery and puffing,
The greatest goose may get his fill of stuffing.

Song – FORTUNIO – *Air* – *'March, March'*

Quack, quack, nothing like quackery,
Humbug, my friends, of the day is the order!
Quack, quack, any gimcrackery
Now will go off with a puff, for the Border.
Pretenders abounding, trumpeters sounding
Every man his own honour and glory;
Truth you're quite right to prize, if you don't wish to rise,
But if you do you must get up a story.
Quack, quack, etc.

Come to the Chambers of Clement's or Gray's Inn,
Come to the Solons who rule in 'the Row',
Come to the ball where the heiress is blazing,
You will find humbug from Bond Street to Bow.
Bills, yellow, green and red, flutter above your head,
Each of some miracle hangs the recorder;
New projects every day melting your cash away,
Till you're obliged to pop over the Border.
Quack, quack, etc. (*Exeunt.*)

SCENE 3. *A Long Walk lined with orange-trees. The winning post and the Judge's chair, with a bell above it. A set piece crosses the stage, over which the runners pass and descend out of view; beyond, the course is continued in perspective, and the figures pass rapidly along grooves up and down. Enter the* EMPEROR, *leading the* PRINCESS VOLANTE, *attired for the race, and followed by the* EMPEROR'S *Court*, LORD CHAMBERLAIN, OFFICERS, GUARDS, *etc.*; FORTUNIO, *with* LIGHTFOOT, *attired for the race, and followed by the other six* SERVANTS.

EMP: This is the spot, the centre of the grove,
Here stands the winning-post. In yon alcove
The judge's chair, where seated I shall be.
The daughter to Matapa here you see,
Fresh as a four-year old – of matchless speed.
FOR: Her make and beauty nothing can exceed.
VOL: Yonder is my antagonist no doubt.
FOR: Fortunio names Lightfoot.
VOL: Trot him out! (LIGHTFOOT *advances and bows.*)

---

the Solons who rule in 'the Row': the wiseacres or arbiters of fashion and taste in Rotten Row, or perhaps Paternoster Row, centre of the publishing and bookselling business.

A scarlet runner, by his legs –

LIGHT: Alack,
Red legs are rarer on the turf than black.

EMP: Come! clear the course. (*Bell rings.*)
Fair daughter, what d'ye say,
To some of our imperial Tokay
Before you start?

VOL: A glass I'll not decline,
To run a race nought helps like racy wine!

EMP: Some Tokay for her Highness.

LIGHT: And for me.

EMP: For thee!

VOL: It is but fair.

EMP: So let it be!
Give him a bumper! Harkye!

(*To* PAGE *and whispers*. PAGE *bows and goes out; returns with goblet, which he hands to* LIGHTFOOT.)

FOR: I misdoubt!
They'll doctor him! (*to* LIGHTFOOT) Take care what you're about.

EMP: Our Chamberlain shall start you when you're ready.

VOL: Come on then –

LIGHT: (*aside*) Well that stuff is rather heady!
(*aloud*) Where do we start from?

VOL: Yonder in the hollow.

LIGHT: Then lead the way.

VOL: And keep it?

LIGHT: That don't follow!

FOR: Now, Lightfoot, mind you run for your existence!

EMP: Once round the course, remember, and a distance.

(*Music. The* EMPEROR *takes his seat in the Judge's chair. Bell rings.* CHAMBERLAIN *stands on the ridge and drops a flag.* VOLANTE *and* LIGHTFOOT *ascend the slope at the back of the stage and disappear behind it.*)

ALL: They're off! they're off!

OFF: I'll bet a thousand to one
'Gainst Lightfoot.

FOR: Sir, I take you.

OFF: Done, sir.

FOR: Done.

(VOLANTE *and* LIGHTFOOT *reappear running*, VOLANTE *rather in advance.*)

CHAM: The Princess makes the running.

EMP: All my own is.

---

scarlet runner: a runner bean, or possibly a Bow Street police officer (Partridge).
black: blackleg was the term applied to a turf swindler (Partridge).
Tokay: Hungarian sweet wine.

CHAM: Six to four on her Highness.
FOR: Done, in ponies.
(*Exeunt* VOLANTE *and* LIGHTFOOT.)
MARKS: Lightfoot is holding in.
TIP: A pretty race!
ALL: Lightfoot is beaten!
CHAM: He can't live the pace.
FOR: They're out of sight.
EMP: And will be so, until
They reach the walk a-top of yonder hill;
But as my daughter runs five miles a minute,
It won't be long before you see her in it.
(*Bell rings as the figure of* PRINCESS *is seen at the top of the hill.*)
OFF: And there she is –
FOR: Alone, as I'm a sinner!
EMP: Hurrah! I'll bet my crown I'll name the winner.
CHAM: No takers.
(*The figure descends the hill rapidly, and disappears behind the rise of the stage.*)
FOR: Where on earth can Lightfoot be?
Listen, good Fine-ear; Marksman, haste and see.
FINE: Where'er he is, he's fast asleep, for I
Can hear him snore.
MARKS: Ha! there the rogue I spy,
Stretched out beneath a tree, full three miles off.
FOR: Of all the empire I shall be the scoff!
Our lives are forfeit, too! Asleep! plague take him!
MARKS: Nay, don't despair, good master, this shall wake him.
(*Lets fly an arrow.*)
FOR: What have you done?
MARKS: (*looking out*) Just touched his ear, I vow.
He's up and off.
(*The figure of* LIGHTFOOT *appears at the top of the hill, and descends with incredible swiftness, disappearing behind the rise in the stage.*)
FOR: He comes! He'll beat her now!
(PRINCESS *appears on the ridge of the stage, closely followed by* LIGHTFOOT.)
COURTIERS: Blue! Blue wins easy!
FOR. *and his* MEN: (*as* LIGHTFOOT *appears*) Scarlet, go it, Scarlet!
EMP: Volante!
(LIGHTFOOT *bounds by* PRINCESS *and passes the post.*)
FOR. *and his* MEN: Lightfoot! Lightfoot!
EMP: (*coming out of the chair*) Curse the varlet!
FOR: Won in a canter.
EMP: Scarlet? – I'm done brown!

---

ponies: bets of £25.
done brown: worsted, 'completely swindled' (Partridge).

FOR: Take care again, sir, how you bet your crown.
GOR: The knowing ones are done this time, I say.
TIP: There'll be long faces upon settling day.
FOR: O Lightfoot, what a time to sleep you chose!
LIGHT: I felt so drowsy, I laid down to doze,
Thinking by sleep refreshed to run the quicker!
I ne'er was overtaken, save by liquor!
FOR: It was a narrow 'scape for me, 'tis clear.
LIGHT: Mine was an arrow 'scape, sir! just look here.
(*Shows* MARKSMAN*'s arrow sticking in his ear*.)
FOR: Your Majesty no longer can refuse.
EMP: Our Majesty can do whate'er we choose.
But 'tis a debt of honour, we admit;
And therefore we to pay it *do* think fit.
But in our Court no longer shall you tarry;
So as much treasure as *one man* can carry
We do permit you from our stores to bear.
FOR: One man?
EMP: We've said it. Take more if you dare!
FOR: I humbly take my leave.
EMP: You show your sense.
FOR: Strongback, you hear the Emperor's order.
EMP: Hence!
(*to* CHAMBERLAIN) You, sir, look after them and see it done.
STRONG: (*to* FORTUNIO) I'll carry, sir, enough for any one.
(*Music. Exeunt* FORTUNIO *and* ATTENDANTS, *with* CHAMBERLAIN.)
VOL: I'm so provoked, papa, that I could cry;
At Tattersall's the favourite was I.
EMP: I'm so enraged, Volante, I could roar!
I never knew you be behind before.
VOL: Beneath a tree, asleep I left him, fast;
How could he manage to be first at last?
(*Enter* CHAMBERLAIN *hastily*.)
CHAM: Where is the Emperor? Oh, sire, sire, sire!
EMP: Now what's the matter? Is the town on fire?
CHAM: No, sire, but all your palace sacked and plundered
Of gold and silver statues full five hundred –
The costly mirrors and the massive plate –
The jewelled harness and the coach of state –
Treasure untold, in bullion, bars and cash –
All by one man are carried off – slap-dash!
EMP: All by one man? Impossible! No, no!

Tattersall's: famous London horse-market, popularly identified with the headquarters of racing and betting.

CHAM: Let me endure your wrath if 'tis not so.
I saw him move the goods.
EMP: If thou dost lie,
Upon the next tree shall thou hang as high
As they can swing thee. If the truth it be,
I care not if, instead, they tuck up me.
Is this a time to stand and stare about?
You rogues and vagabonds – arm – arm, and out!
If this which he avouches doth appear,
We may write up 'Unfurnished lodgings here'.
Ring the alarum bell until it crack!
At least we'll have our coach and harness back.
(*Exeunt* EMPEROR, PRINCESS, CHAMBERLAIN, *etc. Alarum bell, etc.*)

SCENE 4. *The Banks of a River. Music. Enter* STRONGBACK, *carrying an enormous pile of treasure of every description on his shoulders, followed by* FORTUNIO *and his other* SERVANTS.
FOR: Run, Strongback; we're pursued – 'tis my belief.
FINE: Yes, master, I can hear them call 'Stop thief'.
FOR: Now is the time your aerial coach to try.
LIGHT: It's built – we've only got to make it fly!
FOR: A trifle merely – yet I almost doubt
If we can wait whilst that is brought about.
MAR: Here comes the Emperor with all his guard!
FOR: What's to be done?
BOIST: I'll breathe a little hard;
And they'll be so completely blown, – I doubt
Their running an inch further on this route.
FOR: Dear friend, to you we'll owe our preservation,
And wait your coming at the railway station!
(*Music. Exeunt* FORTUNIO *and all but* BOISTERER. *Enter* EMPEROR *and* GUARDS.)
EMP: Upon them! – charge!
(BOISTERER *blows, and they are all whirled off stage.*)
Oh, here's a precious breeze! (*as he goes*)
BOIST: That is the 'puff direct', sir, if you please. (*Exit.*)

SCENE 5. *Interior of* KING ALFOURITE*'s Palace, as in* ACT I.
Enter KING *and* MINISTER.
KING: Talk not of comfort to a wretch like me!
My Court is now a Court of Bankruptcy.

---

tuck up: hang (*OED*).
puff direct: allusion to one of Mr Puff's categories of 'puffing' in Sheridan's *The Critic*, produced at Drury Lane in 1779.

Not Mr Lover, who, as you're aware,
Audits accounts of every Irish heir –
Which, for arithmetic, his fame advances,
Could find a cure for my impaired finances.

Air – KING – *'I love her, how I love her'*

E'en Lover! Samuel Lover!
Though he's a dab at L.S.D.
'Twould puzzle to discover
One penny in my treasury.

A tyrant beyond measure
Has walked off all my treasure;
And thinks it quite a pleasure,
To have so diddled me.

(*Enter* LIGHTFOOT.)

LIGHT: Hail to your Majesty.
KING: You come to use
Your tongue – your office quickly – what's your news?
LIGHT: Great news, great King. My Lord Fortunio's near,
With all your treasure!

(*Enter* PRINCESS.)

PRIN: What is this I hear?
KING: With all my treasure!
LIGHT: Sire, the truth to tell,
You'll find some of the Emperor's as well.
We hadn't time to pick and choose, in fact;
So took it as it came.
KING: Judicious act!
PRIN: (*aside*) What, of my vengeance am I baulked again?
KING: How is he coming?
LIGHT: By a special train.
I saw him start, and then ran on before
To give you notice. (*shouts without*) Hark, he's at the door!
KING: Conduct him to our presence – quickly – fly!

(*Exeunt* MINISTER *and* LIGHTFOOT.)

PRIN: (*aside*) I'll crush him yet, or know the reason why.
KING: He comes! he comes! With shouts the people greet him!
Don't stand there, sister, let us haste to meet him.
PRIN: It is not meet we should; he wants your crown,
So pull him up before he pulls you down.
KING: Fortunio false! then never man was true!
Some wicked wag has sure been hoaxing you.

Mr Lover: Samuel Lover, Irish novelist, playwright, lyricist and poet, whose novel *Treasure Trove: the First of a Series of Accounts of Irish Heirs* was originally published in 1844 under the title of *£.s.d.*

PRIN: I tell you, brother, I can prove his guilt.
KING: He was a gentleman on whom I built
An absolute trust.
PRIN: And so did I until
He dared propose your Majesty to kill,
And marry me!
KING: And marry you! Alack,
He must, then, be a monomaniac!
PRIN: Brother!
KING: I mean that such prodigious vanity
Is the best proof of the young man's insanity.
PRIN: I tell you he's a foe you must beware of.
KING: Let him be taken, pray, the greatest care of;
For though he might not run his sovereign through,
He may be mad enough to marry you.
But wherefore spoke you not of this before?
PRIN: I was in hopes he would return no more;
But he's come back, laden with fame and treasure,
And all the people's heads he'll turn with pleasure,
And they'll dethrone you and crown him instead,
Unless you puzzle them to find *his* head.
KING: Ah, me! I haven't got the heart to do it.
PRIN: Then leave the whole to me – I'll pull you through it.
(*Exeunt.*)

SCENE 6. *The Royal Gardens; night. The recovered treasure is pitched at the back of the stage, and occupies the whole centre of the scene.* STRONGBACK *and the other* SERVANTS *discovered. Enter* FORTUNIO.

STRONG: There, sir, I've pitched the whole load in the garden,
For there's no other place will hold it.
FOR: Pardon
Me, friend, but I am full of grief and care;
I cannot find my Comrade anywhere.
STRONG: Your horse? – is he not in the stable?
FOR: No.
And I am on the rack! My Comrade, ho!
Answer! you can, unless you are a corse.
'My horse! my horse! a kingdom for my horse!'
(*Enter* KING *and* PRINCESS *attended by* MINISTER, *and followed by two* GUARDS.)
The Princess!
PRIN: Aye, you tremble, and with reason.
Sir, I accuse Fortunio of high treason.
Arrest him, gentlemen. (*The* GUARDS *seize him.*)
FOR: Arrest! pray stay;

At Court, it seems, this is a collar day.
'Tis shameful, sire –
PRIN: Almost as bad, young mister,
As kill a king and marry with his sister.
FOR: As kill a king?
PRIN: Aye, traitor! 'twas my word.
FOR: And marry with his sister? – how absurd!
Since it has come to this, I must speak out.
Madam, pray tell me, for I almost doubt –
Are *you* a lady?
PRIN: Do you hear him, brother?
FOR: Because, if you are one, – why *I'm another*.
ALL: A lady!
FOR: Yes, a female woman, daughter
Of Baron Dunover.
KING: I always thought her
Too pretty for a man – unless 'twas me –
'The fair, the chaste, the inexpressive she!'
PRIN: Exposed – defeated! I shall burst with spite!
Oh! (*Falls in* MINISTER*'s arms.*)
MIN: Sire! – She's choking!
KING: Verdict – Serve her right.
(MINISTER *carries out* PRINCESS.)
(*to* FORTUNIO) A crown you merit.
FOR: Half a one, I'd rather.
KING: Will you share mine?
FOR: Sir, you must ask my father.
KING: Oh, let us fly to seek him!
VOICE: (*without*) There's no need.
(*Music. The pile of treasure gradually opens, and discovers a magnificent Fairy Chariot, drawn by twenty-four sheep with golden fleeces, in which is the* FAIRY. *In front of the chariot is* COMRADE.)
FAIRY: He to your union has with joy agreed;
And I have hastened, in my own post-carriage,
To give consent and lustre to your marriage.
KING: (*aside*) A carriage drawn by four-and-twenty sheep
With golden fleeces! – That's the flock to *keep*!
FAIRY: They shall be yours – the dower of your bride.
KING: (*aside*) She heard me. (*aloud*) Madam, I'm quite horrified.
FAIRY: Oh, no apologies! They're ewes and rams,
And will breed millions.
KING: Oh, the precious lambs!
FAIRY: (*to* FORTUNIO) Had *you* not helped *me*, all this had been marr'd.
But kindly actions ever meet reward.

---

collar day: a day of court ceremonial when knights are required to wear the collar of their Order (*OED*), punning with a day of execution (Partridge).

Finale – Air – 'Here's to the maiden'

FOR: Here then our curtain we hasten to drop, –
Our folly indulgently view, sirs;
Don't for a moment to criticise stop,
For that would be folly in you, sirs.
Let the piece pass,
One of its class
At Easter may find an excuse with the mass.
CHORUS: Let the piece pass, etc.
Curtain

THE GOLDEN FLEECE; OR, JASON IN COLCHIS, AND MEDEA IN CORINTH

A classical extravaganza in two parts

First performed at the Theatre Royal, Haymarket, on Monday, 24 March 1845, with the following cast:

JASON IN COLCHIS

ÆETES, *King of Colchis, possessor of the original Golden Fleece*	Mr James Bland
JASON, *commander of 'The Argo' and son of Æson, the deposed King of Iolchos*	Miss P. Horton
ANONYMOUS, *captain of the Royal Guards*	Mr Caulfield
MEDEA, *daughter of Æetes, an enchanting creature*	Madame Vestris

ARGONAUTS, COLCHIAN NOBLES, SAGES, GUARDS, etc.

MEDEA IN CORINTH

CREON, *King of Corinth*	Mr James Bland

(*Who, by particular desire, and on this occasion only, has most obligingly consented to be twice the King he usually is at this festive season.*)

JASON, *married but not settled, exceedingly classical, but very far from correct*	Miss P. Horton
MEDEA, *Jason's lawfully wedded wife and mother of two fine boys, both likely to do well, which is more than can be said of their parents*	Madame Vestris
MERMEROS, } *the two fine boys aforesaid*	Master Elder
PHERES, }	Master Younger
PSUCHE, *a good old soul, nurse to the two fine boys aforesaid*	Miss Carre

CORINTHIANS, GUARDS, etc.

N.B. The public is respectfully informed that, in order to produce this grand classical work in a style which may defy competition in any other establishment, the lessee has, regardless of expense, engaged

Mr Charles Mathews

to represent the whole body of the Chorus, rendering at least fifty-nine male voices entirely unnecessary.

The stage, which has been constructed after the approved fashion of the revived Greek theatre, will be partially raised, but the prices of admission remain exactly as before. It is also requisite to observe that, frequent change of scene being contrary to the usage of the ancient Greek drama, several of the most Splendid Pictorial Effects will be left entirely to the imagination of the audience.

Scenery by Mr G. Morris and assistants
Dresses by Miss Cherry, Miss Barnett and assistants
Machinery by Mr C. Adams and assistants
Properties by Mr T. Ireland and assistants

IV *The Golden Fleece*. Charles Mathews as the Chorus.

PART I: JASON IN COLCHIS

SCENE. *The Palace of* ÆETES, *King of Colchis. Three doors in centre, upon a raised stage, a large arch on each side. As the curtain rises the ship Argo comes into port.* ÆETES, *attended, enters and takes his seat.* JASON *and the* ARGONAUTS *enter. Enter* CHORUS *in front of the raised stage, stopping* ÆETES, *who is about to speak.*

CHORUS: Friends, countrymen, lovers, first listen to me,
I'm the Chorus; whatever you hear or you see
That you don't understand, I shall rise to explain –
It's a famous old fashion that's come up again,
And will be of great service to many fine plays
That nobody can understand now-a-days;
And think what a blessing, if found intervening,
When the author himself scarcely knows his own meaning.
You may reap from it, too, an advantage still further;
When an actor is bent upon marriage or murther,
To the Chorus his scheme he in confidence mentions,
'Stead of telling the pit all his secret intentions;
A wondrous improvement you all will admit,
And the secret is just as well heard by the pit.
Verbum sat – To the wise I'll not put one more word in,
Or instead of a Chorus, they'll think me a burden,
But just say, this is Colchis, and that's King Æetes,
And this is young Jason, he coming to meet is;
And there are the forty odd friends of young Jason,
And that's their ship Argo, just entering the bason.
At the end of each scene I shall sing you some history,
Or clear up whatever is in it of mystery,
But I can't tell you why – unless English I speak,
For this very plain reason – there's no Y in Greek. (*Retires.*)

ÆETES: Ye who have dared to tread on Colchian ground
Who and what are ye? whence and whither bound?

JASON: Hail, great Æetes, if you are no less;
My name is Jason, now perhaps you'll guess
My errand here.

ÆETES: We are not good at guessing;
Speak and remember whom you are addressing!
Sun of the Sun, and grand-son of the Ocean,
Of anything like nonsense we've no notion!

Air – JASON – *'I am a brisk and lively lad'*

I am a brisk and lively lad,
As ever sailed the seas on,
Cretheus was old Æson's dad,
And I'm the son of Æson!
With a yeo, yeo, yeo, yeo, etc.

Verbum sat: enough said.

A martyr to rheumatic gout,
    A feeble king was he, sir;
So uncle Pelias kicked him out,
    And packed me off to sea, sir.
        With a yeo, yeo, yeo, yeo, etc.

And now I've with a jolly crew,
    Sailed in the good ship Argo,
To rub off an old score with you,
    Then back again to pa go.
        With a yeo, yeo, yeo, yeo, etc.

ÆETES: 'Yeo! yeo! yeo! yeo!' I never heard such lingo.
    Speak in plain words, you rascal, or by Jingo –
JASON: In one word, then, you killed my cousin Phryxus,
    And we are come for vengeance!
ÆETES: (*aside*) There he nicks us!
    (*aloud*) My good young man, it is so long ago,
    I scarce remember if I did or no;
    Some little circumstance may have occurred
    Of that description, but upon my word –
JASON: Nay, no evasion, you owe reparation.
ÆETES: I plead the statute, then, of limitation.
JASON: Of limitation, in a case of murther?
ÆETES: Why pursue such a subject any further?
JASON: Pursue a subject! I pursue a king,
    And to the grindstone mean his nose to bring.
ÆETES: (*aside*) Bring my nose to the grindstone! Father Phœbus!
    There is no 'modus' in this fellow's 'rebus';
    He looks determined, bullying's no use,
    To save my bacon, I must cook his goose!
    (*aloud*) What reparation, then, may purchase peace?
JASON: The restoration of the Golden Fleece,
    Of which you fleeced my cousin!
ÆETES: Pray be cool!
    All this great cry for such a little wool!
    To take it if you can, sir, you are free,
    No difficulty will be made by me;
    But there are some obstructions in the way,
    Which must all be surmounted in one day.
JASON: To them I beg immediate introduction.
ÆETES: Two bulls are one!
JASON: One bull, or one obstruction?

---

statute . . . of limitation: statute specifying the time within which a legal action must be brought (*OED*).
no 'modus' in this fellow's 'rebus': no limit to his presumption.

ÆETES: Two savage bulls, that breathe out fire and smoke;
You'll have to catch and break them to the yoke.
Then plough four acres, yonder crag beneath,
And sow them with a set of serpent's teeth,
From which will spring of soldiers a fine crop,
Whose heads, to save your own, you off must chop;
Then if the dragon set to guard the treasure
Will let you, you may take it at your pleasure.
JASON: In one day this must all be done?
ÆETES: Just so.
JASON: Anything else in a small way?
ÆETES: Why, no.
There's nothing else occurs to me at present.
JASON: What will occur to me is most unpleasant.
ÆETES: It's optional, you know, you needn't do it
Unless you like.
JASON: Honour compels me to it.
OFFICER: The Princess!
(*Enter* MEDEA.)
JASON: Gods! a goddess, sure, I gaze on.
ÆETES: My daughter, sir – Medea, Mr Jason! (*Introduces them.*)
Quartetto – JASON, MEDEA, ÆETES, *and* ANONYMOUS – *'Donna del Lago'*
JASON: *To Kalon*, to sail on
In quest of, who would deign now?
Eureka! to seek a
Supremer bliss were vain now!
Pros Theōn! my knee on
I sink before such beauty!
Medea, to thee a
Poor Grecian pays his duty.
MEDEA: (*aside*) O Jason, thy face on
I wish I ne'er had looked, sir!
So spicy and nice he
Is – I'm completely hooked, sir!
His glances like lances,
Right through my heart he throws, O!
Enraptured! I'm captured
By that fine Grecian nose, O!
ÆETES: (*aside*) By Jupiter Ammon!
If me he thinks to gammon,
Despite of his mettle
His hash I soon will settle;
I'll hang at least forty

To Kalon: the beautiful, the good (philosophically speaking).
Pros Theōn: by the gods.

Of these bold Argonautæ,
I'll scuttle the Argo
And confiscate the cargo!
MEDEA: (*aside*) Sure there ne'er was such a duck, sir!
Down he seems upon his luck, sir!
I will cheer him – safely steer him;
And for him will run a muck, sir.
Teach him how to plough and sow.
JASON: (*aside*) Overboard my cares I'd chuck, sir,
If to Greece with me she'd go.
ÆETES: (*to* JASON) Pray walk in, and take pot luck, sir,
(*aside*) For full soon to pot you go!
Staring like a pig that's stuck, sir,
To the ground he seems to grow!
ANON: (*aside*) Down he seems upon his luck, sir,
To a goose he can't say 'boh!'
(*Exeunt* ÆETES, JASON *and* ARGONAUTS.)
MEDEA: Too lovely youth! would I had ne'er set eyes on him!
Papa had better mind what tricks he tries on him.
O Eros! vulgarly called Cupid, oh!
Thou God of Love! in all the Greek I know,
And that's not much, I will apostrophise thee!
In vain the heart of mortal woman flies thee!
I, even I, feel sure that very soon I
Shall be on that young man exceeding spoony!
Air – MEDEA – *'John Anderson'*
You wanton son of Venus,
My heart in twain you've rent;
Against no other maiden,
Could your wicked bow be bent?
It may seem very bold, but
I love young Jason so;
If he were to pop the question, I
Don't think I could say, 'No.'
If you wool gathering go, love,
My wits the wool shall gather –
In one boat we will row, love,
In spite of wind and weather;
And if to Davy Jones, love,
We hand in hand should go,
We'll sleep together in the old
Boy's locker down below.
(*Exit* MEDEA. CHORUS *advances*.)
CHORUS: Young ladies, I'm sure you need no explanation
Of the cause of Medea's extreme perturbation;
And yet he's so handsome – this young Grecian swain,
You'll none of you say that the cause is too plain.

However, my business at present is merely
To tell what may not have appeared quite so clearly;
The cause of the voyage, which in the ship Argo
Young Jason has taken; and why this embargo
Is laid on the fleece, which lies here on the shelf;
And as I'm the Chorus, I'll sing it myself.

Song – CHORUS – *'The Tight Little Island'*

There reigned once on a time, o'er Bœotia's clime,
A King (Athamas he's known by name as);
He packed off his first wife, and thought her the worst wife,
Till the second the first proved the same as.
The second was Ino, who, you know,
Was very displeasing to Juno,
And a shocking step-mother the children of t'other
Found her to their cost pretty soon, oh!

She threatened with slaughter her step-son and daughter,
But a ram with a fine golden fleece, sir,
Flew up thro' the sky, with them so very high,
They could not see the least spot of Greece, sir!
They got in a deuce of a fright, sir,
Poor Helle, she couldn't hold tight, sir!
She fell in the sea, but the young fellow he
Came over to Colchis all right, sir!

What do you think this nice man did, as soon as he landed
And found himself safe, the young sinner?
He saw the King's daughter, made love to, and caught her,
And had the poor ram killed for dinner.
'Twas very ungrateful you'll say, sir,
But, alas! of the world it's the way, sir,
When all a friend can you have done for a man,
He'll cut you quite dead the next day, sir.

But his father-in-law, who the Golden Fleece saw,
Thought, 'Oh, oh! two can play at that game, sir.'
And so one fine morning, without any warning,
He served Master Phryxus the same, sir.
Before they knew what he was at, sir,
He killed him as dead as a rat, sir.
He stuck him right thro' – 'twas a wrong thing to do,
But kings don't stick at trifles like that, sir.

Well, to finish my song, which is getting too long,
He hung up his famed Golden Fleece, sir,
On a tree in his park, and, by way of a lark,
Set a dragon to act as police, sir;

If Medea don't help him, you see, sir,
Sharp work it for Jason will be, sir;
The Altar of Hecat'
They're coming to speak at,
But of course that's betwixt you and me, sir. (*Retires.*)
(*Enter* MEDEA, *bearing a small golden box, followed by* JASON.)

JASON: Turn, fair enchantress, too bewitching maid!
A doating lover supplicates your aid;
A thousand charms all own that you possess,
Spare one to get me out of this sad mess.
Lo, I implore you, sinking on my sad knee –
Remember Theseus and Ariadne;
To thread the labyrinth a clue she gave him,
And from the beast (half bull, half man) to save him,
Went the whole hog.

MEDEA: She did, I don't deny it,
And brought her pigs to a fine market by it.
Deceiv'd, deserted, on destruction's brink,
She rushed to Bacchus – that is, took to drink.
To draw a parallel – should Fate decree
As A to B, so C would be to D.

JASON: If I be C, and D my friend in need,
When C proves false to D, may C be D—d!

MEDEA: Great Hecate! hear my ditto to that oath,
And for the same dark journey book us both.
If true to Jason I do not remain,
Send me to Hades by the first down train.
Now mark this box of ointment, do not doubt –
Whate'er your foes, this salve will sarve 'em out.
With it anointed, you may boldly take
Bulls by the horns, nor fear a bull to make.
Thro' the hard soil 'twill speed the plough, and bear,
In all thy labours, more than the plough's share.
When sown the serpent's teeth, prepare to fight;
It's no use showing teeth if you can't bite.
But as the soldiers rise, first take a sight at 'em;
Then pick up the first stone and shy it right at 'em,
On which, each thinking it was thrown by t'other,
They'll all draw swords and cut down one another.
An easy victory you thus may reap.
As to the dragon pa has set to keep
Watch o'er the fleece, so vigilant and grim,
I'll mix a dose that soon shall doctor him.

---

a bull to make: to utter 'an expression containing a manifest contradiction in terms or involving a ludicrous inconsistency unperceived by the speaker' (*OED*); also called an Irish bull and often associated with stage Irishmen.

JASON: My dear Medea! O Medea, my dear!
How shall I make my gratitude appear?
If I succeed, I swear, to Greece I'll carry you,
And there, as sure as you're alive, I'll marry you.
MEDEA: Enough, I take your word, and you my casket.
My heart was Jason's ere he came to ask it.
But oh, beware! I give you early warning.
If, your pledged faith and my fond passion scorning,
You with another venture to philander,
To the infernal regions off I'll hand her,
And lead you such a life as on my word will
Make e'en the cream of Tartarus to curdle.

Duo – JASON *and* MEDEA – *'Ebben a té ferisce'*

JASON: Ye gods and little fishes
Record my vows and wishes;
If from the walls of Æa
Thou'lt fly with me, Medea,
To fair Thessalia's shore,
Thee will I wed.
By Luna! thy mother,
And Phœbus! her brother.
JASON: Thee will I } marry! { thee will I } marry lawfully!
MEDEA: Me will he } { me will he }
The charmer – the charmer – { I adore!
{ he adores!

Air – *'Giorno d'orrore'*

BOTH: Bulls loudly roaring on mischief bent, O!
Broke to the yoke shall be in one moment, O!
Scores of old grinders drawn out for glory,
The unctuous spell shall quickly quell!
And grease for Greece fight *con amore*!
Oh, how, then, crow will { he over papa!
{ I o'er her papa!
MEDEA: Then serenely to distant Thessalia,
Colchian Medea the sea will cross o'er;
JASON: There a queen, in all her regalia,
She a palace will reign in once more.
MEDEA: Oh, an Alpha Cottage with thee, love,
I could share, nor deem it a bore!
JASON: And with thee content I could be, love,
In the poorest attic floor!
But 'tis time that off I went, O!
Soon we meet to part no more!
MEDEA: Be this charm a sweet memento

---

cream of Tartarus: cream of tartar, the crystalline deposit of fermented grape-juice, conflated with the infernal regions of Greek mythology.

Of the maid whom you adore! (*Exit* JASON.)
He's gone! and yet his god-like form before us
Appears to hover. (CHORUS *advances*.) Ah, my gentle Chorus,
You, the impartial confidant of all –
You, to whom every Colchian great or small,
Imparts his hope or fear on this sad stage,
Have I done wrong with Jason to engage
In this great struggle 'gainst my royal sire?

CHORUS: It's rather –

MEDEA: Silence, sir, I don't require
To be told that, whatever it may be
You were about to say; but answer me,
Have I done wrong?

CHORUS: You –

MEDEA: Interrupt me not.
Have I done wrong, I ask? if so, in what?

CHORUS: I –

MEDEA: Ah! your silence answers me too plainly.

CHORUS: But –

MEDEA: And you offer consolation vainly.
'Gainst Fate's decree to strive, who has the brass?
For what must be comes usually to pass.
So let me haste and pack up my portmanteau –
I've got that horrid dragon to enchant, too!

CHORUS: If I might ask –

MEDEA: How that I mean to do?
In confidence, I don't mind telling you.
This dragon is a very artful dodger,
And sleeps with one eye open – the sly codger!
Now, as we daren't approach, a stick to pop in it,
The only chance is if he gets a drop in it;
For though notoriously a scaly fellow,
He's not the least objection to get mellow,
At any one's expense, except his own.
He's partial to an ardent spirit, known
By several names, and worshipped under all;
Some 'Cupid's eye water' the liquor call,
'White Satin' some, whilst others, wisely viewing
The baneful beverage, brand it as 'Blue Ruin'.
A plant called juniper the juice supplies,
And oft beneath Hyperborean skies,
A bowl-full, mixed with raisins of the sun,
Gay youths and maidens set on fire for fun,
And call it 'snap-dragon'. Now, my specific

Blue Ruin: gin (Partridge).
snap-dragon: a Christmas game consisting of snatching raisins from a dish of burning spirit.

Is this – I'll brew a potent soporific,
And in it steep a branch of this fell tree,
Which, when the dragon sniffs, with eager glee,
He'll fall o'erpowered by its strong aroma,
Into what doctors call a state of coma,
And if into his eyes he gets a drop,
'Twill change the coma into a full stop.
Then off with Jason and the Golden Fleece,
I fly to Thessaly, as 'slick as grease.'

Duet – French Air

MEDEA *and*	CHORUS.
Now farewell, for I must go,	Oh!
To invoke my magic ma,	Ah!
Then to pack my portmanteau,	Oh!
Ere I plunder poor papa.	Ah!
When from Colchis far away,	Eh?
With the only Greek I know,	Oh!
To my Jason I will say –	Eh?
'Zoe mou sas agapo'	Oh!

(*Exit* MEDEA.)

CHORUS: Æetes comes, looking as black as thunder,
And when you hear the cause you'll say 'no wonder;'
For Jason, aided by Medea's spell,
Has done the trick, and done the King as well.
You'll think, perhaps, you should have seen him do it,
But 'tisn't classical – you'll hear, not view it.
Whatever taxed their talent or their means,
These sly old Grecians did *behind* the scenes;
So fired with their example, boldly we
Beg you'll suppose whate'er you wish to see.

(*Enter* ÆETES, *attended, and* JASON.)

Song and Chorus – JASON, ÆETES, OFFICER *and* CHORUS – *Heiterersinn Polka*

ÆETES: / OFFICER: / & CHORUS: { Here's a precious row, sir!
What { shall we / will you } do now, sir?

He takes the bulls
And down he pulls,
And yokes them to the plough.
He tills the acres four, sir,
And what's the greater bore, sir,
The teeth he sows,
And down he mows,

'Zoe mou sas agapo': 'my life, I love you' (the sort of modern Greek that Madame Vestris might well have been expected to know in view of her scandalous past!)

{ My / Your } soldiers by the score!

JASON: Glorious Apollo! the victory's mine!
Out of your son I have taken the shine;
Spite of his teeth and his troops of the line,
Cock of the walk am I!

ÆETES: / OFFICER: / & CHORUS: } Here's a precious row, sir, etc.

JASON: Lo! King of Colchis, all my tasks are done,
And yet o'er Caucasus behold the sun.

ÆETES: Still from the dragon you the fleece must win,
Ere out of this you get in a whole skin.
Wound up, you'll find his watch he'll always keep,
You sooner might a weasel catch asleep,
And shave his eyebrow – so about it go;
If he don't eat you, call and let me know. (*Exit*.)

JASON: So, then, I've worked the whole day like a nigger,
To cut at last this mighty silly figure!
Like a Lord Chancellor, compell'd to pack,
I've lost the wool, and only got the sack.
For where's Medea, with her magic flagon –
The dose that was to doctor that deep dragon?
She's chang'd her mind, she neither comes nor sends,
And fate cries, 'Kick him, he has got no friends.'
Embasian Phœbus, thou ungrateful sun!
Was it for this a salted Sally Lunn
We offered thee, the night before the day
The Minyans left the Pegasœan Bay?
Wilt thou descend behind Promethean Caucasus,
Forgetful that on earth such creatures walk as us?
Deaf on the shores of Amaranthine Phasis,
To him who made thy altars burn like blazes!
And vowed to roast whole oxen to thee, more
Than ever hailed a son and heir before.
Magnus Apollo *thou*? Pooh! go to bed,
In Tethis' lap hide thy diminished head.
No sun of mine! – to say it I am glad;
But were I Zeus, thy immortal dad,
I would myself the world, without a blush, light,
And cut thee off without a farthing rushlight.

Air – JASON – *'Then farewell, my trim-built wherry'*

Embasian: favouring embarkation.
Sally Lunn: a light teacake, served hot (*OED*).
Amaranthine Phasis: Colchian river said to rise in the Amaranthine mountains.
Tethis' lap: the sea (from the sea-goddess of that name).

Now, farewell, my trim-built Argo –
Greece and Fleece, and all farewell;
Never more, as supercargo,
Shall poor Jason cut a swell!

To the dragon, quite a stranger,
All alone, I'm left to go;
And to think upon my danger,
Makes me feel extremely low.

My catastrophe too plain is;
Hecate's daughter seals my doom!
Come, the friends, to Jason's *manes*,
Sacrifice a hecatomb!

What do I see? Oh, Sol, I ask your pardon,
I've been too hasty – Yonder, through the garden,
Medea comes to save her doating Jason.
(*Enter* MEDEA, *carrying a bowl of lighted spirits, and in the other a branch of juniper*.)
What's that she carries burning in a bason?

MEDEA: A dainty dish to set before the dragon.
His scaly shoulders how his head will wag on,
When first the odour of this branch he twigs;
But if a drop out of this bowl he swigs,
Deeming it gin – all is not gold that glitters –
To him 'twill prove a dose of gin and bitters.

JASON: Matchless Medea! I'm all admiration.

MEDEA: Silence, whilst I commence my gin-cantation.
Song – MEDEA – *'The Mistletoe Bough'*
The juniper bough to my aid I call.
Its spirit of millions has worked the fall;
And the dragon is longing snap-dragon to play,
Like a boy on a Christmas holiday.
Above him, behold my father's pride –
The beautiful fleece – the golden ram's hide.
But stop till the monster asleep you see,
For he's mighty awkward company.
Wave the juniper bough,
Wave the juniper bough. (*Exit, waving the bough*.)

JASON: Arise, ye Minyans. (*Enter* ARGONAUTS.) If again ye'd scan
Thessalia's shore, make all the sail you can.
For 'pris'ners base' you'll soon be, with your skipper,
If once her dad is roused to 'hunt the slipper'.
(*Exeunt* ARGONAUTS. *Re-enter* MEDEA.)

MEDEA: Behold the monster, overcome by sleep,
Nods to his fall, like ruin on a steep;
'Tis done! He sinks upon the ground, supine,

His end approaches, make it answer thine.
Hence! With bold hand the fleecy treasure tear
Down from this beech, and hasten to that there.

(*Music.* JASON *goes off, re-enters with the fleece, and exit with* MEDEA.)

CHORUS: With her bold Argonaut Medea flies,
Though, 'Ah, go not!' the voice of duty cries.
With golden wool her ears sly Cupid stops,
And, like a detonator, off she pops,
In peace to pass, with Jason, all her days,
Till he or she the debt o' natur' pays. (*Retires.*)

(*Distant shout. Enter* ÆETES.)

ÆETES: My mind misgives me – wherefore was that shout?
What ho! my slaves within! – my guards without!

(*Enter* GUARDS *and* SAGES.)

We are betrayed! robbed! murdered! See – oh, treason!
Yonder he goes, that young son of – old Æson.
He's killed my dragon – stolen my Golden Fleece –
To arms, my Colchians! Stop thief! Police!

(*Exeunt* GUARDS.)

CHORUS: (*advancing*) Be calm, great King, – 'tis destiny's decree.
ÆETES: How dare you talk of destiny to me!
What right have you with such advice to bore us?
CHORUS: Sir, I'm the chorus.
ÆETES: Sir, you're indecorous.
Where is my daughter?
CHORUS: Hopped off with the skipper.
ÆETES: Impious Medea! may the furies whip her
At the cart's tail of Thespis. (*Enter* OFFICER *and* GUARDS.) Now, your news?
OFFICER: Your son, Absyrtus –
ÆETES: Speak –
OFFICER: My lips refuse
Almost, O King, to tell the horrid tale.
ÆETES: My heir apparent?
OFFICER: Dead as a door nail!
ÆETES: Say in what manner hath his spirit fled?
OFFICER: The fist of Jason punched his royal head.
Upon the shores of rapid-rolling Ister,
The youthful prince o'ertook his faithless sister,
When Pelian Jason, on his knowledge box,
Let fly a blow that would have felled an ox –
Black'd both his precious eyes, before so blue,
And from his nose the vital claret drew.
ÆETES: Ah, me! That blow has fallen on my pate.
CHORUS: In Jason's fist behold the hand of fate.

ÆETES: I do – I do! that hits me right and left.
My daughter's stolen what I gained by theft.
Phryxus I slew – my son is now a shade;
Put me to bed, ye Colchians, with a spade.
That fatal punch – I feel it in my noddle.
And down to Pluto I but ask to toddle.
CHORUS: Have patience, man, and learn this truth sublime –
You can't go even *there* before your time!
(*Thunder and lightning. The Palace sinks, and the Argo is seen under sail, with* JASON, MEDEA, *and the* ARGONAUTS.)

PART II: MEDEA IN CORINTH

SCENE. *The Palace of* CREON, *Corinth. On one side the country; on the other side the city, with* MEDEA*'s house. Enter* CHORUS.
CHORUS: The bills have informed you, some years have passed by,
Since we parted in Colchis; then Colchian was I;
Now in Corinth, of course, I'm Corinthian, in order
To hold in this city the place of recorder.
Imprimis. – The King of this state is called Creon.
By the way, no relation to him whom you see on
The throne of old Thebes, the car celebrated
By Antigone check'd and Eurydice mated;
No, this is another guess sort of a person,
Whose daughter, fair Glauce's, a girl to write verse on.
Now it happens, you see, that Medea and Jason,
Whose conduct in Greece has brought both some disgrace on,
Came hither to court, and the libertine saucy
Begg'd Creon's permission to come to court Glauce,
And got it, by this very shameful duplicity –
Disturbing Medea's connubial felicity,
In a manner that really is most reprehensible
In a family man – in short, quite indefensible –
And in one so well knowing the lady's vivacity,
An act which says little for Jason's sagacity;
But here comes the Nurse, who is hired to take care of
The boys, which Medea has brought him a pair of.
She's a querulous, gossiping, ancient Greek gammer,
In matters of this sort as down as a hammer.

---

car: no recognised meaning of the word seems quite appropriate here and one is tempted to consider it a misprint for 'cad', except that 'car' appears in the manuscript licensing copy as well as all three printed editions (1845, 1862 and 1879). The reference here is to Creon, brother of Laius, who assumed the throne of Thebes after the latter's death and again after the abdication of Oedipus.
guess: kind of (*OED*).

(*Enter* NURSE.)

NURSE: Oh, that the hull of that fifty-oared cutter – the Argo,
Between the Symplegades, never had passed with its cargo!
Indeed, I may say that I wish, upon Pelion, the pine trees,
Of which it was built had remained, as they were, very fine trees;
For had there been never a boat in which man could have brought her,
My poor ill-used missis had never come over the water;
Nor – having, for that wicked Jason, cut all her connections –
Seen another young lady possessing her husband's affections.

CHORUS: Good woman, you seem in a terrible taking!
May I ask you if any more mischief is making?
Is there anything new, pray, respecting the scandal
To which our friend Jason is giving a handle?

NURSE: As I was a-walking, just now, by the fount of Pirene,
I heard an old file say to another 'I'll bet you a guinea
That Creon, in order to bring about his daughter's marriage,
Will pack off Medea and both her brats in a second class carriage,
Clean out of the kingdom.'

CHORUS: And does she suspect his intention?

NURSE: I don't know, and to her I don't fancy the matter to mention;
She's half wild as it is, and quite crazy I think it would drive her,
To be passed to her parish without, in her pocket, a stiver.

MEDEA: (*within*) O me! alas! alack, and well-a-day!

NURSE: Hush, that's her voice – she's in a precious way!

CHORUS: Persuade her here awhile in verse to spout;
She seems in famous voice for singing out.

NURSE: I'll do my best – but, when so loud you hear her,
It's rather dangerous to come a-near her. (*Exit.*)

CHORUS: She'll comb young Jason's wig – and serve him right!
I'll bet five talents he's been out all night.

(*Enter* MEDEA.)

MEDEA: O! mighty Theseus and adored Diana!
How long must I be treated in this manner?
The wretch to whom my virgin faith was plighted;
To whom, in lawful wedlock, I'm united,
Has gone and popped the question to another,
And left me of two chopping boys the mother!

Song – MEDEA – *'The Fine Young English Gentleman'*

I'll tell you a sad tale of the life I've been led of late,
By the false Bœotian Boatswain, of whom I am the mate:
Who quite forgets the time when I pitied his hard fate,
And he swore eternal constancy by all his gods so great;

---

file: fellow, cove (*OED*).
stiver: penny (Partridge).
comb young Jason's wig: scold him, or thrash him (*OED*).

Like a fine young Grecian gentleman
One of the classic time!

Now he lives in a fine lodging, in the palace over there,
Whilst I and his poor children are poked up in a back two pair;
And though he knows I've scarcely got a second gown to wear,
He squanders on another woman every farthing he's got to spare
Like a false young Grecian gentleman,
One of the classic time.

He leaves me to darn his stockings, and mope in the house all day,
Whilst he treats her to see 'Antigone', with a box at the Grecian play,
Then goes off to sup with Corinthian Tom, or whoever he meets by the way,
And staggers home in a state of beer, like (I'm quite ashamed to say)
A fine young Grecian gentleman,
One of the classic time.

Then his head aches all the next day, and he calls the children a plague and a curse,
And makes a jest of my misery, and says, 'I took him for better or worse';
And if I venture to grumble, he talks, as a matter of course,
Of going to modern Athens, and getting a Scotch divorce!
Like a base young Grecian gentleman,
One of the classic time. (CHORUS *advances*.)

MEDEA: (*to* CHORUS) Oh, thou Corinthian column of the nation,
Behold a woman driven to desperation.
CHORUS: Unhappy one! But you won't stand it, surely?
MEDEA: No! I will be revenged on all most purely,
But whatsoe'er my project, be thou dumb
As doleful Dido.
CHORUS: Madam, I am mum!
All decent people sure your side must be on –
But Creon comes to act a new decree on.
(*Enter* CREON, *attended*.)
CREON: Madam, 'tis –
CHORUS: (*to* CREON) Stop! Though in another wig,
D'ye think the public won't Æetes twig?
You, Creon?
CREON: Now I am, and you should know it;
I play two parts tonight.

---

back two pair: a rear lodging on the second floor (*OED*).
'Antigone': it was a performance of Sophocles' play at Covent Garden earlier in 1845 that prompted Planché to burlesque its style of presentation.
modern Athens: Edinburgh.
Scotch divorce: before 1857 divorce in the strict sense was not possible in England except by recourse to act of parliament, but judicial divorce enabling the parties to re-marry was available under Scottish law.

CHORUS: Oh, well then, go it.
'Twas to prevent confusion – don't be nettled.
CREON: The bills already have the matter settled;
Therefore, thou most inveterate of praters,
Close up the trap through which you put your taters.
(*to* MEDEA) Madam, 'tis not my custom to mince matters,
So have the goodness to pack up your tatters;
And, with your brats, pack off, in less than no time.
MEDEA: Banished! (*aside*) But I'll dissemble, and gain so time.
(*aloud*) May I of this new crotchet ask the reason?
CREON: We do suspect that you are up to treason;
And, as to cut our throat you might incline,
We take a stitch in time that may save nine.
MEDEA: Who can believe such thought I ever nurst?
I, kill a king?
CREON: It wouldn't be the first.
Remember Pelias!
MEDEA: A vile aspersion!
His daughters killed him.
CREON: That's a mere assertion.
MEDEA: I swear it.
CREON: Poo, poo, you know well enough.
MEDEA: Indeed, great sir, they gave him the wrong stuff.
CREON: By your prescription.
MEDEA: Granted, – but his case
They had mis-stated, and had then the face
To throw on me the guilt of their omission;
So patients die, and blamed is the physician.
I brought from home with me a drug which some
Call (as I come from Colchis) Colchicum;
Arrived in Greece, as you have heard no doubt,
I found old Æson, crippled with the gout;
Because I cured him with this novel physic,
They drenched a man with it who'd got the phthisic;
And when I recommended venesection,
They slashed away at him in each direction;
Truth is, he'd made his will, his daughters knew it,
Thought that he'd cut up well, and chose to do it.
CREON: Supposing all you've said the truth to be,
I've made up my mind you shan't physic me;
You are a dab, I know, at hocus pocus,
But off this point you'll find it hard to choke us,
So quit the building without more ado.

Colchicum: a medicine for gout and rheumatism derived from the plant of that name.
venesection: the cutting or opening of a vein.

MEDEA: Good gracious, Creon! this is not like you.
A sovereign none would change, whilst they could own one!
The most gallant of monarchs fate has shown one!
The capital of this Corinthian order!
CREON: Begone, I charge you, none of your soft solder;
Your downy words don't weigh with me a feather.
MEDEA: Grant me a week to get my traps together?
CREON: To set your traps, you mean, to catch your prey;
I think I catch myself –
MEDEA: Then but a day –
One little day, to get the boys some shoes,
You are yourself a father, don't refuse.
Their own unnatural daddy doesn't care for 'em;
And fit to travel in, I've not a pair for 'em;
Have pity on such little soles as theirs,
Nor see them bootless as their mother's prayers!
CREON: Well, for their sakes I'll grant that brief delay,
You can't much mischief make in one short day.
MEDEA: (*aside*) Can't I?
CREON: 'Tis folly in me to retract,
But I'm too tender-hearted, that's a fact;
So mind, till sunset you may go a-shopping,
But after dark, Medea, you'd best be hopping;
For here if but another sun has seen 'em,
I'll hang the two you have, and you between them.
Trio – CREON, MEDEA, *and* CHORUS – *'Midas'*
CREON: Would you live another day, ma'am,
I'd advise you off to trot;
If you like it better – stay, ma'am,
If you like it better – stay, ma'am,
But if you do – you'd better not.
Fol de rol de rol, etc.
MEDEA: Fol de rol de rol, etc.
CHORUS: Fol de rol de rol, etc.
MEDEA: (*to* CREON) From you I can hope no quarter,
So to move I can't refuse.
(*aside to* CHORUS)
But I think I see his daughter –
But I think I see his daughter –
Standing in Medea's shoes!
Fol de rol de rol, etc.
CHORUS: (*aside to* MEDEA) Fol de rol de rol, etc.
ALL: Fol de rol de rol, etc.
(*Exit* CREON, *attended*.)

---

soft solder: flattery.

MEDEA: Now for revenge! Here comes perfidious Jason,
I wonder he can dare to look my face on.
(*Enter* JASON.)
JASON: So, madam, not content with me abusing,
The royal family you've been traducing;
Your foolish jealousy has wrecked you quite,
I'm sorry for you, but it serves you right.
MEDEA: And this to me, to thy devoted wife!
To me, who saved thy honour and thy life;
When between two mad bulls, 'twas but a toss up?
To me, who made of all thy friends the loss up?
Who doomed the dragon to a fate forlorner
Than any dragon fête at Hyde Park Corner;
Who, for thy sake, all filial love could smother,
Who suffered thee to lick her little brother?
Ungrateful Greek, false, flirting, perjured Jason!
The earth there lives no mortal wretch so base on.
JASON: It pains me that a person of condition
Should of herself make such an exhibition;
I own you got me out of some few hobbles
But I'm quite sick of these domestic squabbles,
And have no talent for recrimination;
My lawyer's drawn a deed of separation,
And if you'll sign it, and not make a noise,
I'll settle something handsome on the boys.
MEDEA: My boys; ah, there you touch a mother's heart;
Well, when folks can't agree, 'tis best to part.
Be mine the punishment, as mine the sin is –
Why should it fall upon the piccaninies?
JASON: *A la bonne heure* – now, madam, you talk sense
I'm vexed you gave my friend, the King, offence.
And as to Glauce –
MEDEA: Oh, don't name that creature!
I heard her say, 'If your wife bores you, beat her.'
JASON: You quite mistook her – the reverse meant she –
Beta, in Greek, you know, is 'Letter B'.
MEDEA: I stand corrected, and am all submission,
And to prove how sincere is my contrition,
Some relics of my former rank and station,
Which now to look upon were but vexation,
I'll beg her to accept in recollection
Of one who once possessed your heart's affection.
The splendid polka, richly bordered o'er,

---

dragon fête: fête at the Chinese exhibition held in Hyde Park in 1841–3.
hobbles: awkward or perplexing situations (*OED*).
polka: 'woman's tight-fitting jacket' (*OED*).

Which at our last grand fancy ball I wore,
And a galvanic ring, of virtue rare,
From all rheumatic pains to guard the fair!
JASON: But, silly woman, why give them away?
MEDEA: What now to me are rings or rich array?
What right, what heart have I to cut a splash?
JASON: But you might pop them if in want of cash.
MEDEA: Pop them? –
JASON: Of course, tho' cast off by your father,
Your uncle might assist you.
MEDEA: I would rather
Perish than pawn such precious things, or see
The pride of one ball made the spoil of three!
JASON: If you are bent on it, why be it so.
MEDEA: Farewell.
JASON: You'll sign the deed before you go?
MEDEA: Trust me. We part in peace?
JASON: Oh, by all means;
I don't bear malice, and I can't bear scenes;
I'll send my lawyer to you with the papers.
(*aside*) I vow the woman's given me the vapours!
MEDEA: (*aside*) I'll burn the writings, cut off thro' the sky,
And leave them all in their own Greece to fry. (*Exit*.)
JASON: I feel, this morning, I'm not quite the thing;
At supper, last night, with my friend the King,
I made too free with his old Chian wine –
It really is particularly fine! –
And toasted Glauce till I scarcely know,
Whether I hadn't better – leave her too.

Song – JASON – *'Vivi tu'* – *'Anna Bolena'*

Leave her too! I'm not quite sure, O!
Do men do so? – Ay, ten in twenty!
Leave her too – the thought abjure, O!
Prudence whispers, 'She's cash in plenty.'
The sweet soul, O 'twere best secure, O
Sign and seal, O! – you won't repent ye!
Tho' you've had a queer wife to start with,
Not Medeas all women are.
No, by Juno! but first, her I'll part with,
Of whom in terror I've been so far.
Fell Medea may form some plan, sir,
To cut short fair Glauce's reign, ah!

---

pop them: pawn them.
uncle: pawnbroker.
Anna Bolena: opera by Donizetti, performed at His Majesty's in 1831.

None to me could cause more pain, ah!
None a fiercer foe could fear,
I'll watch o'er her while I can, sir,
And before the furies arm her,
Packing send the Colchian charmer,
With a huge flea in her ear. (*Exit.*)
(*Enter* MEDEA.)

MEDEA: Go, vile deceiver, now in turn deceived –
To be bereft by her thou has bereaved
Of all thy faithless heart now holds most dear –
Psuche, my soul!
(*Enter* NURSE.)
Conduct the children here,
And from my old portmanteau let them bring
The crimson polka and the magic ring.

NURSE: Madam, I go. (*aside*) Some one will catch a Tartar. (*Exit.*)

CHORUS: (*advancing*) Madam, what are you at? What are you arter?

MEDEA: A bridal gift for Glauce I'm preparing.

CHORUS: And one, no doubt, she'll be the worse for wearing.

MEDEA: You may say that, with your own ugly mug,
But not aloud, for all must be kept snug,
Till the revenge hatched in this brain creative
Flares up sky-high! astonishing each native!
(*Enter* NURSE, *with the two* CHILDREN, *the ring, and the mantle.*)
Ah, they are here! My darlings, oh, my pets!
Your mother into fiddle-strings it frets,
To think how hard a rod Fate has in pickle;
'Toby, or not Toby' soon made to tickle.
Be ye the bearers of these gifts to Glauce,
Make your best bows, and be by no means saucy;
Beg her to wear them for Medea's sake.
They'll fit her for her pains, and no mistake!
Away –
(*Exit* NURSE, *with* CHILDREN *and presents.*)
Now fast around my spells shall fall
And soon play up old gooseberry with all.
Air – MEDEA – *'Irish Quadrille'*
A row there'll be in the building soon,
For I'll burn the palace and bolt the moon.
The rogues shall dance to a pretty tune,
Or I've no more *nous* than will fill a spoon.

---

catch a Tartar: 'tackle one who unexpectedly proves to be too formidable' (*OED*).
Toby, or not Toby: apart from the obvious Shakespearean echo, this phrase is liberally allusive in its own right, 'toby' being a Victorian word for a young child, a euphemism for the buttocks and, of course, the dog in a Punch and Judy show.
play up old gooseberry: play havoc, the deuce (*OED*).

The wench my wicked husband's toasted,
Soon shall be like an apple roasted.
Of Sisyphus's race I'll take a rise out.
And if you interfere, (*to* CHORUS) I'll tear your eyes out!
Row, row, row,
Won't I make a row,
For I'm in a precious humour,
Now, now, now.
CHORUS: Row, row, row,
Murder, here's a row!
Ain't she in a precious humour,
Now, now, now. (*Exit* MEDEA.)
As good as her word she will be, I've no doubt,
And that is as bad as she can be about;
And all this is owing to that rascal, Cupid,
Who, 'men, gods, and columns', turns raving or stupid.
If I were his father, I'd break all his bones,
Or send him to sea, like that other boy Jones;
For peace upon earth to expect is all stuff,
Whilst he plays at 'Blind Man,' in a full suit of buff.
Song – CHORUS – *'Fall of Paris'*
Lovers who are young, indeed, and wish to know the sort of life
That in this world you're like to lead, ere you can say you've caught a wife;
Listen to the lay of one who's had with Cupid much to do,
And love-sick once, is love-sick still, but in another point of view.
Woman, though so kind she seems, will take your heart, and tantalize it –
Were it made of Portland stone, she'd manage to M'Adamize it.
Dairy maid or duchess,
Keep it from her clutches,
If you'd ever wish to know a quiet moment more.
Wooing, cooing,
Seeming, scheming,
Smiling, wiling,
Pleasing, teasing,
Taking, breaking,
Clutching, touching,
Bosoms to the core.
O Love, you've been a villain since the days of Troy and Helen,
When you caused the fall of Paris, and of very many more.

Sisyphus's race: descendants of Sisyphus, legendary king of Corinth, who murdered all travellers entering his realm.
boy Jones: a persistent intruder into Queen Victoria's private apartments, who had been packed off to sea to keep him out of mischief.
Portland stone: high quality building stone quarried in the Isle of Portland.
M'Adamize it: break it up into small pieces, after the system of road-making devised by John McAdam (1756–1836) in the early years of the nineteenth century.

Sighing like a furnace, in the hope that you may win her still,
And losing health and appetite, and growing thin and thinner still;
Walking in the wet before her window or her door o' nights,
And catching nothing but a cold, with waiting there a score o' nights;
Spoiling paper, by the ream, with rhymes devoid of reasoning,
As silly and insipid as a goose without the seasoning.
Running bills with tailors,
Locking up by jailors,
Bread and water diet then your senses to restore.
Sighing, crying,
Losing, musing,
Walking, stalking,
Hatching, catching,
Spoiling, toiling,
Rhyming, chiming,
Running up a score.
O Love, you've been a villain, etc.
Finding all you've suffered has but been the sport of jilting jades,
And calling out your rival in the style of all true tilting blades;
Feeling, ere you've breakfasted, a bullet through your body pass,
And cursing, then, your cruel fate, and looking very like an ass.
Popped into a coffin, just as dead as suits your time of life;
Paragraphed in papers, too, as 'cut off in the prime of life'.
When the earth you're under
Just a nine days' wonder.
And the world jogs on again, exactly as before.
Jilting, tilting,
Calling, falling,
Swearing, tearing,
Lying, dying,
Cenotaphed and paragraphed,
And reckoned quite a bore.
O Love, you've been a villain, etc. (*Retires.*)

(*Re-enter* NURSE, *with* CHILDREN, *meeting* MEDEA.)

NURSE: Oh, missis, missis, you must cut and run!
MEDEA: Why, what's the matter?
NURSE: We are all undone!
MEDEA: Does Glauce spurn my gifts?
NURSE: Oh, would she had –
She took 'em in, as you have her.
MEDEA: I'm glad
To hear it. Tell me all, how do they fit her?
NURSE: Fit her! she's frying in them, like a fritter.
MEDEA: She stole my flame, and now in flames she lingers,
And with my wedding ring she's burnt her fingers.
The tyrant, Creon, too, does he not frizzle?

NURSE: He does – and so will you, unless you mizzle,
For all the palace now begins to blaze.
Oh, jump into a jarvey or a chaise,
A boat, a barge, a cab, or anything;
But don't stay here, unless you'd burn or swing.
MEDEA: Fly – save thyself; I've still a deed to do
No mortal eye may see, save my own two. (*Exit* NURSE.)
Yes, my poor children – yes, it must be done,
Your fate it is impossible to shun.
CHORUS: What would you do to them? Say, I implore.
MEDEA: (*drawing a rod from out the sheath of a dagger*)
That which I never did to them before.
CHORUS: Whip 'em? Oh, wherefore? Is the woman mad?
What is their crime?
MEDEA: They are too like their dad!
(*Snatches up* CHILDREN *and exit*.)
CHORUS: 'Tis plain her wrongs have driven her wild, or will.
Help, Jason, help!
(*Enter* JASON.)
JASON: How now? What more of ill
Has Jason now to dread? The King's a cinder;
My match is broken off – my bride is tinder;
And I am left, a poor, unhappy spark,
To go out miserably in the dark.
Where is the wicked worker of these woes?
CHORUS: Inflicting, now, the heaviest of blows
Upon thy children.
JASON: On my children – where?
CHORUS: Behind, of course.
CHILDREN: (*within*) Oh, mother, mother!
CHORUS: There!
You hear them?
JASON: (*Rushes to door*.) Paralysed with awe I stand –
Medea, hold, oh, hold thy barbarous hand;
The door is fast, where shall I find a crow?
CHORUS: You have one –
JASON: Where?
CHORUS: To pluck with her, you know.
JASON: I mean an iron crow, to force the gate
Which she has bolted.
MEDEA: (*within*) Fool, thou art too late!
JASON: Too late, by Jove! She's bolted, too – despair!

---

mizzle: decamp, 'depart slyly' (Partridge).
jarvey: a hackney-coach (*OED*).
a crow . . . to pluck with her: a bone to pick with her.

NURSE: (*entering*) Gone in a dragon-fly, no soul knows where.
JASON: A dragon-fly! How dare she so presume!
A witch's carriage ought to be a broom.
CHORUS: I said that she was flighty, and she's fled.
(*Thunder, etc. The Palace sinks, and* MEDEA *is seen in a chariot drawn by two fiery dragons, amidst the clouds*.)
The palace sinks – behold her there instead.
JASON: Thou wicked sorceress – thou vile magician!
Come out, I say, and meet thy just punition.
MEDEA: I told you I would play the very devil,
If to another you should dare be civil;
I've done the deed – didst thou not hear a noise?
JASON: Barbarian, I heard you flog the boys.
MEDEA: I didn't flog 'em – I but made believe.
CHORUS: Oh, shame! the very Chorus to deceive.
MEDEA: Stand up, my darlings. (*Shows* CHILDREN.) See, thou traitor, here is
Thy eldest, Mermerus – thy youngest, Pheres;
I bear them to the land of Erectheus,
By special invitation of Egeus.
To a Greek grammar school he means to send them,
And pay a private tutor to attend them.
Now hear the fate, false Jason, which shall fall
Upon thy head, thou wicked cause of all;
A timber of the Argo, that old barque,
Now rotting there, above high-water mark,
Clean out thy dull Bœotian brains shall dash.
JASON: Shiver my timbers, that will be a smash!
MEDEA: So shall the craft, of which thou wert the master,
Punish the craft that caused all my disaster.
JASON: And what will be thy fate, thou cruel fury?
MEDEA: My fate depends alone on the grand jury,
To whom the bill presented is tonight;
I fairly own I'm in an awful fright.
But if against me they don't find a true bill,
The Manager may not soon want a new bill.
(*to Audience*) Do you but smile, 'The Golden Fleece' we win.
'One touch of nature makes the whole world *grin*.'
Finale – 'Post Horn Galop'
CHORUS: Off she goes, sir – off she goes, sir!
Highty-tighty! highty-tighty!
Goodness knows, sir, all her woes, sir,
Made her flighty, made her flighty.

---

true bill: in criminal assizes 'a bill of indictment found by a Grand Jury to be supported by sufficient evidence to justify the hearing of a case' (*OED*).
'One touch of nature . . .': misquoted from Shakespeare's *Troilus and Cressida* (III.iii).

Calm her fury, gentle jury,
    Thus to end were most improper;
As they scream aboard a steamer –
    'Back her! ease her! stop her!'

MEDEA: (*to her* CHILDREN)
Now, my darlings, off we go;
Gee up! gee oh! gee up! gee oh!
    With your mammy pammy you
        Shall coachee poachee ride in.
If they wish us here to stay,
They know the way – they know the way
    To keep the peace, and give us too
        This merry house to bide in.

CHORUS: Off she goes, etc., etc.

JASON: (*to* AUDIENCE)
In your hands our cause we place,
    You alone can keep the peace, sirs;
If with you we but find grace,
    We have won the Golden Fleece, sirs.

CHORUS: Off she goes, etc.

ALL: Let not so Medea go!
Gee up! gee oh! gee up! gee oh!
    But with Jason and his crew,
        The Golden Fleece take pride in.
Say you wish us all to stay,
You know the way – you know the way
    To keep the peace, and give us too
        This merry house to bide in.

MEDEA (*in chariot*)

CHORUS. JASON.

Curtain

THE CAMP AT THE OLYMPIC

An introductory extravaganza and dramatic review in one act

First performed at the Olympic Theatre on Monday, 17 October 1853, with the following cast:

MATTER-OF-FACT PERSONS

THE NEW LESSEE, *a notorious Fact*	Mr Alfred Wigan
HIS WIFE, *an absolute Fact*	Mrs Alfred Wigan
STAGE CARPENTER, *a plain Fact*	Mr Deal
A BOY, *in fact*	The Call Boy

PERSONS OF IMAGINATION

FANCY, *on her way to a Fancy Ball*		Mrs T. G. Reed
TRAGEDY		Mrs Chatterley
COMEDY		Mrs Stirling
BURLESQUE	*The*	Mr F. Robson
OPERA		Miss Corri
BALLET	*Play-Household*	Miss Wyndham
MELODRAMA		Mr Sanders
PANTOMIME	*Brigade*	Miss Stevens
HIPPO-DRAME		Miss E. Turner
SPECTACLE		Mr Emery
GHOST OF THE OLD ITALIAN OPERA, *bearing a great bodily resemblance to a celebrated Basso*		Signor Galli
HARLEQUIN		Mr Franks
CLOWN		Mr H. Cooper
PANTALOON		Mr Lindon
COLUMBINE		Miss Henderson
THE TRUE BRITISH SAILOR		Mr Morton
SYLPHIDES		Mdlles Howard & Graham

The Tents of Real Canvas, painted, as well as the other Scenes (if not better) by Mr Dayes

The Gentlemen's Uniforms by that uniformly Civil though occasionally Military Tailor, Mr Brown

The Ladies to 'dress up' under the command of Mrs Curl

The Accoutrements by Mr Moreland

The Machinery by Mr Sutherland, of the Royal Olympic Engineers

SCENE. *The Stage at the Olympic Theatre. Enter* MR *and* MRS WIGAN, *arm-in-arm*.

MR W: Well, come what may, at least behold us here!
I hope you're satisfied? (*to* MRS WIGAN)
MRS W: So far, my dear,
The house is ours. We've nothing now to do
But –
MR W: Fill it. Do you call that nothing, too?
MRS W: Well, it's not much. The theatre is small,
And Lord John Clapham said he'd take –
MR W: A stall!
MRS W: Well, love, that's one – and one –
MR W: (*checking her*) '*Friend*', you would say,
'Makes many'. I devoutly wish it may,
However, we are in for it, and so
It's no use *talking*, we must *act*!
MRS W: I know
We must act, and I come resolved to play –
MR W: All the best parts.
MRS W: If they are in my way.
MR W: And yours is such a taking way, my dear.
MRS W: Come, Mr Impudence, you needn't sneer,
There *was* a time, to which I *could* allude –
MR W: Nay, don't be angry.
MRS W: Then don't you be rude.
MR W: I'd not the least intention. Don't let's squabble!
But as you've got me into such a hobble –
MRS W: *I* got you
MR W: Well, no matter then, since *we*
Have got into it, let us, pray, agree
Upon some plan, at least, to get well out of it.
You think we shall succeed?
MRS W: I've not a doubt of it!
MR W: Bless the dear women! They're such sanguine souls!
Whilst men in doubt stand scratching their dull polls,
They, by mere force of will, their ends achieve!
'*Ce que femme veut, Dieu veut*', I do believe!
And so at once to business. I have got
An opening piece, of which I like the plot.
(*Takes MS out of his pocket.*)
(*reading title*) 'The Camp at Chobham'.

Lord John Clapham: perhaps a reference to Lord John Russell, then the leader of the House of Commons and erstwhile prime minister, a man of pronounced literary and theatrical sympathies ('clap 'em'?); or, more tenuously still, to some pro-theatre Quaker whose traces have not survived in the publications of the Society of Friends.

Ce que femme veut, Dieu veut: 'what woman wills is God-willed' (French proverb).

The Camp at Chobham: farce by Mark Lemon produced in June 1853.

MRS W: Law! Why, that's been done
At the Adelphi!
MR W: *A* piece – not this one.
MRS W: But the same titles –
MR W: More attractive make 'em.
When titles are so catching people take 'em
Just as they do the measles – from each other.
And 'bout this Camp there has been such a pother,
The name alone is money sure to bring.
So here, you man! fly-catching at the wing –
(*A* CARPENTER *advances from between wings.*)
Show us a pair of flats.
(CARPENTER *smiles*) What do you mean
By grinning? Get me out, sir, a tent scene!
(*aside*) Of flats, I'll swear, that rascal meant to say
We were the biggest pair he'd seen today.
(*A tent scene is put on.*)
What's this?
CAR: King Richard's tent, sir.
MR W: That will do.
It's so old that it's actually new.
'Methinks the ghosts of all who've Richard murthered'
Arise before me! Our cause won't be furthered
Much by such actors. (*to* CARPENTER) Two chairs, if you've got 'em!
(CALL BOY *brings forward two old broken chairs.*)
One with three legs – the other with no bottom!
'This is a sorry sight!'
MRS W: 'A foolish thought
To say a sorry sight' – you rather ought
To think it a good omen here.
MR W: How so?
MRS W: If we can't *sit* we *must stand*!
MR W: Oh! oh! oh!
You've got the inventory of the dresses;
What regimentals are there in the presses?
MRS W: (*producing a paper and reading from it*)
'Uniform coats, one red, one green, one blue.'
MR W: I don't call that quite uniform. Do you?
MRS W: (*continuing*) 'Three guns, two bayonets, one sword and belt.'
MR W: How about hats?
MRS W: Ah, there the pinch is felt!
Only one cocked hat!
MR W: Humph, that won't go far
To carry on, as we may say, the war;

---

flats: greenhorns or fools (Partridge), punning with the theatrical term for pieces of stage scenery.

Although at Astley's half-a-dozen horses
And twenty men play all the British forces!
MRS W: I'll tell you what, we'll have *one* man well dressed,
And let the audience fancy all the rest.
MR W: Ah, if we could bring Fancy to our aid!
(FANCY *rises from trap, in a jester's costume.*)
FAN: Fancy you can. It's done as soon as said.
MR W: 'Angels and ministers of grace defend us!'
What does this novel stage effect portend us?
MRS W: 'Be thou a spirit of health or goblin' –
FAN: Hum!
MR W: 'Bring with thee airs from heaven or blasts from' –
FAN: Mum!
I'm Fancy.
MRS W: Only fancy that!
MR W: Who'd guess,
In such a habit –
FAN: It's a fancy dress.
MRS W: A fool's – saving your presence.
FAN: You forget
That Fancy plays the fool with sense, and yet
Without some fancy Sense would be a frump,
While without sense Fancy's not worth a dump!
Their happy union makes for youth and age
The choicest entertainments of the stage,
(For which I have the greatest partiality)
And give to every scene I touch reality.
MR W: Then pray touch some of mine up, and I'd name
This tent for one.
FAN: With that intent I came.
Air – FANCY – *'La Donna è mobile'*
Fancy her magical
Influence lending,
Mortals befriending,
As much as befooling,
Comical – Tragical –
Classic – Romantic;
Aping each antic –
Every sense ruling –
As you request her,
Comes as a jester,
Gaily to test her
Influence here.

Astley's: Astley's Amphitheatre, renowned for performances of equestrian melodrama and similar spectacles.
dump: small amount.

On each sensorium,
Wild airs essaying –
Fancy sets playing
The world at 'supposes'.
From her emporium,
Fashion proceeding –
All the town leading
By their own noses.
Her stage direction
Baffles objection;
Fancy perfection
Can make it appear.
But not at Chobham shall my camp be found –
The common there is now too common ground
To be brushed up by even Fancy's wing.
'The Camp at the Olympic' is the thing!
Here all the Drama's forces we'll review,
And see what troops will flock her standard to.
At Fancy's call, the Play-Household Brigade
Shall turn out for inspection on parade!
(*to* MR WIGAN) You as Field-Marshal shall command in chief.

(MR WIGAN *retires through tent, and immediately re-enters in a Field Marshal's uniform with bâton*.)

(*to* MRS WIGAN) You as 'White Sergeant' come with the relief.

(MRS WIGAN *goes off, and re-appears in white dress*.)

Changing that horrid every day dress
For one which may your brevet rank express
In Fancy's Army. Here begins my reign;
Current I make 'the coinage of the brain',
And General Orders issue from this station,
Now the Head-Quarters of Imagination.

Trio – FANCY, MR *and* MRS WIGAN – *'Rat-a-plan'*

Rat-a-plan! Rat-a-plan! Rat-a-plan!
To arms! to arms! ye mighty spirits muster!
Here pitch your tents – your standards here unfold.
To arms! to arms! the British Drama's lustre,
At Fancy's call shed round us as of old!
To arms! the Drama's cause uphold!
Rat-a-plan! Rat-a-plan! Rat-a-plan! Rat-a-plan!

A new campaign the Drama here prepare for,
With souls in arms and eager for the fray,
Your fights are all sham fights, you know, and therefore

---

brevet rank: in military parlance, an acting (unpaid) rank (Partridge).
'the coinage of the brain': from Shakespeare's *Hamlet* (III. iv).

At soldiers sure you can't object to play.
To arms! the magic call obey.
Rat-a-plan! Rat-a-plan! etc.

(*Scene changes to the Camp of the Combined British Dramatic Forces; on one side are the characteristic tents of* TRAGEDY, MELODRAMA, *and* OPERA: *on the other those of* COMEDY, FARCE, *and* PANTOMIME. *In the centre is the large and splendid pavilion of* SPECTACLE.)

(*Music (grand march). Enter* TRAGEDY *from her tent in the costume of LADY MACBETH, 1753, a letter in her hand.*)

FAN: First in the field, old English Tragedy
In stately hoop and train 'comes sweeping by!'
As in the British Drama's palmy day,
When people took an interest in the play!
MR W: A letter in her hand! Why, then the dame is –
FAN: The wife of the ambitious Thane of Glamis!
MRS W: Lady Macbeth! In Dollalolla's dress!
TRA: (*reading the letter*) 'They met me in the day of my success.'
MR W: That must have been a hundred years ago,
To judge from a costume so rococo!
TRA: (*indignantly*) In my day, sir, judgment, and power, and feeling,
With confidence to public taste appealing,
Received the crown – no matter what its fashion,
It *was* the crown!
MR W: Well, don't be in a passion.
TRA: Not in a passion! when I see the state
Of Denmark rotten! When I hear the fate
Which hath befallen both the classic domes,
'Neath which my votaries once found their homes!
Where Garrick, monarch of the mimic scene,
His sceptre passed from Kemble down to Kean;
Where Cibber's silver tones the heart would steal,
And Siddons left her mantle to O'Neil!
The Drama banished from her highest places
By *débardeurs* and 'fools with varnished faces',
Sees foreign foes her sacred ruins spurning,
Fiddling like Neros while her Rome is burning!
FAN: The times have changed; but there is still a stage,
And one on which Macbeth has been the rage!

LADY MACBETH, 1753: Hannah Pritchard, who played the part opposite Garrick and is so portrayed in Zoffany's famous painting of the dagger scene.
Dollalolla: the queen in Fielding's burlesque tragedy *Tom Thumb*, first performed at the New Haymarket Theatre in 1730.
'They met me . . .': allusion to Macbeth's letter relating his encounter with the witches.
both the classic domes: the two erstwhile patent theatres, Covent Garden and Drury Lane.
débardeurs: carnival revellers in garish costume.

TRA: Macbeth! Is't possible! O, hie thee here,
That I may pour my spirit in thine ear!

(*Music. The pavilion opens and discovers 'The Blasted Heath', same as at the Princess's Theatre, with the Three Witches, MACBETH and BANQUO in the costume worn at that theatre. Temp. 1853.*)

FAN: Behold, he comes!
TRA: 'Great Glamis! worthy Cawdor!'
Can that be he?
FAN: In heavy marching order.
Not as when Garrick used to meet the witches –
In gold-laced waistcoat and red velvet breeches;

(*GARRICK appears as MACBETH with the daggers.*)

Nor as in Kemble's time, correct was reckoned,
Accoutred like 'the gallant forty-second',

(*KEMBLE appears as MACBETH, with target and truncheon.*)

But as a Scottish chieftain roamed scot-free –
In the year one thousand and fifty-three.

Trio – MR *and* MRS WIGAN *and* FANCY – *'Auld Lang Syne'*

My auld acquaintance I've forgot,
If ever he was mine;
Is that the way they clad a Scot
In days o' Lang Syne?
For Auld Lang Syne, my dear,
For Auld Lang Syne,
We'll look on him wi' kindness yet
For Auld Lang Syne!

TRA: 'My countryman – and yet I know him not!'
MR W: More like an antique *Rum'un* than a Scot!
TRA: A Scotchman, and no kilt?
MRS W: Don't Macbeth say,
'We've scotch'd the snake, not kilt it!'
MR W: Oh, don't pray!

(*Scene closes.*)

Air – FANCY – *'The Bonnets of Bonny Dundee'*

Through their habits conventional managers broke,
To make old plays go down they new habits bespoke;
The old-fashioned Scotchman no longer we see,
Except as a sign for the sale of rappee.
So pack up your tartans, whatever your clan,
And look a new 'garb of old Gaul' out, my man;
For the stage in its bonnet has got such a bee,
It's all up with 'The Bonnets of Bonny Dundee'.

FAN: But see, where brilliant Comedy appears,

---

the gallant forty-second: the Black Watch (Royal Highland) Regiment.
rappee: coarse, strong-flavoured snuff.

(*Music. Enter* COMEDY *from her tent, in the costume of LADY TEAZLE.*)

Blooming as brightly as in former years,
Invincible, with powder, paint, and patches,
Loaded and primed – her eyes the lighted matches –
Ready to play upon a yawning pit,
She brings up the artillery of wit!

COM: Wit! oh, my dear, don't mention such a thing!
Wit on the stage what wit away would fling?
There are so few who know it when they hear it,
And half of those don't like so much as fear it.
Wit! If to theatres for wit they'd come,
Would Farquhar, Congreve, Wycherly be dumb?
Or even the poor devils now-a-days,
Who can't help scribbling, hawk their hapless plays
From house to house, to hear the sentence chilling,
'Your piece is clever, but won't draw a shilling.'

MR W: Then, what will draw?

COM: O mercy! Tell me, pray,
What horse will win the Derby, sir? You may,
I'm sure, as easily as I tell you
What the dear British public will come to!
Just what they like – whatever that may be –
Not much to hear, and something strange to see.
A Zulu Kaffir, with his bow and quiver;
A Pigmy Earthman, from the Orange River;
An Aztec Lilliputian, who can't say a
Word, from the unknown city Iximaya.
Any monstrosity may make a hit,
But no one's fool enough to pay for wit!
Or if he be, in theatres why seek
For jokes, when *Punch* is but a groat a week!

MR W: No wonder that in such a situation
Your spirits flag!

COM: My only consolation
Is that all sorts of folks are now so funny,
My dullness will be soon worth any money.
E'en Tragedy – my sister there – sad soul,
Has recently become so very droll,

LADY TEAZLE: leading character in Sheridan's *The School for Scandal*, produced at Drury Lane in 1777.
Zulu Kaffir: Kaffirs had featured in the London 'African exhibition' of 1850 and in another at St George's Gallery, Hyde Park Corner, earlier in 1853, which purported to show 'the whole of Caffre life'; a pair of pygmy 'Earthmen' from South Africa and two 'Aztec Lilliputians' from Central America had also drawn great crowds when exhibited during the summer of 1853.
groat: fourpence, which was the price of *Punch* for country readers in 1853; in London it cost threepence.

That the judicious few her acts who see,
Laugh at her more than at poor Comedy!
TRA: (*advancing on her*) Madam! This irony! –
COM: Oh, lud! she'll bite!
MR W: Part them! they are incensed!
FAN: A jest so light
Should not to any serious censure doom her;
Like Mr Sulky – she 'will have her humour'.
TRA: Will she, indeed? Then I'll forgive her gladly,
For lately she has wanted humour sadly.
COM: Now who's ironical, dear sister, pray?
'Oh, sister, sister! sister ev'ry way!'
MR W: Come, come, be friends! The Drama's foes to rout,
The word should be 'fall in' and not 'fall out'.

Air – MR WIGAN – *'We have been friends together'*
You have been friends together,
Together money made –
When tragedies and comedies
To crowds were nightly played!
And though the word may make you start,
The fact you must allow,
You have been – damned together!
Shall a light word part you now?

MRS W: Talking of humour – where on earth has fled
Our broad old English Farce? or is he dead?
FAN: No, but too homely for this polished age,
He's lately taken French leave of the stage;
But there's a substitute still more grotesque
We often find for him – he's called Burlesque.
TRA: Don't name the wretch! I hate him with a hate
Known only on the stage! He mocks my state;
Mimics my voice; my words mis-quotes, mis-matches,
A vice of kings! a king of shreds and patches!
(*Flourish of penny trumpets heard.*)
FAN: He comes! I know his trumpet!
TRA: Too! too! too –
Well I remember it! Support me, do!
MR W: Tragedy! show me where's the actor strong enough?
TRA: Then I shall fall! (*Sinks into a chair.*)
MRS W: Alas, I've thought so long enough!
(*Charivari. Enter* BURLESQUE *in the costume of KING ARTHUR in 'Tom Thumb'.*)
BUR: 'Call up our cavalry from Horselydown!'
Queen Tragedy, I'll fight you for a crown!

Air – BURLESQUE – *'Such a fine King as I!'*
Such a fine King as I,
Don't care for your frowns a fig!

Folks laugh till they're ready to die
At the wisdom that's in – my wig!
For Burlesque is up! up! up!
And Tragedy down! down! down! O!
Pop up your nob again!
And I'll box you for your crown, O!
Toll rol der rol loll, etc.
Your Hamlet may give up his Ghost,
Your Richard may run himself through,
I'm Cock-of-the-Walk to your cost,
And I crow over all your crew!
For Burlesque is up! up! up!
And Tragedy down! down! down! O!
Pop up your nob again,
And I'll box you for your crown, O!
Toll rol der rol loll, etc.

TRA: Avaunt, and quit my sight! let the earth hide thee
Unreal mockery, hence! I can't abide thee!
BUR: Because I fling your follies in your face,
And call back all the false starts of your race
Show up your shows, affect your affectation,
And by such homœopathic aggravation,
Would cleanse your bosom of that perilous stuff,
Which weighs upon our art – bombast and puff.
MR W: Have you so good a purpose then in hand?
BUR: Else wherefore breathe I in dramatic land?
MRS W: I thought your aim was but to make us laugh?
BUR: Those who think so but understand me half.
Did not my thrice-renownèd Thomas Thumb,
That mighty mite, make mouthing Fustian mum?
Is Tilburina's madness void of matter?
Did great Bombastes strike no nonsense flatter?
When in his words he's not one to the wise,
When his fool's bolt *spares* folly as it flies,
When in his chaff there's not a grain to seize on,
When in his rhyme there's not a ray of reason,
His slang but slang, no point beyond the pun,
Burlesque may walk, for he will cease to run.
MR W: Although your trumpet, sir, is but a penny one,
You blow it, I confess, as well as any one!
COM: I vow the wretch to common sense pretends!

Fustian: bombast, rant, and hence a writer or speaker thereof; the tragedy-author is so named in two of Fielding's satirical pieces, *Pasquin* and *Tumble-Down Dick*.
Tilburina: the heroine of Mr Puff's tragedy, *The Spanish Armada*, in Sheridan's *The Critic*.
Bombastes: the general in Rhodes's burlesque, *Bombastes Furioso*.
penny one: a toy trumpet, or 'petty boasting' (*OED*).

BUR: Don't mention it, I beg, e'en among friends.
Like Mr Snake, though here the truth I own,
I should be ruined if abroad 'twere known.
I live as that same worthy does aver
Upon the badness of my character.
If once of common sense I was suspected,
I should be quite as much as you – neglected.
TRA: 'That's wormwood!'
(*music*)
MR W: Hark! what means that prelude grand?
(*Enter* ENGLISH OPERA *as Mandane in 'Artaxerxes', with a German Band.*)
FAN: 'Tis English Opera!
MRS W: With a foreign band!
FAN: She takes the best her music book that suits.
She always had French horns and German flutes.
COM: Has she forgot her native wood-notes wild?
FAN: She hasn't chirped them since she was a child.
TRA: You mean 'When music, heavenly maid, was young,
And first in early Greece – she – she – '
BUR: (*prompting her*) 'Gave tongue.'
(TRAGEDY *sits down disgusted*.)
FAN: But not in Opera like that before us,
The Greeks had none.
TRA: They'd Tragedy!
MR W: And Chorus!
FAN: Yes! *spoken*, so that you heard every word;
A sort of chorus now that's never heard.
MR W: But let us hear what Opera has to say,
Or rather sing, in her own cause to-day.
OP: (*Sings.*) 'The soldier tired of war's alarms', etc.
MR W: (*interrupting her*) Thank you! that's quite enough! Oh dear! Oh dear!
BUR: That old style don't agree with the new y(ear)!
MRS W: It was a stile I hoped she had got over!
OP: Of English Opera you wished a 'Prova';
And that's about the best in English still.
MR W: Except 'the Beggar's'.
OP: That's a vaudeville!
MR W: Have you no new and great airs on your shelves?
OP: The greatest airs the singers give themselves!
FAN: And while they do so there is little chance
Of seeing English Opera advance;

Mr Snake: character in Sheridan's *The School for Scandal*.
Artaxerxes: opera by Arne, performed at Covent Garden in 1762.
Prova: demonstration, or rehearsal.

The only compositions her proveditors
Have lately gained by have been with their creditors.
MR W: Then Bishop, Balfe, and Barnett, where are they?
MRS W: Wallace! Macfarren!
TRA: (*wildly*) 'Rivers! Vaughan! Grey!'
OP: Madam!
FAN: Poor soul! Her wits are going fast,
She has not seemed quite right for some time past
And now Burlesque completely has upset her.
TRA: I shall weep soon, and then I shall be better!
MRS W: Suppose you take a nap?
COM: Aye, sister, do;
Your audience sleep sometimes, why shouldn't you?
MRS W: (*to* COMEDY) You're too severe upon your sister muse.
(*to* OPERA) This interruption, madam, pray excuse.
OP: Sir, I'm accustomed to a few bars' rest.
MR W: You spoke of airs by which you were oppressed.
OP: Oh, e'en my foreign rivals on that score
Suffer as much as I do, if not more;
One has already given up the ghost.
FAN: See where it walks!

(*Ghost music from 'Don Giovanni'. The* GHOST *of Her Majesty's Theatre appears, having a great bodily resemblance to Signor Lablache.*)

Once in itself a host!
The last, but not the least by any means,
Of the great stars that lighted up her scenes.
MR W: What, old acquaintance! could not all that flesh
Keep in a little life? Mine ears refresh
With choice Italian. Speak, 'Ore rotundo!'
Enormous artist! Great basso profundo!

Ensemble from 'Don Pasquale'

Solo – GHOST OF OLD ITALIAN OPERA
Pacing yon colonnade

---

proveditors: purveyors of works.
Bishop, etc.: Henry Bishop (1786–1855), Michael Balfe (1808–70), John Barnett (1802–90), Vincent Wallace (1812–65) and George Macfarren (1813–87) were all contemporary composers of opera and theatre music and collaborators with Planché at one time or another.
'Rivers! Vaughan! Grey!': three adversaries whom Richard III had imprisoned and executed at Pomfret Castle in order to secure his accession to the throne; the line itself derives either from Queen Margaret's 'revenge' speech in Act IV of Shakespeare's play or, more probably, from three successive exclamations by the Duchess of York and Queen Elizabeth in Cibber's version, conflated no doubt to emphasise Tragedy's distracted state.
Signor Lablache: Luigi Lablache, famous basso and star of the Italian Opera at Her Majesty's until it closed to opera at the end of the disastrous 1852 season.
'Ore rotundo!': in well-rounded speech, from Horace's *Ars poetica*: 'Graiis ingenium, Graiis dedit ore rotundo/Musa loqui . . . (ll. 323–4).
Don Pasquale: opera by Donizetti, performed at Her Majesty's in 1843.

Most melancholy,
Humming the serenade –
From 'Don Pasquale';
Nightly I wander – sighing and sulky,
No more in Figaro, brilliant as bulky!
Dull is thy valet now,
Gay Don Giovanni!
What trump shall rally now
'I Puritani'?
My Impresario
Plays 'Belisario',
Grisi and Mario
Partiti son!
Trio – MR WIGAN, FANCY, ENGLISH OPERA
Bravo, bravo! Don Pasquale!
Can no magic flute recall ye,
Whose superb recitativo
Could this great basso relieve O?
Caro mio, let this trio –
So enchanting, so bewitching,
Bring a moment back to Fancy,
The great rôle you were so rich in!

GHOST: Bene, si!
Now fortissimo!
Now pianissimo!
Bravo, bravissimo –
Bene, si.

TRIO: But while we strive
Once more alive
To fancy Don Pasquale,
We find, alas,
The shadow pass,
And so as a finale,
Regretting one so great should e'er
Be forced to sing so smally,
Addio, addio, unhappy Buffo say!

GHOST: To the shades I must away,
There a deeper part to play!
(GHOST *retires*.)

I Puritani: opera by Bellini, performed at Her Majesty's in 1835.
My Impresario/Plays 'Belisario': the proprietor of the Italian Opera at Her Majesty's, Benjamin Lumley, whose managerial endeavours had made him virtually bankrupt in 1852.
Grisi and Mario: the soprano, Giulia Grisi, and her partner for many years, the tenor Giovanni Mario, became regular members of the Italian opera company at Covent Garden.
Partiti son: have departed.

BUR: Poor Buffer!
MRS W: Buf*fo*.
MR W: In his situation
'Buffer's' the more expressive appellation.
(*to* FANCY) 'Our cause, my friend, is in a damn'd condition',
The Drama's perishing of inanition,
In all its branches, foreign and domestic.
Tragedy halting in her march majestic;
Poor Comedy with nothing left to spout;
Farce only fit to play the people out;
The English Opera completely prostrate,
And the Italian taken up to Bow Street.

Air – MR WIGAN – *'Oft in the stilly night'*

When I remember all
The talent brought together,
I've seen in 'Don Pasqual –
E', and in such high feather –
I grieve, I own, that he alone
Should haunt that stage deserted,
Whose lights are fled, and garlands dead,
And all but he – departed;
Still on an opera night,
When other voices wound me –
Fond memory brings the light
Of all those stars around me!

MRS W: And whither has the once gay Ballet hopped?
FAN: Like the poor sylphide when her wings were cropped,
Behold her shorn of all her magic power,
Denied to dance upon a single flower.

(*Enter* BALLET *'à la Sylphide', with her* CORYPHÉES. *She expresses her altered state in action to* MR WIGAN.)

MR W: What does she mean? I'm stupid, I've no doubt,
But I could never make a ballet out.
With diplomatic notes take rank they should,
The most successful when least understood
BAL: Oh I could tell you, sir, in words as well,
But if the Ballet talk'd it mightn't tell.
FAN: She tells you, fallen from her high estate,
On her last legs she's taken now to skate
Like a bold wench, resolved at any price
To cut a figure, though it's but on ice.

Bow Street: the site of Covent Garden Theatre, which had become the London home of Italian opera after its (temporary) demise at Her Majesty's in the previous year.
sylphide: in the romantic ballet *La Sylphide*, first danced in London by Marie Taglioni in 1832, the sylph sheds her wings and dies when a magic shawl which would bind her to earthly life is placed on her shoulders.

(*Music. Scene at back opens and shows the skating scene from 'Le Prophète', as at the Italian Opera, Covent Garden.*)

Air – BALLET – *Skating Music in 'Le Prophète'*

We slide and glide and slip and trip,
And wheel and reel through snow and sleet,
These are bad days when Coryphées
Are puzzled to keep their feet!
We colds have caught and chilblains brought,
To spite our light fantastic toes!
And vile Jack Frost perhaps may cost
Poor Ballet her lovely nose!

(*Scene closes.*)

MR W: Cold comfort this for a new speculator!
MRS W: For a house warming – a refrigerator!
MR W: A drama must be found, or we are undone,
With spirit in it to stir up all London!
FAN: Oh, if you want a piece with spirit in it,
I'll call up Melodrama in a minute.
His efforts supernatural have told,
When all things else have failed. Appear!

(*A chord.* MELODRAMA *comes through his tent as 'the Monster', in 'Frankenstein'.*)

Behold!

MR W: What monster's this?
FAN: The one from 'Frankenstein'.
He reads a lesson to folks in your line.
How many a manager I've seen a stew in,
Making a monster that has been his ruin!
MRS W: He looks of blue ruin the incarnation!
I've no great hopes from his resuscitation!
FAN: There is a spirit of another blue;
He sometimes personates the fine old 'true'!

(*Chord. Enter* WILLIAM *in the melodrama of 'Black-eyed Susan'.*)

FAN: Of 'Black-eyed Susan' there the hero stands,
Into the pit he oft has piped all hands,
And brought the drama up with a wet sail.
BUR: He goes a-head – but thereby hangs – a tail.
COM: All in the Downs the British fleet lay moored,

Le Prophète: opera by Meyerbeer, performed at Covent Garden in 1849.
Frankenstein: the reference is probably to H. M. Milner's adaptation of Mary Shelley's romance, produced at the Royal Coburg in 1823, though other versions existed.
blue ruin: see note to p. 154 above.
blue . . . true: faithful, staunch.
'Black-eyed Susan': melodrama by Douglas Jerrold, produced at the Surrey Theatre in 1829.
with a wet sail: swiftly and successfully (*OED*).
All in the Downs: a fleet anchorage off the Kent coast opposite the North Downs (and the sub-title of *Black-eyed Susan*).

When 'Black-eyed Susan' came the stage on board;
The scene is changed – the fleet is at Spithead,
And our poor stage 'All in the Downs' instead.

FAN: Well, there's another sprite at Christmas time
That oft does wonders – Comic Pantomime!
Spite of blows, tumbles, changes, kicks, and slaps,
She makes her annual trips and sets her traps.

(*Music.* PANTOMIME *enters as 'Mother Goose',* HARLEQUIN, COLUMBINE, PANTALOON, *and* CLOWN *rise up trap, dance, rally, group.*)

BUR: Shade of Grimaldi! who thy loss can know,
That never saw Inimitable Joe!

Quintette – BURLESQUE, FANCY, OPERA, *and* MR *and* MRS WIGAN – *'There's some one in the house with Dinah'*

Solo – BURLESQUE: (*bone accompaniment*)
Old Joe he was an artist great,
There's been nobody like him seen of late;
To Pantomime 'twas a knock down blow
When the curtain fell upon poor old Joe!
Poor dear Joe – was *the* Joe – yes, *the* Joe!

ALL:
Old Joe kicking up behind and before,
The Columbine a kicking up behind old Joe;
There's no one in this house so fine, ah,
Nor any other house I know,
There's no one in that funny line, ah,
Can play the fool like dear old Joe!

MRS W: But though such kickshaws may succeed perchance,
We must have some *'morceau de résistance'*;
And from such fare we're as far off as ever.

MR W: Do help us, Fancy!

FAN: Well, don't I endeavour?
Shall I invoke the genius of the ring?

MRS W: What! from Aladdin?

FAN: Quite another thing;
One who knows how the public in to whip,
And witch the world with noble horsemanship.

(*Music. Enter* HIPPO-DRAME *as a lady attired for the ring,* RIDING MASTER, *etc.*)

FAN: Hither he brought amusement for the million,
When here old Astley first pitched his pavilion.

Air – FANCY – *'I'm the Genius of the Ring'*
He's the Genius of the Ring,
To this house by no means new,

Grimaldi: Joseph Grimaldi (1778–1837), the greatest of all English pantomime clowns.

Horses here could money bring,
    Ere the stage they were put to;
And when fast the stage has stuck,
    As all stages sometimes do,
Horses oft have had the luck
    The poor Drama to pull through.

On Parnassus' highest ground
    Still a wingèd horse one views,
And a horse is to be found
    Wheresoever there's a Mews;
And if Thespis in a cart
    Made the Drama first the rage,
Horses must have played their part
    In that very early stage.

    To the Genius of the Ring
        Then be ev'ry honour due,
    If the Drama's not the thing,
    Try what Hippo-drame can do!

MR W: Soft sawdust! I am proof against soft sawder;
    I've great respect for the equestrian order,
    And hope its members oft my stalls will pay to;
    But horses on the stage I must say nay to.
    To cavalry I own its obligations,
    But there's no field here for its operations;
    The genius of the ring it would but cramp,
    And might put out the genius of the lamp.

FAN: You're very hard to please.

MR W: The town is harder!
    And sadly empty the dramatic larder.
    While army-raising Fancy plays the fairy at,
    I fear she quite forgets the Commissariat!
    The bravest troops that ever took the field,
    If they've no food to fight upon, must yield.

(*Music.* SPECTACLE *appears in splendid fancy dress.*)

SPEC: You're right; and then the food should be well drest,
    Or quite uneatable may be the best.

MR W: Who's this that talks and looks so mighty fine?

FAN: Spectacle! a great friend of mine.

BUR:
OP:
PAN:
MELO:
and
HIPPO: } And mine!

---

soft sawder: see note to p. 163 above.

FAN: You've heard of him, of course!
MR W: And seen him, too,
Till I am almost sick of him! aren't you?
SPEC: Is this your gratitude for all the splash
I've made upon the stage, and all the cash
I've brought into the treasury?
MR W: I doubt
If you bring in as much as you take out.
SPEC: Well, try a piece without me now-a-days;
See if your triumph will be called a blaze!
MR W: The blaze is often only in the bill –
MRS W: Or one that burns the fingers through the till.
COM: Why should a drama that deserves success
Burn blue lights, like a vessel in distress?
TRA: Has not immortal Shakespeare said 'tis silly,
'To gild refinèd gold – to paint the lily?'
SPEC: Immortal Shakespeare! come, the less you say
The better on that head. There's not a play
Of his for many a year the town has taken,
If I've not buttered preciously his bacon.
TRA: More shame, then, for the town!
SPEC: (*to* COMEDY) And you, Miss Prue;
Pray, has Spectacle nothing done for you?
Have I not given you correct costumes,
And furnished splendidly your drawing-rooms!
Ungrateful minx! till my Augustan age
You never saw a carpet on your stage.
Dragging your train through dust of other days,
You envied Tragedy her old green baize;
And all the sticks to muster you were able
Consisted but of two chairs and a table!
COM: You have improved my room, I don't deny,
But you preferred it to my company;
And Lady Townley now, or Lady Teazle,
May starve unless she'll dance, 'Pop goes the weasel!'
FAN: What's to be done when the immortal names
Of Shakespeare and of Byron urge their claims,
In vain to popularity, without
Spectacle march all his contingent out?
Not mere Dutch metal, spangles, foil, and paste,
But gems culled from authority by Taste;
Until, reflecting every bygone age,
A picture-gallery becomes the stage;

---

buttered . . . his bacon: furnished him with extravagant staging (Partridge).
Lady Townley [sic]: leading character in Cibber and Vanbrugh's comedy *The Provok'd Husband*, produced at Drury Lane in 1728.
Dutch metal: cheap imitation gold leaf.

And modern Babylon may there behold
The pomp and pageantry that wrecked the old!
(*Music. The Pavilion of* SPECTACLE *opens and discovers Tableau from 'Sardanapalus'*)
MRS W: It seems, then, that the new way to success
Is, when the Drama halts, to make it dress.
FAN: 'The tailor makes the man', we used to say –
The tailor makes the manager, today.
COM: Oh, if he'd really be our benefactor,
Let him take one stitch more and make the actor!
FAN: Well, Fancy has done all she can to aid you,
And seems more fanciful but to have made you.
You must make up your mind – if you have got one –
Out of all these fair offers is there not one
That you can count on?
TRA: (*to* MR WIGAN) Tragedy restore
To the proud station that she held of yore!
COM: (*to* MR WIGAN) Give Comedy again a chance to play
Where folks may hear what she has got to say.
MR W: Thus Tragedy and Comedy between,
I stand like Garrick – in the print, I mean,
The only way like him that I could stand –
A musing, with a Muse on either hand!
Now swayed by Mirth – now mov'd by Melancholy,
Or, like Macheath, 'twixt Lucy and poor Polly!
Air – MR WIGAN – *'How happy could I be with either'*
How happy could I be with either,
If either were certain to pay,
But really I much question whether
To both I had not better say –
Tol de rol de rol lol de rol loddy, etc.
(TRAGEDY *knocks his hat out of his hand.* COMEDY *picks it up, brushes, and restores it to him.*)
OP: Let native music here, then, weave her spell –
You really sing yourself, sir, pretty well;
Italian Opera can't object to roam (Rome),
For English Opera 'there's no place like home'.
MELO: Try me! I keep all spirits under my lock!
BUR: Try me, my boy, remember Mr Shylock!
PAN: Before you leap, just look at one of mine!

---

modern Babylon: London.
Sardanapalus: tragedy by Byron, produced at Drury Lane in 1834.
'there's no place like home': from Bishop's most successful ballad 'Home, Sweet Home', with words by John Howard Payne, which became the theme-song of their opera *Clari*, produced at Covent Garden in 1823.
Mr Shylock: Robson, playing Burlesque here, had scored a great success at the Olympic earlier in the year in the title role of Talfourd's burlesque *Shylock; or, The Merchant of Venice Preserved*.

SPEC: Without me you can never cut a shine!
BAL: You'll catch no mice without an *entrechat*.
HIPPO: What can you find like horses, pray, to draw?
MR W: I am completely bothered, that's a fact,
And, like some actors, don't know how to act!
TRA: But screw your courage to the sticking place!
MR W: I have – and stuck quite fast – that's just my case.
MRS W: I'll tell you what to do.
MR W: I wish you would.
MRS W: In each of them there's something that is good.
Without committing ourselves here to fix 'em,
Let's take the best and mix 'em.
MR W: Mix 'em!
MRS W: Mix 'em!
MR W: Like pickles? or like physic? what a notion!
D'ye think the town will swallow such a potion?
Why, Tragedy's a black dose of itself!
MRS W: Who talks of taking *all*, you silly elf?
I mean an extract of each spirit – Tragic,
Comic, Satiric, Operatic, Magic,
Romantic, Pantomimic, Choreographic,
Spectacular, Hip –
MR W: Spare that tongue seraphic
Such vain exertion – for they would but call
Your mixture melodrama, after all.
MRS W: With all my heart, I say, I don't care what
It's called, provided always it is not
Of 'the stage stagey' – whatsoe'er we do,
Let there be nature in't –
FAN: And fancy, too,
MRS W: By all means, for with you I quite agree,
Without some Fancy, dull e'en sense would be.
Besides, you know, to vary our diversions,
We must make *supernatural* exertions.
MR W: 'It must be so; Plato, thou reasonest well.'
On second thoughts I think the plan will tell.
Elegant extracts shall be, as you say,
In this, our Camp, the order of the day.
And so – attention! eyes right! dress up there!
I fear it's hopeless to say 'as you *were*';
But as you *are* – on you I will depend,
So 'stand at ease'!
TRA: And you will stand my friend?
MR W: One of the best you ever had on earth;
I wouldn't murder you for all you're worth!

'*It must be so; . . .*': a line from Addison's *Cato* (V. i.), produced at Drury Lane in 1713.

TRA: Then I may take myself off, I suppose?
BUR: 'Do it, nor leave the task to me!'
TRA: Here goes!
MR W: Stay! though I leave Burlesque to cure your bathos,
We'll keep of Tragedy the gentler pathos.
(*to* COMEDY) From you I would extract – you look so arch,
Upon me, I'm afraid, you'll steal a march –
Gay as a lark, and so good-humoured too,
I feel I can't extract too much from you!
(*to* MELODRAMA) Some spirits from your vasty deep I'll call;
Ballet shall help me to keep up the ball,
Opera lend a ballad or romanza,
And Fancy make Burlesque, Extravaganza.
Pantomime teach me how to do the trick;
E'en Hippo-drame may furnish a last kick.
SPEC: Well, try what trick you please to get the tin with,
Spectacle's, after all, the card to win with.
MR W: Yes, *after all*; yet in one sense, my friend,
Spectacle should not be the Drama's *end*.
Where that's the case the satirists may say
It is indeed all over with the play!
But my play's over now, thanks to your stars! (*to* FANCY)
(*to* AUDIENCE) And now I fain would call up your huzzahs,
To keep the ground for us and our review.
I have not told you all I mean to do;
For on that head – as promises may fetter –
The lessee thinks the less he says the better!
But to our Chobham if you will but tramp,
And smile on our experimental Camp,
A gallant corps in time I hope to form,
Which may, some fine night, take the town by storm!
Oh! let me hope that hope's not a forlorn one,
I'm a bold man, if ever there was born one!
Pardon that boldness in my utmost need,
And by your *coups de main* make mine succeed;
Confirming me in this proud situation,
By the command of general approbation.
SPEC: From me to borrow nothing do you mean?
MR W: Perhaps you'll favour me with a last scene,
On this occasion, by your own desire.
SPEC: Then give the word –
MR W: Make ready! – present!
(*Scene changes to a splendid Fairy Temple.*)
Fire! (*Coloured fires are lighted.*)

CHORUS – *Finale* – *'The Sturm Marsch'*
March to support the Drama's small division here;
Into the ranks before us nightly volunteer;

Over 'the roughs' at Chobham you your pleasure took!
Over 'the roughs' you meet with here be pleased to look!
Solo – MR WIGAN
Critics, don't our ardour damp,
Nor compel us to decamp;
Kindly, just as something new,
Pray review our 'Grand Review.'
Solo – FANCY
Only fancy what on earth will Fancy do,
If her fancy sketch you take no fancy to!
In this mighty wise utilitarian age
Leave to Fancy still a little, tiny stage!
CHORUS: March to support, etc.
CHORUS: (*Grand Salute*)
Thus presenting arms before we march away,
        End we our review!
Off with beating drums and flying colours pray,
        Let the piece go too;
Command us by a parting cheer,
Nightly to salute you here!

Curtain

---

roughs: irregular cavalrymen (who figured in *The Camp at Chobham*), here punning presumably with 'roughs' in the sense of things disagreeable or unfinished.

THE DISCREET PRINCESS; OR, THE THREE GLASS DISTAFFS

A new and doubly-moral though excessively old melodramatic fairy extravaganza in one act

First performed at the Olympic Theatre on Wednesday, 26 December 1855 with the following cast;

Character	Description	Performer
GANDER THE STUPENDOUS, *Rex Anserorum semper Agoosetus*		Mr Emery
PRINCESS IDELFONZA	*his three daughters*	Miss Marston
PRINCESS BABILLARDA		Miss F. Ternan
PRINCESS FINETTA		Miss J. St George
THE COUNT OF TOWER AND TAXES, *Prime Minister*		Mr J. H. White
BARON WANDINHAND, *Grand Chamberlain*		Mr E. Clifton
BLOCK	*State Councillors*	Mr Coney
STOCK		Mr Davis
MOCK		Mr Lygoe
HOCK		Mr Thomson
SCHARP, *State Page*		Miss Maynard
HORN, *a messenger*		Mr Franks
PRINCE RICHCRAFT	*sons of Fogrum, King of Nomark*	Mr F. Robson
PRINCE BELAVOIR		Miss Maskell
WOLF	*creatures of Richcraft*	Mr H. Cooper
WORM		Mr Danvers
STAB	*free companions, in the pay of Richcraft*	Mr Barks
GRAB		Mr Green
KNAB		Mr Ball
DAB		Mr Wyx

In the Ancient Uniform of their Corps on the Surrey Side of the Water

Character	Description	Performer
MOTHER GOOSE, *protector of the Royal House of Gander*		Miss Stephens

In the Ancient Costume of Fairy-land, first introduced to England in the Witching Days of Queen Bess

THE POPULATION OF GANDERSHOLM by Messrs A., B., and C. Smith, and Mesdames D., E., and F. Brown.

Scenery by Mr Gray, Mr H. Craven and assistants
Mechanical changes by Mr Sunderland
Appointments and decorations by Mr Lightfoot
Costumes by Mr Dommett and Mrs Curl
Music arranged by Mr Barnard

Tower and Taxes: playful corruption of Thurn und Taxis, the name of a Bavarian aristocratic family.

V Planché as Somerset Herald.

SCENE 1. *The Council Chamber. The* KING *discovered in Council.*

KING: Props of our power and pillars of our State,
Supporting of our government the weight,
Like – I may say without offence – like bricks;
To you King Gander turns, when in a fix,
That as you in your wisdoms may think fit,
You may advise him to get out of it.

MINISTER: My liege, as you sagaciously surmise,
That is exactly what we do advise.

KING: What?

MIN: To get out of it without delay.

KING: But how? By what means? In what kind of way?

1ST COUNCILLOR: Ere we decide, perhaps 'twill please your grace
To favour us by stating first the case.

KING: The case?

2ND COUN: We can't well argue it without
Knowing a little what it is about.

KING: Can't you? Why how do other councils do
That know no more of anything than you?

MIN: But we are not a common council, sire,

KING: Certainly not!

1ST COUN: And if we might inquire –

KING: Well, it won't make much difference, and so
The case is this. Some nineteen years ago
I prayed for three fine boys my name to bear.
Indulgent fortune granted my fond prayer
By sending me three girls.

2ND COUN: Three graces!

1ST COUN: Goddesses!
Not to be matched in Iliads or Odysses.

KING: The eldest, Princess Idelfonza, who
Does nothing –

MIN: As a princess ought to do.

KING: The second, Babillarda, fair as young,
But with no end whatever to her tongue.

1ST COUN: But then so musical each word it drops,
It may be called an organ –

KING: Without stops.
The third – Finetta – who one happy morn,
With a full set of wisdom teeth was born,
So shrewd – so prudent – 'tis our firm impression,
That all her years have been years of discretion.

MIN: A fact almost to make one doubt her sex.

1ST COUN: A fact to please you, sire; and not perplex.

KING: Granted; but there is yet to state another:
Fate has deprived them of their royal mother;
And when I go, as by my vow I'm bound,

The Paynim foe in Palestine to pound,
Like all the ancient Ganders of my race,
Who shall protect them in their parent's place?
How keep them from believing gay deceivers
Whilst I am pummelling the unbelievers?
Answer me that, ye Councillors, who can.

MIN: My liege, methinks I could propose a plan
On which your Majesty might act with ease.

KING: Which is – ?

MIN: To do whatever, sir, you please.

KING: Humph! that idea had occurred to me.
What say you, Baron?

1ST COUN: With humility,
I differ from so learned an authority;
No doubt I shall be quite in a minority –
But still my sense of duty makes me dare,
Dread sire, emphatically to declare
That in a case – permit me the expression –
A case, my liege, affecting the succession,
You're bound to do – not as has been expressed,
Just what you please – but just what you think best;
And we, as loyal subjects, bending low,
Are bound to think what you think best is so.

KING: Courageous Councillor! who ventures thus
To speak his mind, and tell the truth to us!
I'll follow your advice, sir, to the letter,
And let me see the man who dares think better.
Has any one another word to say? (*All shake their heads*.)

MIN: They answer, nothing – in the usual way.
The Council is unanimous.

KING: And so
Am I. (*They rise*.) Accept my thanks before you go,
For having, after grave deliberation,
Confirmed me – in my own determination.
(*Exeunt all but* KING.)
Though what that is, I have not quite decided.
Kind fortune, who has every gander guided,
Since 'twixt the legs of Jove one saved his life
From old Philemon's hospitable knife,
Be to an anxious father of some use,
And to my goslings prove a –
(*Music. The back of the throne opens and discovers* MOTHER GOOSE.)
Mother Goose!

Philemon: poor cottager of Roman legend, who shared his meal with Jupiter in disguise.

Save me, and hover o'er me with your wings!
What would your gracious figure?
MOTHER G: First of kings,
In whom I've ta'en an interest for ages,
Being a special pet of my own pages,
I come to solace your paternal pains,
And with my art supply your lack of brains.
KING: I feel the compliment.
MOTHER G: I know you do.
I read your thoughts, and could your mind look through,
If you had one.
KING: I've half a mind, good mother,
But can't quite make it up, some way or other.
MOTHER G: Yes! to lock up your daughters in a tower!
As if Dan Cupid hadn't got the power
To make in adamantine walls a gap!
Love laughs at locksmiths!
KING: That's a farce.
MOTHER G: Mayhap.
There's but one way the tempter to avoid;
Keep head and hand in honest work employed.
Idleness of all evil is the root.
KING: A fact established quite beyond dispute!
I wrote it in my copy book at school.
MOTHER G: Then make your daughters copy the same rule.
KING: A brilliant thought! 'tis plain whate'er inviting,
They can't be wronging if they're always writing;
I'll order in, of copy books, a van full,
Hundreds of pens, of ink a mighty can full.
MOTHER G: Nay, nay, though goose quills I must needs respect,
Young ladies' hands they sometimes mis-direct.
I'll keep them safer occupation in,
The proper task of spinsters is to spin.
(*Music. Waves her crutch. Three Glass Distaffs rise through the stage.*)
(*Presents them.*) There is a precious gift for each fair lass.
These distaffs are of fine cut fairy glass;
Though force can make upon them no impression,
They shiver at the slightest indiscretion.
KING: Odds bobs! they're ticklish tools for girls to handle!
MOTHER G: But safeguards against violence or scandal.
On your return, if they're produced unbroken,
Of prudence you can't have a surer token.
Farewell! upon my friendship reckon freely.
(*Music.* MOTHER GOOSE *disappears.*)

Love laughs at locksmiths: title of a farce by George Colman the Younger, produced at the Haymarket in 1803, and other anonymous pieces.

KING: No fairy could behave much more genteelly.
Astounding incident! But quick! time presses;
Ho! some one – summon hither the Princesses.
(*Enter* SCHARP.)
SCHARP: One Princess comes unsummoned, gracious sir.
KING: 'Tis well! if so, you need not summon her.
But tell the other two to bring their too –
Too solid flesh to melt into adieu! (*Exit* SCHARP.)
(*Enter* FINETTA.)
FIN: 'Adieu!' in time I come, then.
KING: Ah, Finetta!
Or, as thy mother called thee, Pin Basketta!
Thou always comest *apropos*, my dear.
FIN: It's *apropos de bottes* this time, I fear;
For if the news be true about that's bruited,
By glory spurred, you'll speedily be booted.
KING: The tidings are authentic, daughter mine,
Like brave Dunois, I'm bound for Palestine.
FIN: And wherefore off to Palestine thus bustle men?
KING: We go to Palestine to fight the Mussulmen.
FIN: But why to fight the Mussulmen, in fine?
KING: Because, my love – we go to Palestine.
FIN: That is no answer, sir, my question to.
What have the Mussulmen, pray, done to you?
KING: What have they done to me? – Good gracious, why?
They have done – Pshaw! what can that signify?
If people stopped to ask why out they fall,
There'd be no fighting in the world at all!
Suffice it that for glory I've a passion –
Besides, 'Partant pour la Syrie' 's the fashion.
(*Enter* SCHARP.)
SCHARP: The Princess Babillarda.
(*Enter* BABILLARDA.)
BABIL: Oh, papa!
What's this they tell me – you are going to war?
And not alone – which nobody would mind, sir –
But leaving not an officer behind, sir,
To chat or flirt with – it is much too hard.
Not a young Guardsman to take off his guard –
No Grenadier to form a forlorn hope with –

---

apropos de bottes: apropos of nothing, without reason, and of course a pun on the riding boots her father is about to put on.
brave Dunois: Jean d'Orléans, comte de Dunois, fifteenth-century military commander, largely responsible for the expulsion of the English from France.
'Partant pour la Syrie': anthem composed by Queen Hortense and substituted for *Vive Henri Quatre* and *La Marseillaise* on the accession of Napoleon III as Emperor in 1852.

No Light Dragoon a lady could galope with –
To dance 'The Lancers', not a Lancer near us,
And when we're toasted, no Hussar to cheer us!
It's too bad – all our beaux off thus to walk too,
And leave us not a single soul to talk to!
I –

KING: Hold your tongue!

BABIL: I can't! I never could!
And is it likely in this case I should!
I've got a thousand things to you to say.

KING: Well, tell me all then – when I'm gone away.

BABIL: But –

Song – BABILLARDA – *Air, 'Domino Noir'*

I must today, sir, have my say,
Before you go away;
And so I beg you'll stay,
And hear me, pray.
For not a word as yet I've heard
Of what has just occurred,
That doesn't seem absurd, say what you may.
If go you must for glory's sake, sir,
There's no reason you should take, sir,
All the nice young men in town, sir,
Who don't care about renown, sir;
And would rather here at home at soldiers play.
It's folly, quite, to go and fight,
When at your ease you might
Be morning, noon, and night – says Mr Bright.
And I'd agree with that M.P.,
If folks would let you be!
But then they won't, you see – despite advice:
Yet still, I think, if you'd but send
To them, some 'honourable friend',
Who to practise what he preaches,
Would do nothing but make speeches,
They'd be glad to buy his peace at any price.

KING: Silence!

FIN: Dear sister! Pray obedient be –
Or, if you can't stop talking – talk to me. (*They go up stage talking aside.*)

(*Enter* SCHARP, *preceding* IDELFONZA.)

SCHARP: (*announcing*) The Princess Idelfonza!

KING: So! At last –
You haven't made much haste!

Domino Noir: opera by Auber, performed (in English) at Covent Garden in 1838.
Mr Bright: John Bright, M.P. for Manchester and staunch Quaker, who had spoken forcefully in the Commons against the Crimean War and urged Palmerston to make peace with Russia.

IDEL: I can't walk fast –
You know, papa, it puts me in a flurry.
Where are you going, sir, in such a hurry?
KING: To Palestine, to gather laurels!
IDEL: Law!
Why can't you gather laurels here, papa?
Or send somebody – though it cost you double –
To gather 'em and save you all the trouble?
KING: The trouble is a pleasure!
IDEL: Well, I vow,
I can't think trouble pleasure – any how.
KING: You must be taught to think so, daughter. See
Here are three distaffs.
(FINETTA *and* BABILLARDA *come down*.)
IDEL: There then let them be.
KING: Nay, they are presents from a learned friend –
There's one for each – and, girls, you may depend
During my absence you'll find great enjoyment
In this serene and primitive employment.
BABIL: I spin!
KING: Why not? you love to spin a yarn.
IDEL: You'll tell us next our stockings we should darn.
FIN: Nay, sister, history and fable show
Princesses used to spin some time ago;
And Babillarda knows such occupation
Is no impediment to conversation.
BABIL: Well, that's some comfort certainly and though –
KING: Let me get one more word in, ere I go,
And then talk till you're tired, if you can.
IDEL: Let me sit down, then, there's a dear good man.
For I am tired. (*Sits*.)
KING: Hear me, girls, all three!
Through these glass distaffs you don't clearly see.
They have been made by magic.
THREE PRINCESSES; Magic!
KING: Magic!
And your ends may be tragic.
THREE PRINCESSES: Tragic!
KING: Tragic!
If by misconduct you should chance to break 'em!
BABIL: Then what a shame of you to go and make 'em!
KING: I didn't.
FIN: No, he told us just before
They're made by magic. Pa's no conjuror!
KING: Not I! But to proceed. They will protect you
Whilst you behave as prudence should direct you.
But if you swerve the least from her dictation,
You'll find 'em brittle as your reputation.

BABIL: Do you suspect us, sir, of –
KING: Heaven forbid!
But I shall treat you just as if I did,
And upon this score to feel quite at ease,
Make you your own 'material guarantees',
By wisely locking up the stable door,
Not after the steed's stolen – but before!
BABIL: What! Lock us up! 'Twill be my death, sir!
FIN: Pshaw!
Papa's not going, child, to lock your jaw.
With work and books it won't be so distressing.
IDEL: Well, I shan't have to move, and that's a blessing!
BABIL: And where's this hateful prison, pray, to be?
KING: In the Round Tower, which I go to see
Prepared for your reception. You safe in it,
On my own tour I set out the next minute.

Quartette – KING, BABILLARDA, FINETTA *and* IDELFONZA – *'Goosey Gander'*

KING: Like a gallant Gander,
Ere hence I wander,
You three
I'll see
Safe in the Tower yonder.

THREE PRINCESSES: If any young man
Drops in unawares?
KING: There's a policeman
Ready, if he dares!
To take him by the right leg,
Take him by the left leg,
Take him by both legs,
And drop him – down stairs.

ALL: Like a gallant Gander,
Ere hence { I / he'll } wander
{ You / Us } three
{ I'll / He'll } see
Safe in the tower yonder.

(*Exeunt* KING *and* PRINCESSES.)

SCENE 2. *Exterior of the Round Tower. Music.* WORKMEN *enter, and employ themselves in fixing a crane and pulleys (to which are attached a rope and basket) to Tower.* STONE-MASONS *enter with materials for walling up the door,* GRAND CHAMBERLAIN *superintending.*

Air and Chorus – GRAND CHAMBERLAIN *and* WORKMEN – *'Bartlemy Fair'*

Come bustle, boys, about,
It is time you'd all cleared out;
Get the crane and pulley ready,
And the basket to make steady,
Select a very sure rope.
Don't the balance lose of your rope,
Or you'll find it an awkward affair, O!

Work away – no delay
Scrub and burnish – paint and furnish;
By the drumming, the King's coming!
If he find you all behind, you
Will sing, hey down, ho down,
Derry derry down,
To a very, very different air, O!

Flourish. Enter PEASANTS, *preceding* GUARDS, PAGES, LADIES OF HONOUR, *then enter the three* PRINCESSES, *with their* PAGES, *and the* KING, *attended by his* MINISTER *and* COUNCILLORS.

KING: The hour is come, when from my dearest daughters
I must depart for foreign country quarters,
But first secure 'gainst Cupid's artful dodgings,
I'll place you in genteelly furnished lodgings;
You'll find in them your own linen and plate,
And as upon yourselves you'll have to wait,
There'll be no extra charges for attendance.

IDEL: And upon what, sir, can we place dependence,
For board, as well as lodging, pray?

BABIL: I hope
You'd not have us depend upon a rope!

KING: No, not without a basket at the end on't.
But by these simple means you may depend on't,
You'll be provided with three meals a day,
'Provided always', as the lawyers say,
You turn a button you'll find in the wall,
As you would have the basket rise or fall.
I've given strict orders to my Major Domo,
And he alone, of all the *genus homo*,
Will have with you intercommunication –
All persons else by Royal Proclamation,
Are warned from coming even near this spot,
On pain of being sent to instant pot.

BABIL: Only the Major Domo! Cruel whim!
But I may say whate'er I please to him?

---

sent to instant pot: cut to pieces, destroyed.

KING: Whate'er you please, without the slightest fear,
For he's as deaf as the door post.
BABIL: Oh dear!
But shan't we be allowed to take the air?
KING: Upon the top you'll find a garden fair,
Laid out in plots, where you may walking go.
And laugh to scorn plots laid for you below.
Thus, armed at all points, do I take my leave.
FIN: 'Tis too late to prevent you, I perceive,
You've ta'en your place already in the mail,
And fate alone has power to turn the scale.
KING: True! But although I've steel'd this manly breast,
To which, for the last time, perhaps, thou'rt pressed,
While all the father in my bosom warms,
I feel myself again a child in arms! (*Weeps.*)
Snivelling! O shame! A Gander and in tears!
Brush off fond drops, and you, my pretty dears,
Brush in.
THREE PRINCESSES: Good-bye, papa!
(*The* KING *embraces them as they pass, then all* THREE PRINCESSES *enter the tower.*)
KING: Farewell! Once more!
They've entered! Men of stone, block up the door!
(MASONS *busy themselves in building up door.*)
Adieu, my people! When I'm far away,
Remember me, and punctually pay
Your taxes. You'll be gratified to learn
They will be doubled until I return –
Which, though of parting it increase the pain,
Ensures you joy to see me back again.
Strike up, my drums, and let my trumpets bray!
Like a good knight, I wish you all good day!
(*March. Exeunt* KING, *followed by* MINISTER, COUNCILLORS, GUARDS, PAGES, LADIES, PEASANTS *and* WORKMEN.)
(BABILLARDA *appears at window of tower.*)
BABIL: Heigho! What will become of me now! There
Is Idelfonza sunk in an arm-chair
And half asleep already – Sister Fin
In her own room has gone to sit and spin,
No mortal creature, not e'en a poor bird,
With whom I can exchange a single word.
Well, I must talk then to myself until
Somebody passes, but nobody will!
The horse patrol would stop 'em on the high road,

Brush in: hurry indoors.

And this bye-road is not a passing-by-road.
Yet sure there's something moving on it now!
Is it a man, a donkey, or a cow?
It's an old beggar woman, I declare!
Who looks as if just come out of Rag Fair.

(*Music. Enter* RICHCRAFT, *as an old woman, with basket and long string of ballads.*)

BABIL: Here, here! Good woman! What have you to sell?
RICH: Ballads, my pretty mistress.
BABIL: Ballads! Well
I love a ballad in print. Have you many?
RICH: Three yards of songs, miss – forty for a penny –
Here's 'Old Dan Tucker', 'Will Watch', 'Nelly Bly',
'Love Not', 'Hot Codlings', 'Coming' thro' the Rye'.
'Long ago', 'Mary, I believe thee true',
'I'd be a Butterfly', 'Red, White, and Blue',
'Pop goes the Weasel', 'Far upon the Sea',
'When the Wind blows', 'Then you'll remember me',
'Cheer, boys, Cheer', 'On the Banks of Allan Water',
'Gentle Zitella', 'The Ratcatcher's Daughter'.
BABIL: Oh! The Ratcatcher's Daughter! How I should
Like to hear that. Pray sing it.
RICH: That I would,
But I'm afeard to stop so long, my dear,
I'm told they'll hang me if they catch me here –
Couldn't you let me in? I'm old and poor –
Order your porter, pray, to ope the door.
BABIL: Order our porter! We've no porter here,
To order – if we wanted it – our beer;
No door to open, if we had a porter,
They've gone and blocked it up with stones and mortar.
RICH: Oh dear! To take me in, find some way, do,
I'd try to find some way to take in you.
If you've no servant, you'll want one, no doubt –
And if you'll let me in, I'll serve you (*aside*) out.
BABIL: How can I let you in, when –
RICH: What's to hinder
Your winding me up safely to the winder?
The basket I see hanging to that pulley,
I'm pretty sure would hold me beautifully!

Rag Fair: old-clothes market held in Houndsditch, London (Partridge).
'The Ratcatcher's Daughter': a song by the Reverend E. Bradley which enjoyed considerable popular success at the time and had already been sung at the London music halls by Robson himself and by his great American contemporary, Sam Cowell.
porter: a dark, bitter beer, punning with 'porter' in the sense of attendant.

BABIL: I never thought of that! The very thing!
What fun to trick papa! But where's the spring?
Oh! this must be it – yes; down goes the basket;
My explanation's ready if they ask it –
I've but obeyed his Majesty's commands,
To take up any one found on these lands.
Say when you're ready.
(RICHCRAFT *steps into the basket which has descended.*)
RICH: Now then – that will do,
Haul up! (*aside*) And 'twill be soon all up with you.
(*Music. The basket ascends with* RICHCRAFT. *When it is level with the window* BABILLARDA *helps him in, and the scene changes to*)

SCENE 3. *The Garden at the top of the Tower. Enter* BABILLARDA, *followed by* RICHCRAFT (*as old woman*).
BABIL: One more step, and you're at the top.
RICH: I'm glad
To hear it, for my breath's so very bad.
BABIL: Sit down, and take some fresh then – for no doubt,
You couldn't sing conveniently without.
RICH: Who was the lady fast asleep below?
BABIL: My eldest sister, Idelfonza.
RICH: Oh!
But you've another sister, I've been told.
BABIL: Oh, yes, Finetta! Won't she fume and scold,
When she finds –
(RICHCRAFT *goes to alcove and leaves basket. Enter* FINETTA, *followed by* IDELFONZA *dragging a camp stool.*)
FIN: Ha! my fears then were too true!
BABIL: (*aside*) Oh, my! she's here, and Idelfonza too!
IDEL: Why, Babillarda! who on earth's this stranger?
FIN: Who let her in?
BABIL: I did, and where's the danger?
FIN: There's always danger where there's disobedience.
BABIL: Folks shouldn't drive one, then, to such expedients.
FIN: Your indiscretion will be punished – see
Your distaff's broken!
BABIL: So it is – dear me!
When could I break it?
FIN: When you broke your word.
BABIL: I never gave it, so don't be absurd.
FIN: Alas, more mischief may be brewing!
BABIL: Stuff!
Don't preach. I've done it, child, and that's enough.
What mischief can this poor old body do,
I should just like to know, to me or you?
I brought her in to wait on us.

IDEL: Delightful!
The thought of waiting on one's self is frightful.
BABIL: Besides she can sing songs, and so amuse me!
If you don't like it, you can go.
FIN: Excuse me,
I shan't leave you such company alone in.
BABIL: Well, I don't care, if I'm not left my own in.
So sing, good mother, and don't mind her prosing.
IDEL: Yes, do sing! it's so pleasant while one's dozing.
RICH: What shall I sing? ugh, ugh! I'm rather hoarse.
BABIL: Oh, 'The Ratcatcher's Daughter', dame, of course.
RICH: D'ye know the song?
BABIL: I know the air – no more.
RICH: Then you have never heard these words before?

Song – RICHCRAFT – *Air* – *'The Ratcatcher's Daughter'*

Not long ago there lived, somewhere,
A king who had three fair daughters;
But he didn't quite like to leave 'em there,
While he went t'other side of the waters.
The father smelt rats, for he'd often caught flats,
A prowling about his quarters;
So packed up snug, in a sort of stone jug,
Were these purty little Flatcatcher's Darters.
Singing, Doodle dee, doodle dum,
Didum doodle da.
CHORUS, LADIES – Doodle dee, etc.

But Cupid is a downy cove,
Wot it takes a deal to hinder;
And if you shuts him out o' the door,
Vy he valks in at the winder.
So one day there came a poor old dame,
Who all in rags and tatters,
By an artful dodge, got into the lodge
Of these purty little Flatcatcher's Darters.
Singing, Doodle dee, etc.

Now I have heard since that a rich young prince,
Who had come from a foreign land, O,
Laid a wager that he, out of one of the three,
Would inveigle her lily-white hand, O.
So in this disguise, he flung dust in the eyes,
Of the girls wot he was arter;
And like a sly fox, spite of bolts, bars and locks,
Bolted off with one purty little Darter.
Singing, Doodle dee, etc.

---

flats: see note to p. 175 above.
downy cove: artful or knowing fellow (Partridge).

RICH: In plain prose, I'm the hero of the story,
And thus fling off the mask, like gay Count Ory.
(*Music.* RICHCRAFT *throws off his old woman's disguise.* BABILLARDA *screams and rushes off, followed by* FINETTA. IDELFONZA, *who has gone to sleep during the song, is aroused by the scream, starts up, and is about to follow, but* RICHCRAFT *intercepts her.*)
RICH: Fly not, sweet princess!
IDEL: I don't want to fly;
It's so much trouble, but perforce must try.
RICH: Wherefore?
IDEL: Because 'twould be great impropriety,
For me to stay alone in your society.
RICH: Oh, say not so! For you alone I came,
For you alone I've played this desperate game!
You are alone the prize I have in view.
IDEL: Leave me alone, then – and be quiet, do.
RICH: Not till my passion moves you to compassion.
IDEL: It bores me to be moved in any fashion –
Besides, how can you talk such trash to me?
It was my sister you came here to see.
RICH: What, Babillarda! That eternal chatterer,
Who, to call magpie, would but too much flatter her!
No; 'tis the sloe black of those sleepy eyes!
'Tis Idelfonza that I idolise!
'Tis the delicious languor of that air
That laps me in Elysium! Matchless fair,
I am a Prince – of money I have plenty,
And love, like you, the *dolce far niente*.
Of slaves you will possess a countless band,
Besides your humble servant, to command.
And you shall sit as long as daylight lingers,
Twiddling, in graceful ease, those fairy fingers.
And you shall have not only naught to do,
But your own time to do it in!
IDEL: 'Tis true
You talk this well!
RICH: By Heaven, I'll do this, lady!
Say but to marry me that you are ready –
I've lords in waiting, who in ambush tarry,
To carry you off, if my point I carry.
IDEL: Somebody must, for I will ne'er be married
Unless to church, at any rate, I'm carried.

---

gay Count Ory: the raffish hero of Rossini's opera, who disguises himself as a Mother Superior in order to seduce the Countess Adèle. (The work had opened the 1855 season at Covent Garden.)
dolce far niente: delightful idleness (literally 'sweet doing nothing').

RICH: You shall be, in a litter!
IDEL: Really! Shall I!
You don't mean what you say?
RICH: Yes! Literally.
IDEL: Well, I suppose I ought to ask papa.
RICH: But then your father's gone so very far.
And never may come back again, I'm told.
And by that time we should be both so old.
IDEL: Well, you may take my hand, then.
RICH: Rapture! thus,
Upon my road to bliss, I take a buss!

(*Music. As he kisses her, the glass distaff she carries at her girdle flies into pieces.*)

IDEL: Ah! There's my distaff, now, gone all to shatters!
RICH: (*aside*) That's number two! (*aloud*) Well, dearest, and what matters?
IDEL: Not much, I grant, for I should never use it.
RICH: (*aside*) Now for the third! Time flies! I mustn't lose it!
(*aloud*) The sun is going down, and so must I,
To call my friends up – off with you to hie!
Rest in this bower till 'tis time to start.
IDEL: Oh, I'll rest anywhere with all my heart.
(*aside*) He really is a charming little man! (*Goes into alcove.*)
RICH: (*quickly shutting the door and locking it*)
I have caught you, now catch me if you can!

Song – RICHCRAFT – *Air* – *'Like the lightning'*

Like the lightning, or as slick as grease,
I fly to conquests grander,
And, please the pigs, I'll cook the geese
Of all the race of Gander!
I'm aware that time is fleeting,
But I can't avoid repeating,
That like lightning, or as slick as grease, etc., etc. (*Exit.*)

SCENE 4. *A Room in the Tower. Door in centre with staircase leading to upper part.* FINETTA *and* BABILLARDA *appear at opposite entrances.*

FIN: Ah!
BABIL: Ah!
FIN: It's only me!
BABIL: It's only you!
Are you quite certain? Dear! what shall we do?
FIN: Where's Idelfonza!
BABIL: Haven't the least notion;
So limited her power of locomotion,
It's possible she's still just where we left her.

---

buss: kiss, punning with the common word for omnibus.

FIN: And of her life that wretch may have bereft her,
Following us, I'm sure I thought I heard her.
BABIL: Let's up stairs to the window and scream murder!
Here she comes! No, she doesn't! It is the man!
Where shall we fly to? (*Exit.*)
FIN: You fly where you can!
I will not budge a foot! This Tower shall fly
From its firm base as soon as basely I –
Though I've not here Clan Alpine's warriors true,
I'll do exactly as did Roderick Dhu!
For, as like him, I stumbled here some sacks on,
I fortunately laid my hand this axe on. (*Takes axe from wing and conceals it behind herself.*)

Song – FINETTA – *Air* – *'Di quella Pira'*

Let him appear, ah
Shan't he get toco
For yam as surely
As I stand here!
Oh his base marrow-bones
I with this cleaver,
Will 'Con fuoco'
Play without fear!
Yes, from this chopper
He'll get a topper;
And since with oper—
A plots he makes free,
While of 'Count Ory'
He apes the story,
'Il Trovatore!'
This bold air gives me!

(*Enter* PRINCE RICHCRAFT.)

RICH: So here you are at last! I've had some pains
To find you, Princess.
FIN: If you've any brains
Move not a step, or I shall solve the doubt
By trying if I can knock any out.
RICH: With what? That distaff? You'll excuse my grinning –
FIN: No, something that will set your head a spinning.
Behold! I have a weapon! (*brandishing axe*) A small toy
Left in a corner by some chopping boy.

Roderick Dhu: fierce Highland chieftain of the Clan Alpine in Scott's poem *The Lady of the Lake*.
Di quella Pira: aria from Verdi's opera *Il Trovatore*, performed at Covent Garden earlier in the year.
get toco/For yam: be punished (Partridge).
Con fuoco: with fire or passion.
chopping: big, strapping (*OED*), and an obvious pun.

It has cut blocks as thick as yours.
RICH: The deuce!
You wouldn't make of it so bad a use!
To gain that hand these brains I have been taxing.
FIN: You'll find my hand's not to be had for axing.
RICH: But hear me, Princess!
FIN: I can hear you there.
Where's Idelfonza?
RICH: I don't know or care.
You are the idol that I worship!
FIN: How?
RICH: 'Pon honour!
FIN: Poh! I know your worship, now.
And doubt your honour.
RICH: You know me! Who am I?
FIN: My father's deadly foe – Prince Richcraft!
RICH: (*aside*) Damme!
FIN: Of old King Fogrum, eldest son and heir.
RICH: Discovered! Then I'll candidly declare,
Since I'm found out, that I am Richcraft, and
Delighted to find you at home – your hand.
FIN: Not without this! Some mischief you intend.
RICH: No, with our union let all discord end!
Say you'll be mine, and of your father I
Will henceforth be the good and true ally.
FIN: (*aside*) Exactly! (*aloud*) After such a declaration
There may be grounds for some negotiation;
I will despatch a letter to my father
And let you know his answer.
RICH: Let me rather
Have yours at once.
FIN: But I am not of age,
And can't against his will my hand engage.
I am a minor.
RICH: Say, an under-miner.
Though you're a fine girl, you will find me finer.
I'll wait for no man's will, so don't be silly,
Mine you must be, proud Princess, willy-nilly!
Lay down that axe while I am yet pacific;
And drive me not to acts much more terrific.
FIN: (*aside*) I'll feign a little female hesitation.
(*aloud*) Grant me a short time for consideration.
RICH: I will. It shall be short, as you implore;
I grant you just five minutes, not one more.
If still you hesitate you'll to your cost
Prove that the maid who hesitates is lost;
You can't imagine how uncommon funky

You'll feel, if once you quite put up my monkey!

Song – RICHCRAFT – *Air* – *'The Campbells are coming'*
Not e'en Gordon Cumming – oh, oh, oh, oh!
Not e'en Gordon Cumming – oh, oh, oh, oh!
Has e'er seen a lion,
That you mightn't try on,
More safely your humming – oh, oh, oh, oh!

No tiger Van Amburgh had ever to dare,
No bear ever petted by Labarriere,
Was half so ferocious, rapacious, atrocious!
So, madam, I'd have you beware, beware! (*Exit.*)

FIN: What's to be done? Not Richcraft, I'm afraid;
He is a keen, though badly-tempered blade!
Oh, my poor distaff! Quite of spirits I'm out,
You won't be wanted now to spin the time out!
But till the spinsters three my thread shall sever,
To hold you harmless I will still endeavour!
Heyday! how's this? It made me quite spin round,
And makes a point of pointing to the ground –
(*Trap opens.*)
And a trap opens in it, and displays
One of those horrid cells of other days,
Called 'Oubliettes,' because when in they let you,
Though they would ne'er forgive, they'd quite forget you.
This opens a new prospect of success;
To make it work, I've but this spring to press;
Though Richcraft is a very downy chap,
He may not be quite up to such a trap;
And if he's not up to it – he must be
Down in it – ere he can be down on me!
I hear his step – quick! let me set the trap for him.
(*Touches spring and trap closes.*)
There! it's all right! and I don't care a rap for him!
(*Re-enter* RICHCRAFT.)
RICH: Time's up! Am I to count on your axe-cession?
FIN: Sir, I surrender at my own discretion;
I lay my arms down (*flinging axe away*) and present my hand.

---

put up my monkey: make me angry (Partridge).
Gordon Cumming: big game hunter, whose exhibition of trophies from Africa ran in London from 1850 to 1852 before going on tour.
Van Amburgh: seen note to p. 130 above.
Labarriere: presumably a popular bear-tamer.
spinsters three: the Fates of Greek and Roman mythology, Clotho, Lachesis and Atropos, who were supposed to spin the thread of human life.
downy: see note to p. 208 above.

RICH: On ceremony, then, no more I stand,
But thus –
(*Music. Springs forward to seize her hand, but the moment he steps on the trap he disappears.*)
FIN: You fall! Victoria! That's a case,
I hope, of the right man in the right place!
Recitative – FINETTA
The plot was deep! – the plotter now lies deeper!
Babillarda!
(*Enter* BABILLARDA.)
Duet – FINETTA *and* BABILLARDA – *'Il Trovatore'*
BABIL: Oh, joy! I scarce can trust my eyes!
Alive I thus behold you;
And no 'alarming sacrifice',
To him who thought he'd sold you.
My tongue, in vain, for utt'rance tries,
I want words, I declare, dear,
A want in me so rare, dear,
It adds to my surprise.
FIN: 'Full fathom five', the traitor 'lies',
Like – I forget whose – father;
Those mayn't be 'pearls that were his eyes',
But he a purl had – rather.
BABIL: Huzzah!
FIN: Away, away! if most unwise
To let him in you were, dear;
I've let him in, just there, dear,
Much more to his surprise. (*Exeunt.*)

SCENE 5. *Exterior of the Tower. Night. Music. Enter* WOLF *and* WURM, *cautiously*.
WOLF: Hush!
WURM: Silence!
WOLF: Soft! From yonder turret high
Methought I heard – Nothing!
WURM: And so did I.
WOLF: No signal! Then I fear Richcraft's success
Will not be signal.
WURM: I suspect, no less.
WOLF: Within the Tower, all's as dark as pitch!
WURM: There's something darker rising from that ditch!
(RICHCRAFT *covered with mud, rises slowly out of the ditch.*)
RICH: (*faintly*) Wurm!
WOLF: It's old Bogie! And he's come for you!

---

purl: a heavy fall, a cropper (*OED*).

RICH: Wolf!
WURM: Oh! It must be! For he wants you too!
RICH: Knaves! Don't you know! – the Prince –
WURM: Of Darkness! Oh!
RICH: (*advancing*) Fools! I'm Prince Richcraft!
WOLF: Eh? You don't say so?
WURM: His Highness! Is it possible?
(*They both go to assist* RICHCRAFT *out of ditch and lead him forward.*)
RICH: Too true!
WOLF: All over black!
RICH: I grieve to add – and blue!
WURM: How came you in this pickle – pray explain?
Have you been up a flue?
RICH: No, down a drain!
WURM: Into the Tower, then, you never stole?
RICH: Oh, yes! And went completely through the whole.
Flung through what oft has lost a man his station,
A story utterly without foundation!
The mud I fell in only broke my fall,
But I have spoiled my clothes, both great and small.
WOLF: Take comfort, sir, and change them.
RICH: Never! No!
Like to the Pontic Sea whose icy flow
Ne'er feels retiring ebb, but still goes on tick,
By rushing up the spout to the Propontic
Without a change – even so, behold, I swear
This jacket and etceteras to wear
Till I have washed the stains out in a flood
Of blood! By Jingo! Blood! Blood! Blood! Blood! Blood!
WURM: Whose – gracious sir?
RICH: Finetta's! That false fair's –
If all her hairs were lives –
WOLF: First, catch her hairs!
RICH: In course! So hounds! – I let you slip, and woe
Betide you, if you let her slip, also!
WURM: Footsteps! If it should be the bobbies! Run!
WOLF: It's but a booby! (*looking out*)
RICH: Then you're two to one,
And were he twice a booby – quite his match.
WURM: It's a King's messenger, with some despatch.

---

up the spout: a suitably burlesque image which assimilates the Hellespont, the narrow channel connecting the Aegean with the Propontic or Sea of Marmara, to the goods lift of a Victorian pawnshop, where many distressed Londoners pledged their best clothes in return for 'tick' or credit.
First, catch her hairs: from the French proverb, 'To make a stew, first catch your hare'.

RICH: Dispatch him, then! First knock him gently down,
And then we'll hear – the message from the Crown.

(*Music. They retire. Enter a* MESSENGER. *He approaches the Tower, and raises a horn to his mouth, but before he can sound it he is knocked down by* WOLF. WURM *takes a letter out of the man's pouch, and hands it to* RICHCRAFT.)

RICH: A letter! But of light there's not a spark!
WURM: (*at back*) I've got a lantern, though it's rather dark.
RICH: (*Takes lantern, breaks the seal of letter and reads.*)
What do I read! My eyes deceive me, surely!
King Gander has been taken very poorly,
And feeling in his head a sort of dizziness,
Is coming home on 'urgent private business'.
Accursed chance!
WURM: A happy chance, sir, rather.
Let's give Finetta this note from her father, –
'Twill lure her out.
RICH: O, mischief! thou art quick,
To enter into heads, however thick.
With speed about it! Doff your cloak and cap,
And put on those belonging to this chap;
Then fling his body in the ditch there plump,

(*Music. They act accordingly.*)

Now take his horn, and blow it like a trump.

(WURM *blows the horn.* FINETTA *appears at the window of Tower.* RICHCRAFT *and* WOLF *retire.*)

FIN: What means that mournful blast, mysterious stranger?
WURM: Madam, your royal father's life in danger.
FIN: My father's life in danger! Is he ill?
WURM: Dying! but can't die easily, until
He sees his darling child, Princess Finetta.
FIN: What proof of this?
WURM: An autographic letter.
Drop me a line, sweet maid, and, by return,
The truth you in a line from him will learn.
FIN: You'd get me in a line, insidious knave!
I much suspect this is some barbarous 'shave'.
WURM: I shave a lady! Not with softest soap.
FIN: Send up the line, then – and beware the rope!

(*Music. She lets down the basket.* WURM *throws the note in it.* FINETTA *draws up the basket, takes out the note, and reads it.*)

---

lantern . . . dark: punning allusion to a lantern whose light can be concealed and to a court servant who receives bribes (*OED*).
'urgent private business': a reference to the pretext all too frequently offered by officers for returning home from the Crimean War.
get me in a line: hoax, trick me (Partridge).
'shave': in military slang, a false or unauthenticated report (*OED*).

My father's hand. I can no longer doubt!
But the seal's broken! – how came that about?
Who dared to ope this scroll, thou naughty elf?
WURM: His gracious Majesty's most royal self.
He wanted to add something, but he couldn't,
And so, on second thoughts, he thought he wouldn't.
FIN: How like the circumspection of his race!
WURM: O, hasten to receive his last embrace.
FIN: Where is he?
WURM: Hard by, in the wood; no further
Could he bear carriage! To delay is murther!
FIN: I come!
(*Music.* FINETTA *gets into the basket and descends.*)
WOLF: (*aside*) We have her!
RICH: Seize the jade and gag her.
(*As* FINETTA *steps out of the basket, they obey* RICHCRAFT*'s order by throwing a cloak over her head.*)
Call up your fellows! O'er the border drag her!
(WOLF *hurries out with* FINETTA.)
Would she had forty thousand lives, that I
Might forty thousand ways to take 'em try,
Or that she had but nine lives, like a cat –
But as she has but one, I will take that
In such a way, that no cat of nine tails,
Could ever raise of woe such horrid wails.
Get me a barrel, stick it full of spikes,
So sharp, nobody ever felt the likes!
In it I'll cram the baggage like a ball,
And roll it down the Brockeneckerthal!
Once off, she'll find her way to the bottom. Mizzle! (*Exit* WURM.)
On the hot gridiron of hate I grizzle!
Vengeance, be thou my Lord Mayor; at thy feast,
See if I don't just make myself a beast. (*Exit.*)

SCENE 6. *Summit of a mountain.* WOLF, WURM, *and other* ATTENDANTS OF RICHCRAFT *enter with* FINETTA *prisoner*.
WOLF: Of Gander's kingdom we're safe o'er the border,
And there's the pit to which she'll have an order.
FIN: Are ye banditti? If so, name my ransom,
My father is a king, he'll come down handsome.
WOLF: Will he? If that's your hope it is but small,
'Twouldn't be like his Majesty at all.
FIN: Answer my question, man of features grim!

Mizzle!: see note to p. 169.
order: a pass giving admission to the 'pit' of a theatre.

WOLF: Here comes his Highness, pop it, ma'am, to him.
FIN: His Highness! – this low mudlark?
(*Enter* PRINCE RICHCRAFT.)
Ah, Prince Richcraft!
Alive, and out of limbo – This is witchcraft!
RICH: No, traitress! Deep the craft through which I fell,
But here is trap for trap, and sell for cell.
FIN: No traitress I, but double traitor thou,
Who to two sisters equal love could vow.
RICH: For equal love read henceforth equal hate;
For know I found out in the 'Book of Fate',
And sticking sundry pins in fortune's wheel,
Thy father's kingdom fallen *en quenouille*
Would with my father's to some other pass
By one of those three distaffs made of glass;
If indiscretion caused them not to snap.
Two are in two –
FIN: Too sad is our mishap.
But there is yet a third thou canst not harm
While I am wide awake.
RICH: Despair thy charm!
And let old Mother Goose who manufactured
That distaff, tell thee though it mayn't be fractured,
Richcraft will still be of the crown a winner,
By breaking all to bits the artful spinner.
FIN: Upon the wheel?
RICH: No, in a novel way.
(WURM *beckons on* MEN *with barrel, the inside of which is furnished with steel spikes, hooks, etc.*)
Invention is the order of the day,
And here is my new organ of destruction,
To which you shall have speedy introduction.
FIN: A barrel organ!
RICH: Yes, to grind your bones
At every turn it takes over those stones.
(MEN *take barrel up the mountain.*)
You needn't be afraid of falling out,
The spikes in it will hold you fast no doubt.
FIN: What, chuck me down the mountain?
RICH: Yes, my chuck.
Not long ago you made me run amuck,
Now I'll see how you like it, my fair lady!
FIN: I'll not be cast down.
RICH: You look so already.

---

mudlark: 'one who dabbles, works or lives in mud' (*OED*).
en quenouille: to the distaff side.

FIN: Will no just lightning singe this dirty dog's head?
Mercy!
RICH: No, you shall go the entire hogshead!
(*Music. He drags her up the mountain.*)
First let me see though, there are spikes enough in it,
Before this dainty bit of goods we stuff in it.
(*Music.* RICHCRAFT *mounts on a piece of rock and looks into the barrel.* FINETTA *tipping him over, he falls into it, and the barrel rolls down the hill and disappears, amidst the cries of the* ATTENDANTS, *who rush after it, leaving* FINETTA *to run out unperceived.*)
WURM: (*on rock piece*) Stop! Stop him! Ha! Upon a rocky shelf
He has been good enough to stop himself!
If it had only rolled another yard with him,
Over those stones it had gone very hard with him.
(*Music. Re-enter* WOLF *and the rest, bearing and surrounding* RICHCRAFT, *insensible.*)
WOLF: Gently, boys, gently! Here's a sad disaster,
In a rude spot where there is no court plaster!
Of opodeldoc, not a drop to use!
No spermaceti for an inward bruise!
WURM: If you are dead, sir, speak, and tell us so!
RICH: (*slowly reviving in arms of* ATTENDANTS) I think that I may venture to say, no.
(ATTENDANTS *set him down.*)
Of stout bull's hide my under jerkin, tough,
Kept those vile spikes from working my own buff.
But oh, my back! (*They rub him.*) Upon the other side!
Where is the minx? I'll have her sliced and fried!
The very thought a thrilling joy diffuses,
Like Friar's balsam, over all my bruises!
WURM: Sir, without warning she has dared to quit again.
RICH: Finetta 'scaped! Ah me! then comes my fit again;
And all my pains return – because I've lost 'em!
Who let her 'scape? their dog's ears it shall cost 'em!
WOLF: We couldn't run two ways at once.
RICH: That's true.
What's to be done? for something I must do,
To bar that fatal prophecy's fulfilment.
WURM: Administer some 'leperous distilment!'
Some 'juice of cursed hebanon in a vial!'
WOLF: Or some new pill, that 'only asks one trial!'

---

court plaster: sticking-plaster.
opodeldoc: soap liniment.
spermaceti: ointment.
buff: bare skin (and a pun on buff-leather).
Friar's balsam: tincture of benzoin used as an application for wounds.

RICH: Ha! I remember a low sort of shop,
Where they sold peppermint and lollipop,
And lozenges in boxes by the score,
With this inscription o'er them 'COUGH NO MORE'.
I gazed upon the things, red – green – and blue,
And others of a still more sickly hue;
And thought if one for poison had a whim,
There lived a seedy chap would sell it him;
And prove the truth that brief inscription bore,
For in his coffin he would 'cough no more!'
Ha, ha! I feel unnaturally merry!
WURM: (*to* WOLF) I think his head's a little –
WOLF: (*to* WURM) I think – very.
RICH: My brain is overtaxed! Oh, yes, I feel
Fate has surcharged me, and I must appeal:
They have assessed my wits in schedule D,
As if wit ever was a property!
Now they're distraining on them, I'm done brown.
An undone brother sits upon my crown,
And takes away the use on't! And my scept –
Re – changed to the distaff which Finetta kept,
Is lost and gone! Hah! fiends to Pluto's region
Have come to drag me! Though you were a legion,
Aye, e'en the Foreign Legion, thus I'd fall
Among you, and – and – over-reach you all!
(*Music. The* RETAINERS *rush off alarmed. Business of 'Sir Giles Overreach'.* RICHCRAFT *sinks into the arms of* WOLF *and* WURM, *and they bear him off. Scene closes.*)

SCENE 7. *Interior of* KING GANDER*'s Palace. Flourish and shouts without. Enter* KING GANDER, *leaning on his* MINISTER, *and followed by his* COUNCILLORS *and* PAGES, *bearing his helmet and shield.*

KING: Thanks, countrymen! Thanks, loving friends. Alack!
You're always glad, I know, to see me back!
What! (*to* MINISTER) Have the Masons made my daughters free
Of the Grand Lodge, in which we lodged all three?
(*Loud knocks heard.*)
MIN: My liege, e'en now they're knocking at the door.
KING: It's no use knocking at it any more,
For here, I take it, are our daughters come.

---

schedule D: one of the categories of income tax, which had been reimposed by Peel in 1842.
done brown: see note to p. 138 above.
Business of 'Sir Giles Overreach': Overreach's fit of rage and despair in the last act of Massinger's *A New Way to Pay Old Debts* and one of Edmund Kean's most celebrated pieces of business.
Grand Lodge: pun on a meeting-place or organisation of freemasons (to which no 'daughters' could be admitted!).

MIN: But one, and she is looking rather rum.
(*Exeunt* MINISTER *and* COUNCILLORS.)
(*Enter* FINETTA.)
KING: My child!
FIN: He lives! And I've a parent still!
How fares my gracious father?
KING: Not so ill,
But that we might be worse, yet not so well,
But that we might be better.
FIN: Tell, oh, tell
Thy daughter all. The worst, oh, let me learn!
I fear small profit from this quick return.
KING: You may be a false prophet.
FIN: Aye! indeed?
But you were indisposed?
KING: Yes – to proceed –
Thou shalt know all! Yon moon which rose last night
Round as my shield –
FIN: Which is not round.
KING: Not quite,
Had not quite risen, when with great long bills,
A band of fierce barbarians from the hills,
Rushed on my gallant host. My warriors fled
For safety and for succour. I, instead,
On bended bones – familiarly called marrow,
For quarter sued. When lo! a young cock-sparrow
Flew to my rescue with his bow and arrow.
FIN: A young cock-sparrow! Surely not the sparrow
That killed cock-robin?
KING: No, ingenuous child!
Not the winged hero of that legend wild,
But a young stripling, fair as early dawn!
We fought and conquered ere a sword was drawn!
FIN: Oh, speedy conquest!
KING: Interrupt me not!
I made a vow, if off scot-free I got,
One of my daughters should become the bride
Of that brave youth, and wear my crown beside –
When I have done with it.
FIN: And who's the man, sir?
KING: I asked that question, but received no answer,
But I will know who my deliverer is –
He comes.
(*Music. Enter* PRINCE BELAVOIR.)
FIN: (*aside*) Oh, Cupid! what a charming phys–
Iognomy! If he be marrièd,
My grave is like to be my wedding bed.

KING: Young sir, I think you said you were a knight.
BEL: I'm a knight-bachelor.
FIN: (*aside*) So far all's right.
KING: You want a wife, then?
BEL: Frankly, I declare,
I want just such a one as I see there!
KING: I have two more such, and have sworn that you
Shall take your choice.
BEL: Oh, then allow me to –
KING: Allow you two!
BEL: To take her, this choice fair.
Her eyes are load-stars, and her tongue's sweet air,
More tunable than lark to shepherd's ear.
KING: Why, you've not heard it.
BEL: No, but long to hear.
With one sweet syllable my ear then bless,
And let that sweet one be your sweetest yes.
FIN: Sir, first my sisters let me beg you'll see,
They are much handsomer indeed than me;
If, after that, you still should press me so,
It is just possible I mayn't say 'no'.
KING: (*Embraces her.*) Still of thy sex discreetest, wisest, best –
But ah! I had forgot the magic test,
Thy distaff!
FIN: (*aside*) Heavens!
KING: Thou hast it not? Ha! say!
Is't lost? Is't broken?
FIN: No, it's over the way!
I left it in my haste to fly to you.
KING: Fetch it!
FIN: I will! (*aside*) What will my sisters do?
Ah, here they come, and all must out 'tis clear!
KING: She hesitates!
BEL: What mystery is here?
(*Enter* PRINCESSES IDELFONZA *and* BABILLARDA. *The former has* FINETTA*'s distaff, which she holds behind her.*)
BABIL: } Papa!
IDEL: }
KING: Before I answer to that name,
Your distaffs!
IDEL: (*showing* FINETTA*'s*) Here is mine, sir!
FIN: Oh, for shame!
BABIL: (*to whom* IDELFONZA *has passed the distaff unseen by the* KING) And here is mine – and here is yours, Finetta,
We brought it for you. (*giving it to her*)
FIN: Come, that's rather better.
KING: Humph! Here's some sleight of hand!

FIN: (*aside*) I feel a feather
Would knock me down.
KING: Show all three, both together!
Present arms! Two are absent! Wretched sire!
FIN: (*aside*) 'Tis done, and all the fat is in the fire.
KING: Who is the owner of the one unbroken?
BABIL: Well, then, sir, if the truth must needs be spoken,
It is Finetta's. But my fault was small.
IDEL: And I did nothing, sir, I'm sure, at all.
KING: Both guilty! Six months with hard labour, you. (*to* IDELFONZA)
For you, the silent system! (*to* BABILLARDA)
FIN: Oh, sir, do
Forgive 'em, I implore you, for my sake,
Or else their little hearts they next will break;
They've saved the pieces, let them make their own.
KING: Well, for your sake, but yours shall be my throne,
And as I've sworn, your troth you now shall plight
To this illustrious and renowned knight,
Sir Something – Thingumbob – zounds! What's your name?
Your patronymic you must now proclaim;
For though your modesty mayn't care about one,
You can't be asked in church, you know, without one.
BEL: I dread to name my name, yet must, I know;
I am the son of Fogrum, your old foe.
ALL: The son of Fogrum!
KING: Richcraft!
BEL: No; the other –
Prince Belavoir, his poor and younger brother;
Turned out of doors by that insidious sinner,
And forced to go a hunting for a dinner.
BABIL: The brother of that wicked little man!
IDEL: Oh, no; it can't – oh no; it never can!
FIN: My only love sprung from my only hate,
Too early seen, unknown, and known too late.
KING: O, fatal vow! The son of my worst foe –
The poor one, too! Consarn it – here's a go!
This bitter pill is far too big to bolt;
And yet, my honour! Shall a Gander moult
One feather of his white, unsullied fame?
And for a name – a name – 'What's in a name?'
Yet reputation's called, by the same poet,
'A bubble!' 'sdeath! I could almost say, blow it!
(*A trumpet sounds without.*)
Somebody has blown something. What's the row?

---

silent system: method of prison discipline which imposes complete silence at all times (*OED*).

(*Enter* SCHARP *with a scroll.*)

SCHARP: A letter for the unknown stranger.

BEL: How?

For me? Art sure of that, sir? By what sign?

SCHARP: There's no name on it.

BEL: Then it must be mine. (*Reads.*)

Ah! can I credit what is herein stated?
My brother dead – my father abdicated!
The people call me to the vacant throne.

KING: My son-in-law! – the son I'm proud to own!
King Belavoir, Finetta is thy queen.

BEL: The future, now, will sure be all serene.

FIN: (*aside*) O, happiness, I feel too great to last;
By his shade I cast over – overcast.

Song – FINETTA – *'The Tempest of the Heart'* – *'Il Trovatore'*

Though 'twas in self-preservation
That I threw his brother over!
Still I dread his condemnation,
When the truth he shall discover!
So to me joy brings no gladness –
Pleasure wears the dress of sadness;
Mem'ry with a spoon, like madness,
Stirs the tempest in my heart.

Quintette – KING GANDER, FINETTA, BABILLARDA, IDELFONZA, *and* PRINCE BELAVOIR

Recitative – KING

Away! Prepare
A banquet rare!

BABILLARDA – *'Polka'* – *Allary*

Who'd have thought it? Cunning little puss!
Here's for the *Court Circular* a pretty piece of news, dear!
Our youngest sister married before us,
At the wedding we shall have to dance without our shoes, dear!

IDEL: Why about the matter rave?
It don't seem to me so serious;
I don't dance, and so shan't have
To go without my shoes.

FIN: (*aside*) Wherefore am I pestered thus,
With presentiments mysterious!
In the midst of all this fuss,
I tremble in my shoes.

KING *and* BEL: Here's a splendid day for us;
I with joy shall go delirious!

---

dance without our shoes: a girl whose younger sister marries before her is said to 'dance barefoot' (Partridge).

All my woes are banished, thus!
By this glorious news.
(*Exeunt all.*)

SCENE 8. *Gardens of the Palace by moonlight. Bank, alcove. Enter* PRINCE RICHCRAFT, *enveloped in a mantle, carrying a scroll.*

RICH: After a long succession of short fits,
I have got back a small part of my wits;
Only again the lot well nigh to lose,
At hearing this extraordinary news!
My father has resigned his crown in favour
Of Belavoir; and that smooth-faced young shaver
Is going to be married to Finetta,
And so heal up the deadly old vendetta.
This is the fun fate's book was at me poking;
But fortune's wheel I still may put a spoke in.
I've hoaxed my brother with a *billet-doux* –
He thinks he's coming here to bill and coo;
And now, that upon horrors he may sup,
I'll act the ghost, before I give it up;
E'en such a ghost, so pale, so woe begone,
As I have seen another brother warn.
For a costume, to me now most accessible,
The loss of mine, being all but inexpressible;
(*Throws off his mantle, and appears in his tights and white shirt, like the Ghost in 'The Corsican Brothers'.*)
In this attire, upon him gently stealing,
I'll try to work on his fraternal feeling.
If I can but persuade the simple elf
To kill Finetta – he will kill himself.
Lo, where he comes, in mood the most romantic!
Now to look Corsican and Corsicantic!
(*Powders his face, then resuming his mantle, steals behind a tree.*)
(*Enter* PRINCE BELAVOIR.)

BEL: In a sweet note, than note of wood lark sweeter,
My love, by moonlight begged alone I'd meet her.
I thought she seemed something to have to say
Too tender to be told by light of day.
This is the spot – the centre of the grove;
There stands the oak, and there a snug alcove.

The Corsican Brothers: drama by Boucicault, produced at the Princess's Theatre in 1852; in the closing scene, set in the forest of Fontainebleau, the ghost of Louis dei Franchi 'appears rising gradually through the earth' and places his hand on his twin brother Fabien's shoulder *after* the latter has avenged his death.
elf: 'a (poor, pious) soul' (*OED*).
Corsicantic: a nonce word incorporating 'antic' in the sense of grotesque or clown-like.

(RICHCRAFT *groans*.)
What sound was that? 'twas like some yawning grave
That teems with an untimely ghost; or cave
Through which winds squeeze, like courtiers at a levée;
No matter what: and yet my heart feels heavy.
(*Seats himself on a bank in front of the oak*.)
(*Music*. RICHCRAFT *comes from behind the tree, as the Ghost does in the last scene of 'The Corsican Brothers', and touches him on the shoulder*.)

BEL: (*starting up*) Kings, Queens, and Ministers in place defend us!
Be thou my brother, or a fiend they send us?
Bringing with thee an air from the Princess's
In the most questionable of un-dresses.
I will speak to thee, ask thee, what's the matter?
Oh, answer me! and tell – who is your hatter?
That thus bare-headed he can let you go;
Say, why is this? wherefore do you do so?

RICH: Mark me!

BEL: I will, if you touch me again!

RICH: Bully me not! I rise, sir, to explain.
I am thy brother's spirit! Pray desist
From asking questions, and list, list, oh list!
If ever thou didst thy dear brother love.

BEL: I can't say you were over and above
Affectionate to me; but never mind,
You're dead, and I forgive you.

RICH: Well that's kind.

BEL: What can I do, pray, to oblige you further?

RICH: Revenge my foul and most unnatural murther!

BEL: Murther!

RICH: The most unnatural ever seen.

BEL: Haste me to know it then, that I, as clean
As a new broom, may sweep to my revenge.

RICH: Swear!

BEL: By my head!

RICH: Swear harder!

BEL: By Stonehenge!

RICH: That's hard enough; now hear – 'tis given out,
That slipping on a mountain here about,
I cracked my cranium; but that's rank abuse;
For know that she who cooked thy brother's goose
Would share thy crown.

BEL: Oh, my prophetic soul!
Finetta!

RICH: Aye, she gave me such a roll!
Oh, brother! what a falling off was there!
But soft! methinks I scent the morning air! (*Music, piano*.)

So, as I always was – brief let me be!
Adieu! Adieu! Adieu! Remember, *She*! (*Exit.*)

BEL: Remember she! I wish I could forget her!
But I have sworn – and off I must not let her –
She's here! Confusion! I've forgot my dagger!
Back to my chamber for it, I must stagger!
But though her gruel, I am bound to give her,
I'll take another oath – I won't outlive her! (*Exit.*)

RICH: (*who has peeped and listened*) Hurrah! The work goes bravely on! I've tricked him!
And here, in good time, comes the other victim! (*Retires.*)

(*Enter* FINETTA.)

FIN: Some mischief's in the wind. – Some wicked folks
Have played upon my Belavoir a hoax.
I found a little note he dropped, inviting
Him to meet me here – but 'tis not my writing –
My mind misgives me! It is only Richcraft
Who could be up to anything like sich craft –
So for myself I've brought a substitute –

(*Goes to wing and returns with a milliner's doll's head and dummy figure, dressed like herself.*)

And trust once more to circumvent the brute!

Song – FINETTA – *Air* – *'Meet me by moonlight'*

I'll meet him by moonlight alone,
And then I will tell him a tale
Of a tub, which I managed, I own,
To tumble down into the dale.
I must say, if Richcraft's not dead,
That he certainly ought to have been;
But no more on that – or this head,
Till the object more clearly I've seen,
Of this meeting by moonlight alone!
Lie there, my double! (*placing figure on bank*) If there's aught to dread,
This plan must surely bring it to a head.
Meanwhile to foil my foe, and guard my love,
I'll bide the issue in this dark alcove. (*Hides in alcove.*)

(*Re-enter* PRINCE BELAVOIR, *with a dagger.*)

BEL: What would make some men drunk, has made me bold!
I've drained a full pint of 'Tom', called 'the old',
And now I must fulfil the pint of honour!
Lo! Where she sleeps! I dare not look upon her!

(*stabbing the doll, as he turns away his face*)

Thus! thus! I keep my oath! (FINETTA *screams.*)

---

gruel: punishment.
'Tom', called 'the old': strong gin (Partridge).

O cruel brother!
Thou art avenged!
RICH: (*aside*) One's gone! Now for the other! (*Retires.*)
BEL: I swore I'd not survive her, and I won't!
Thus! thus! I follow thee! Eh! No I don't!
(*Looks at the dagger, which has changed into a bunch of roses.*)
What potent power my stern will opposes?
My dagger's changed into a bunch of roses!
RICH: (*advancing*) The deuce it is! And I have none to lend him!
FIN: (*entering*) And if you had, I'm here, sir, to defend him!
BEL: Finetta living! Yet Finetta dead!
FIN: I backed myself, and beat him by a head!
(MOTHER GOOSE *enters.*)
MOTHER G: Yes, but there's few can beat me at a tale,
So I'll wind this up!
FIN: I hope without fail!
(*Music.* MOTHER GOOSE *waves her crutch, and the scene changes to*)

SCENE 9. *Fairy Palace of the Golden Eggs.* FAIRIES *discovered at back. One* FAIRY *in centre with three glass distaffs. The* PRINCESSES BABILLARDA *and* IDELFONZA, *with* KING GANDER, MINISTER, COUNCILLORS, GUARDS, PAGES, *and* LADIES OF HONOUR *discovered.*
MOTHER G: (*joining the hands of* BELAVOIR *and* FINETTA)
Here crown'd and wedded happy may you be.
RICH: Well, but I say, what's to become of me?
Of crown – of queen – of vengeance all bereft.
MOTHER G: Without 'em for the moral you are left.
RICH: Me! Well, I shan't be the first rogue of quality
Who at the last has taken to morality;
(*to audience*) We've all been guilty of a deal of folly,
But then it was to make our young friends jolly,
And teach them, too, some lessons often told,
But not at all the worse for being old;
And first the Author owns he's made strange use,
Of these thrice golden eggs of Mother Goose:
But you'll observe he humbly hopes and begs,
Some reason in this roasting of her eggs.
As idleness of evil is the root,
So safety is, of prudence, the rich fruit;
We've not been idle, that I think you'll own –
Whether we have been prudent will be shown
By your decision; if a kind one, we
To golden eggs shall change the distaffs three!

---

roasting of her eggs: rough treatment of the original tale from *Mother Goose* (which Planché took to be this story's source).

Finale – Air – 'The Ratcatcher's Daughter'

FIN: At Christmas time, whate'er the rhyme,
It should convey a moral;
For giving you a piece with *two*,
With us you will not quarrel.
So may distress, through idleness,
Ne'er make your children smarters;
But prudence still ensure success
To your pretty little sons and daughters.
Singing, Doodle dee, etc.

BABIL: The 'Yellow Dwarf' to Easter ran,
And a very long time arter;
And our Princess may do no less,
If you'll but kindly start her;
Then from east and west, come here, and just
Make these your winter quarters;
And every night, we'll strive to delight,
All your pretty little sons and daughters.
Singing, Doodle dee, etc.

RICH: Wych Street's not fur from Westminster,
As you come up the Strand, O;
And here we are, at Temple Bar,
With the City close at hand, O.
There are buses vot run to Islington,
And t'other side of the water;
So we trust you'll bring, every mother's son,
With his purty little father's *darter*.
To sing, Doodle dee, etc.

FAIRY
FAIRIES FAIRIES
LADIES PAGES PAGES LADIES
GUARDS GUARDS
COUNCILLORS COUNCILLORS
BABIL KING IDEL RICH MOTHER G. FIN P. BEL

Curtain

The 'Yellow Dwarf': Planché's highly successful fairy extravaganza, produced at the Olympic for the previous Christmas season.
Wych Street: site of the Olympic Theatre, demolished to make way for Aldwych.

APPENDIX: Some Variants

The most common source of variation between successive editions of Planché's plays lies in the songs that accompanied their performance. For reasons of topicality or because of changed theatrical circumstances these were not infrequently amended or totally substituted on the occasion of a revival.

A case in point is Beauty's song to a 'Nigger Melody' in Act I of *Beauty and the Beast.* In the original version of 1841 Madame Vestris sang a parody of the song 'Happy Land' incorporating an allusion to James Bland who played Sir Aldgate:

Father bland, Father bland!
　　Blander none could ever be.
Come again, come again,
　　And bring a rose to me.

This was replaced by 'Susannah don't you cry' for the 1849 revival (in which Bland did not appear), no doubt to take account of the vogue for minstrel shows which had developed in the mean time. The licensing copy, incidentally, contains no mention of any song at this point, a not uncommon feature of the versions submitted to the Lord Chamberlain, indicating at how late a stage of rehearsal musical interpolations were finalised.

An intriguing disparity occurs in the first part of *The Golden Fleece* at the point where the dragon is disposed of. The text of the first edition places Medea's speech beginning 'Behold the monster, overcome by sleep' immediately after her song to the tune of 'The Mistletoe Bough' and keeps her on stage throughout the scene; only Jason makes an exit, to retrieve the fleece, but does so before, rather than after, he has summoned the Argonauts. The whole sequence reads:

MEDEA: . . . Wave the juniper bough.
　Behold the monster, overcome by sleep,
　Nods to his fall, like ruin on a steep;
　'Tis done! He sinks upon the ground, supine,
　His end approaches, make it answer thine.
　Hence! With bold hand the fleecy treasure tear
　Down from this beech, and hasten to that there.
　　　(*Exit* JAS. *and returns with fleece.*)
JAS:　Arise, ye Minyans. (*Enter* ARGONAUTS)
　　　　　　　　　　　If again ye'd scan
　Thessalia's shore, make all the sail you can.

For 'pris'ners base' you'll soon be, with your skipper,
If once her dad is roused to 'hunt the slipper.'

Medea then has the speech beginning 'With her bold Argonaut Medea flies' (which is not attributed to Chorus until the 1864 edition), and this is followed by a stage direction: '*Exeunt. The Argo is seen leaving the Port. Shouts. Enter* ÆETES.' The whole sequence makes perfect sense, even if it does presuppose that the monster can be overpowered by remote control, as it were. The licensing copy goes still further by apparently situating '*Music & business with Dragon*' on stage and making the entire text (with some modifications) a monologue for Medea up to the entry of Æetes.

The licensing copy of *The Discreet Princess*, too, shows some interesting divergences. The march for the king's departure in Act I is specified as 'Il brociato' and the '*Exeunt Omnes*' is followed by a further stage direction: '*The Princesses appear at the Window of the Tower and wave their kerchiefs to the King as he goes out and then retire. As soon as the Stage is clear, Babillarda returns to the window*.' Richcraft's ascent in the basket is accompanied by an eight-line duet to the air of 'There was an old woman', and his first exchange with Finetta has some additional dialogue:

RICH: . . . And drive me not to acts much more terrific.
'Bury the Hatchet!' as the Indians say
And smoke the pipe of peace with me to-day.
FIN (*aside*): I smoke him – and will bury no such thing,
But as we say, 'the Hatchet gently fling',
And feign . . .

His reading of the messenger's letter also has somewhat different business and dialogue to match:

RICH: . . . A letter! But of light there's not a spark
To read it by – so I'm still in the dark.
WOLF: I've German Tinder!
WURM: I've a piece of wax!
(*They light a Candle end.*)
RICH: Good! That will throw some light upon the facts.
What do I read? . . .

THE PLAYS OF J. R. PLANCHÉ

Amoroso, King of Little Britain, with music by Tom Cooke. Drury Lane, 21 April 1818.

Rodolph, the Wolf; or, Columbine Red Riding-Hood. Olympic Theatre, 21 December 1818.

The Troubadours; or, Jealousy Outwitted. Olympic Theatre, 9 February 1819.

Abudah; or, The Talisman of Oromanes, with music by Michael Kelly. Drury Lane, 13 April 1819.

The Czar; or, A Day in the Dockyards, adapted from *Le Bourgmestre de Sardam* (Mélesville, Merle & Boirie). Sadler's Wells Theatre, 21 June 1819.

The Caliph and the Cadi; or, Rambles in Bagdad. Sadler's Wells Theatre, 16 August 1819.

Fancy's Sketch; or, Look Before You Leap. Adelphi Theatre, 29 October 1819.

Odds and Ends; or, Which is the Manager? Adelphi Theatre, 19 November 1819.

The Vampire; or, The Bride of the Isles, from *Le Vampire* (Carmouche, Nodier & de Jouffroy), with music by William Reeve, M. Moss and Hart. Lyceum Theatre, 9 August 1820.

A Burletta of Errors; or, Jupiter and Alcmena, from *Amphitryon* (Dryden). Adelphi Theatre, 6 November 1820.

Who's to Father Her? or, What's Bred in the Bone Won't Come Out of the Flesh. Adelphi Theatre, 13 November 1820.

The Deuce is in Her! or, Two Nights in Madrid. Adelphi Theatre, 27 November 1820.

Zamoski; or, The Fortress and the Mine. Adelphi Theatre, 11 December 1820.

Dr Syntax; or, Harlequin in London. Adelphi Theatre, 26 December 1820.

Giovanni, the Vampire; or, How Shall We Get Rid of Him? Adelphi Theatre, 15 January 1821.

Kenilworth Castle; or, The Days of Queen Bess, from Scott. Adelphi Theatre, 9 February 1821.

Lodgings to be Let. Adelphi Theatre, 19 February 1821.

Half-an-Hour's Courtship; or, La Chambre à Coucher. Adelphi Theatre, 27 February 1821.

Sherwood Forest; or, The Merry Archers. Adelphi Theatre, 12 March 1821.

The Mountain Hut; or, The Tinker's Son. Sadler's Wells Theatre, 23 April 1821; revived at Olympic Theatre, 25 November 1822.

Peter and Paul; or, Love in the Vineyards. Haymarket Theatre, 4 July 1821.

The Witch of Derncleuch, from Scott's *Guy Mannering*, with music by William Reeve. Lyceum Theatre, 30 July 1821.

Capers at Canterbury. Adelphi Theatre, 1 October 1821.

The Corsair's Bride; or, The Valley of Mount Etna. Adelphi Theatre, 22 October 1821.

Marplot in Spain, from Susanna Centlivre. Adelphi Theatre, 7 November 1821;

revived as *Too Curious By Half*, with music by William Reeve, Lyceum Theatre, 27 August 1823.

Love's Alarum. Adelphi Theatre, 8 November 1821.

Le Solitaire; or, The Unknown of the Mountain. Olympic Theatre, 24 November 1821.

The Pirate, from Scott. Olympic Theatre, 14 January 1822.

Henri Quatre and the Fair Gabrielle, with music by Barham Livius. Lyceum Theatre, 19 June 1822; revived as *The Fair Gabrielle*, 6 September 1822.

All in the Dark; or, The Banks of the Elbe, from *Hasard et Folie* (Victor), with music by Barham Livius. Lyceum Theatre, 10 July 1822; revived at Royalty Theatre, 21 November 1861.

Ali Pacha; or, The Signet Ring, from J. H. Payne. Covent Garden, 19 October 1822.

Maid Marian; or, The Huntress of Arlingford, from Peacock, with music by Henry Bishop. Covent Garden, 3 December 1822.

Clari; or, The Maid of Milan (songs only), with music by Henry Bishop. Covent Garden, 8 May 1823.

I Will Have a Wife!, with music by William Reeve. Lyceum Theatre, 7 August 1823.

(Hernando) Cortez; or, The Conquest of Mexico, with music by Henry Bishop. Covent Garden, 13 October 1823.

St Ronan's Well, from Scott. Adelphi Theatre, 19 January 1824.

Military Tactics, from *Les Projets de mariage*, with music by William Reeve. Lyceum Theatre, 6 July 1824.

The Frozen Lake, from *La Neige; ou, Le Nouvel Eginard* (Scribe & Delavigne), with music by William Reeve. Lyceum Theatre, 3 September 1824.

Der Freischütz; or, The Black Huntsman of Bohemia, from J. F. Kind's text to Weber's music, arranged by Barham Livius. Covent Garden, 14 October 1824.

A Woman Never Vext; or, The Widow of Cornhill, from Rowley. Covent Garden, 9 November 1824.

The Coronation of Charles X of France. Covent Garden, 11 July 1825.

Lilla. Covent Garden, 21 October 1825.

Jocko; or, The Brazilian Monkey. Covent Garden, 8 November 1825.

Success; or, A Hit If You Like It. Adelphi Theatre, 12 December 1825.

Oberon; or, The Elf-King's Oath, from Wieland, with music by Weber. Covent Garden, 12 April 1826.

Returned Killed, from *Le Mort dans l'embarras*. Covent Garden, 31 October 1826.

All's Right; or, The Old Schoolfellow. Haymarket Theatre, 15 June 1827.

Pay To My Order; or, A Chaste Salute. Vauxhall Gardens, 9 July 1827; revived, as *The Chaste Salute*, at Olympic Theatre, 19 January 1831; and at Sadler's Wells Theatre, 26 December 1832.

The Rencontre; or, Love Will Find Out the Way, with music by Henry Bishop. Haymarket Theatre, 12 July 1827.

You Must Be Buried, from *La Veuve du Malabar* (Scribe). Haymarket Theatre, 11 August 1827.

Paris and London; or, A Trip Across the Herring Pond. Adelphi Theatre, 21 January 1828.

The Merchant's Wedding; or, London Frolics in 1638, from *The City Match* (Mayne) and *Match Me at Midnight* (Rowley). Covent Garden, 5 February 1828.

Carron Side; or, The Fête Champêtre, with music by Giovanni Liverati. Covent Garden, 27 May 1828.

A Daughter To Marry, from *Une Demoiselle à marier; ou, La Première entrevue* (Scribe & Mélesville). Haymarket Theatre, 16 June 1828; revived, as *My Daughter, Sir!*, 9 October 1832.

The Green-Eyed Monster, from *Les Deux jaloux*. Haymarket Theatre, 18 August 1828.

The Mason of Buda, from *Le Maçon* (Scribe), with music by Auber, arranged by George Rodwell. Adelphi Theatre, 21 October 1828.

Charles XII; or, The Siege of Stralsund, from Voltaire. Drury Lane, 11 December 1828.

Thierna-na-Oge; or, The Prince of the Lakes, with music by Tom Cooke. Drury Lane, 20 April 1829.

The Partisans; or, The War of Paris in 1649, from *La Maison du rampart; ou Une Journée de la ronde*. Drury Lane, 21 May 1829.

Manoeuvring, from *L'Ambassadeur* (Scribe & Mélesville). Haymarket Theatre, 1 July 1829; revived at Sadler's Wells Theatre, 24 August 1846.

Der Vampyr, from W. A. Wohlbrück's text to Marschner's music, arranged by William Hawes. Lyceum Theatre, 25 August 1829.

The Brigand Chief, from *Le Bandit*, with music by Tom Cooke. Drury Lane, 18 November 1829.

The National Guard; or, Bride and No Bride, from *La Fiancée* (Scribe), with music by Auber. Drury Lane, 4 February 1830.

The Dragon's Gift; or, The Scarf of Flight and the Mirror of Light, with music by Tom Cooke. Drury Lane, 12 April 1830.

Hofer; or, The Tell of the Tyrol, from *Guillaume Tell*, with music by Rossini, arranged by Henry Bishop. Drury Lane, 1 May 1830.

The Jenkinses; or, Boarded and Done For. Drury Lane, 9 December 1830; revived at Lyceum Theatre, 6 December 1852.

Olympic Revels; or, Prometheus and Pandora (with Charles Dance). Olympic Theatre, 3 January 1831.

The Romance of a Day, with music by Henry Bishop. Covent Garden, 3 February 1831.

My Great Aunt; or, Where There's a Will. Olympic Theatre, 5 March 1831.

The Legion of Honour, from *Le Centenaire*. Drury Lane, 16 April 1831.

A Friend at Court. Haymarket Theatre, 28 June 1831.

The Army of the North; or, The Spaniard's Secret. Covent Garden, 29 October 1831.

The Love Charm; or, The Village Coquette, from *Le Philtre* (Scribe), with music by Auber, arranged by Henry Bishop. Drury Lane, 3 November 1831.

Olympic Devils; or, Orpheus and Eurydice (with Charles Dance). Olympic Theatre, 26 December 1831.

The Compact. Drury Lane, 5 April 1832.

His First Campaign. Covent Garden, 1 October 1832.

Little Red Riding-Hood; or, The Fairy of the Silver Lake. Clarence Theatre, 26 December 1832.

The Paphian Bower; or, Venus and Adonis (with Charles Dance). Olympic Theatre, 26 December 1832.

Promotion; or, A Morning at Versailles in 1750. Olympic Theatre, 18 February 1833; revived at Queen's Theatre, 23 April 1835.

Reputation; or, The Court Secret. Covent Garden, 4 March 1833.

The Students of Jena; or, The Family Concert, from *La Table et le logement* (Gabriel & Dumersan), with music by Chélard. Drury Lane, 4 June 1833.

The Court Masque; or, Richmond in the Olden Time, from *Le Pré aux clercs* (de Planard), with music by Hérold, arranged by William Hawes. Adelphi Theatre, 9 September 1833.

High, Low, Jack and the Game; or, The Card Party (with Charles Dance). Olympic Theatre, 30 September 1833.

Gustavus III; or, The Masked Ball, from Scribe's text to Auber's music, arranged by Tom Cooke. Covent Garden, 13 November 1833.

The Deep, Deep Sea; or, Perseus and Andromeda (with Charles Dance). Olympic Theatre, 26 December 1833.

The Challenge (with H. M. Milner), from *Le Pré aux clercs* (de Planard), with music by Hérold, arranged by Tom Cooke. Covent Garden, 1 April 1834.

Secret Service, from Mélesville and Duveyrier. Drury Lane, 29 April 1834.

The Loan of a Lover. Olympic Theatre, 29 September 1834; revived, and revised, as *Peter Spyk*, Gaiety Theatre, 22 August 1870.

My Friend, the Governor. Olympic Theatre, 29 September 1834.

The Regent, from *Le Moulin de Javelle* (Scribe & Mélesville). Drury Lane, 18 October 1834.

The Red Mask; or, The Council of Three, from *Il Bravo* (Berrettoni), with music by Marliani, arranged by Tom Cooke. Drury Lane, 15 November 1834.

Telemachus; or, The Island of Calypso (with Charles Dance). Olympic Theatre, 26 December 1834.

The Court Beauties. Olympic Theatre, 12 March 1835; revived at Lyceum Theatre, 4 June 1851.

The Travelling Carriage. Drury Lane, 26 October 1835.

The Jewess, from *La Juive* (Scribe), with music by Halévy, arranged by Tom Cooke. Drury Lane, 16 November 1835.

Chevy Chase, with music by George Macfarren. Drury Lane, 3 March 1836.

Court Favour; or, Private and Confidential, from Carmouche. Olympic Theatre, 29 September 1836.

The Siege of Corinth, from Byron and *Le Siège de Corinthe* (Soumet & Balochi), with music by Rossini, arranged by Tom Cooke. Drury Lane, 8 November 1836.

The Two Figaros, from *Les Deux Figaro; ou, Le Sujet de comédie* (Richaud-Martelly). Olympic Theatre, 30 November 1836.

Riquet with the Tuft (with Charles Dance), from *Riquet à la houppe* (Sewrin & Brazier). Olympic Theatre, 26 December 1836.

A Peculiar Position, from *La Frontière de Savoie* (Scribe & Bayard). Olympic Theatre, 3 May 1837.

Norma, from F. Romani's text to Bellini's music. Drury Lane, 24 June 1837; revived at Covent Garden, 2 November 1841.

The New Servant. Olympic Theatre, 29 September 1837.

The Child of the Wreck, with music by Tom Cooke. Drury Lane, 7 October 1837.

Caractacus, from *Bonduca* (Fletcher), with music by Michael Balfe. Drury Lane, 6 November 1837.

Puss in Boots (with Charles Dance). Olympic Theatre, 26 December 1837.

The Magic Flute, from E. Schikander's text to Mozart's music, arranged by Tom Cooke. Drury Lane, 10 March 1838.

The Drama's Levée; or, A Peep at the Past. Olympic Theatre, 16 April 1838.

The Printer's Devil. Olympic Theatre, 11 October 1838.

The Queen's Horse; or, The Brewer of Preston (with M. B. Honan). Olympic Theatre, 3 December 1838.

Blue Beard (with Charles Dance). Olympic Theatre, 2 January 1839.

Faint Heart Ne'er Won Fair Lady. Olympic Theatre, 28 February 1839.

The Garrick Fever. Olympic Theatre, 1 April 1839.

The Fortunate Isles; or, The Triumphs of Britannia, with music by Henry Bishop. Covent Garden, 12 February 1840.

The Sleeping Beauty in the Wood. Covent Garden, 20 April 1840.

The Spanish Curate, from Fletcher and Massinger. Covent Garden, 13 October 1840.

Harlequin and the Giant Helmet; or, The Castle of Otranto, from Walpole. Covent Garden, 26 December 1840.

The Captain of the Watch, from *Le Chevalier du guet* (Lockroy). Covent Garden, 25 February 1841.

The Embassy. Covent Garden, 22 March 1841.

Beauty and the Beast. Covent Garden, 12 April 1841; revived at Lyceum Theatre, 31 October 1849.

The Marriage of Figaro, from Da Ponte's text to Mozart's music. Covent Garden, 15 March 1842.

The White Cat, with music by J. H. Tully. Covent Garden, 28 March 1842.

The Follies of a Night, from *Charlot* (Lockroy, Anicet, Bourgeois & Vanderburch), with music by Tom Cooke. Drury Lane, 5 October 1842.

The Way of the World, from Congreve. Haymarket Theatre, 17 December 1842.

Fortunio and his Seven Gifted Servants. Drury Lane, 17 April 1843; revived at Sadler's Wells Theatre, 22 April 1851.

Who's Your Friend?; or, The Queensberry Fête, from *Trianon* (Bayard & Picard). Haymarket Theatre, 22 August 1843.

The Fair One with the Golden Locks. Haymarket Theatre, 26 December 1843; revived at Sadler's Wells Theatre, 13 April 1857.

Grist to the Mill, from *La Marquise de Carabas* (Bayard & Dumanoir). Haymarket Theatre, 22 February 1844.

The Drama at Home; or, An Evening with Puff. Haymarket Theatre, 8 April 1844.

Somebody Else. Haymarket Theatre, 4 December 1844.

Graciosa and Percinet. Haymarket Theatre, 26 December 1844.

The Golden Fleece; or, Jason in Colchis and Medea in Corinth. Haymarket Theatre, 24 March 1845.

A Cabinet Question. Haymarket Theatre, 23 September 1845.

The Bee and the Orange Tree; or The Four Wishes. Haymarket Theatre, 26 December 1845.

The Irish Post. Haymarket Theatre, 28 February 1846.

'The Birds' of Aristophanes. Haymarket Theatre, 13 April 1846.

Queen Mary's Bower, from *Les Mousquetaires de la reine* (St Georges). Haymarket Theatre, 10 October 1846.

Spring Gardens. Haymarket Theatre, 15 October 1846; revived there 2 October 1875.
Story-Telling; or, Novel Effects. Haymarket Theatre, 16 December 1846.
The Invisible Prince; or, The Island of Tranquil Delights. Haymarket Theatre, 26 December 1846.
The New Planet; or, Harlequin out of Place. Haymarket Theatre, 5 April 1847.
The Jacobite. Haymarket Theatre, 12 June 1847.
The Price of the Market. Lyceum Theatre, 18 October 1847.
The Golden Branch. Lyceum Theatre, 27 December 1847.
Not a Bad Judge. Lyceum Theatre, 2 March 1848.
Theseus and Ariadne; or, The Marriage of Bacchus. Lyceum Theatre, 24 April 1848.
The King of the Peacocks. Lyceum Theatre, 26 December 1848.
A Romantic Idea. Lyceum Theatre, 8 March 1849.
Hold Your Tongue. Lyceum Theatre, 22 March 1849.
The Seven Champions of Christendom, from Richard Johnson. Lyceum Theatre, 9 April 1849.
A Lady in Difficulties. Lyceum Theatre, 15 October 1849.
The Island of Jewels. Lyceum Theatre, 26 December 1849.
Fiesco; or, The Revolt of Genoa, from Schiller. Drury Lane, 4 February 1850.
Cymon and Iphigenia, from *Cymon* (Garrick), with music by Arne. Lyceum Theatre, 1 April 1850.
My Heart's Idol; or, A Desperate Remedy. Lyceum Theatre, 16 October 1850.
The White Hood. Lyceum Theatre, 11 November 1850.
A Day of Reckoning. Lyceum Theatre, 4 December 1850.
King Charming; or, The Blue Bird of Paradise. Lyceum Theatre, 26 December 1850.
The Queen of the Frogs. Lyceum Theatre, 21 April 1851.
The Prince of Happy Land; or, The Fawn in the Forest. Lyceum Theatre, 26 December 1851.
The Mysterious Lady; or, Worth Makes the Man. Lyceum Theatre, 18 October 1852.
The Good Woman in the Wood. Lyceum Theatre, 27 December 1852.
Mr Buckstone's Ascent of Mount Parnassus. Haymarket Theatre, 28 March 1853.
The Camp at the Olympic. Olympic Theatre, 17 October 1853.
Harlequin King Nutcracker. Strand Theatre, 26 December 1853.
Once upon a Time There Were Two Kings. Lyceum Theatre, 26 December 1853.
Mr Buckstone's Voyage Round the Globe (in Leicester Square). Haymarket Theatre, 12 April 1854.
The Knights of the Round Table, from *Les Chevaliers de Lansquenet*. Haymarket Theatre, 20 May 1854.
The Yellow Dwarf and the King of the Gold Mines. Olympic Theatre, 26 December 1854.
The New Haymarket Spring Meeting. Haymarket Theatre, 9 April 1855.
The Discreet Princess; or, The Three Glass Distaffs. Olympic Theatre, 26 December 1855.
Young and Handsome. Olympic Theatre, 26 December 1856.
An Old Offender. Adelphi Theatre, 22 July 1859.
Love and Fortune, from *La Ceinture de Vénus*. Princess's Theatre, 24 September 1859.
My Lord and my Lady; or, It Might Have Been Worse, from *Un Mariage sous Louis XV* (Dumas). Haymarket Theatre, 12 July 1861.

Love's Triumph, with music by Vincent Wallace. Covent Garden, 3 November 1862.

Orpheus in the Haymarket, from *Orphée aux enfers* (Crémieux), with music by Offenbach. Haymarket Theatre, 26 December 1865.

Queen Lucidora, the Fair One with the Golden Locks, and Harlequin Prince Grateful; or, The Carp, the Crow and the Owl. Sadler's Wells Theatre, 24 December 1868.

King Christmas. Gallery of Illustration, 26 December 1871.

Babil and Bijou; or, The Lost Regalia (songs only). Covent Garden, 29 August 1872.

SELECT BIBLIOGRAPHY

EDITIONS

The only collected edition of Planché's work is the testimonial edition of his *Extravaganzas* in five volumes, published in London by Samuel French in 1879. Edited by T. F. Dillon Croker and Stephen Tucker, it contains prefaces specially written by Planché for all the constituent pieces together with a virtually complete list of his plays.

Fortunio and his Seven Gifted Servants and *The Island of Jewels* are included, with annotations, in volume v of Michael Booth's *English Plays of the Nineteenth Century* (London: Oxford University Press, 1976). An abridged version of *The Vampire* appears in Michael Kilgarriff's *The Golden Age of Melodrama: Twelve 19th Century Melodramas* (London: Wolfe Publications, 1974).

ARTICLES, ETC., ON PLANCHÉ

Anon., 'James Robinson Planché', *The Critic*, 5 November 1859.

'A Theatrical Reformer (J. R. Planché)', *The Stage*, 16 and 23 September 1915.

Dircks, P. T., 'Planché and the English Burletta Tradition', *Theatre Survey*, 17 (1976), 68–81.

Granville-Barker, Harley, '*Exit* Planché – *Enter* Gilbert', *The Eighteen-Sixties*, ed. John Drinkwater, Cambridge, 1932, pp. 102–48.

MacMillan, Dougald, 'Planché's Early Classical Burlesques', *Studies in Philology*, 25 (1928), 340–5.

'Some Burlesques with a Purpose, 1830–1870', *Philological Quarterly*, 8 (1929), 255–63.

'Planché's Fairy Extravaganzas', *Studies in Philology*, 28 (1931), 790–8.

Planché, J. R., 'Extravaganza and Spectacle', *Temple Bar*, 3 (1861), 524–32.

Recollections and Reflections. A Professional Autobiography, 2 vols., London, 1872.

Reinhardt, Paul, 'The Costume Designs of James Robinson Planché (1796–1880)', *Educational Theatre Journal*, 20 (1968), 524–44.

Simpson, J. Palgrave, 'James Robinson Planché', *The Theatre*, 2 (August 1880), 95–9.

Troubridge, St. Vincent, 'Gilbert and Planché', *Notes and Queries*, 179 (1940), 442–3; 180 (1941), 200–5; 181 (1941), 17–18.

Vinson, James (ed.), *Great Writers of the English Language: Dramatists*, London, 1981, pp. 470–6.

Wells, Stanley, 'Shakespeare in Planché's Extravaganzas', *Shakespeare Survey*, 16 (1963), 103–17.

MEMOIRS AND CRITICAL STUDIES OF THE VICTORIAN THEATRE

Adams, W. Davenport, *A Book of Burlesque*, London, 1891.

Baker, H. Barton, *The London Stage, 1576–1888*, 2 vols., London, 1889.

Booth, Michael R., Introduction to *English Plays of the Nineteenth Century, vol. V: Pantomimes, Extravaganzas and Burlesques*, Oxford, 1976.

Victorian Spectacular Theatre, 1850–1910, London, 1891.

Booth, Michael R. *et al.*, *The Revels History of Drama in English, vol. VI: 1750–1880*, London, 1975.

Brown, Eluned (ed.), *The London Theatre, 1811–1866: Selections from the Diary of Henry Crabb Robinson*, London, 1966.

Bunn, Alfred, *The Stage, Both Before and Behind the Curtain*, 3 vols., London, 1840.

Burnand, F. C., *Records and Reminiscences, Personal and General*, London, 1904.

Clinton-Baddeley, V. C., *The Burlesque Tradition in the English Theatre after 1660*, London, 1952.

Coleman, John, *Fifty Years of an Actor's Life*, 2 vols., London, 1904.

Players and Playwrights I Have Known, 2 vols., London, 1888.

Dickens, Charles (ed.), *The Life of Charles James Mathews, Chiefly Autobiographical*, 2 vols., London, 1879.

Donaldson, Walter, *Fifty Years of Green Room Gossip, or Recollections of an Actor*, London, 1865.

Donne, William Bodham, *Essays on the Drama*, London, 1863.

Fitzball, Edward, *Thirty-Five Years of a Dramatic Author's Life*, 2 vols., London, 1859.

Fitzgerald, Percy, *Principles of Comedy and Dramatic Effect*, London, 1870.

Halliday, Andrew, *Comical Fellows, or the History and Mystery of the Pantomime*, London, 1863.

Hollingshead, John, *My Lifetime*, London, 1895.

Hudson, Lynton, *The English Stage, 1850–1950*, London, 1951.

Lennox, Lord William Pitt, *Plays, Players and Playhouses, at Home and Abroad*, 2 vols., London, 1881.

[Mackintosh, Matthew], *Stage Reminiscences: Being Recollections, Chiefly Personal, of Celebrated Theatrical & Musical Performers during the Last Forty Years. By an Old Stager*, Glasgow, 1866.

Mayer, David, *Harlequin in his Element: The English Pantomime, 1806–1836*, Cambridge, Mass., 1969.

Morley, Henry, *Journal of a London Playgoer, 1851 to 1866*, London, 1866.

Nicoll, Allardyce, *A History of English Drama, 1660–1900*; vol. IV: *Early Nineteenth Century Drama, 1800–1850*; vol. V: *Late Nineteenth Century Drama, 1850–1900*, 2nd edn, Cambridge, 1955 and 1959.

Pascoe, Charles E., *The Dramatic List*, London, 1879.

Reynolds, Ernest, *Early Victorian Drama, 1830–1870*, Cambridge, 1936.

Rowell, George, *The Victorian Theatre, 1792–1914*, 2nd edn, Cambridge, 1978.

Theatre in the Age of Irving, Oxford, 1981.

Scott, Clement, *The Drama of Yesterday and Today*, 2 vols., London, 1899.

Scott, Clement and Howard, Cecil (eds.), *The Life and Reminiscences of E. L. Blanchard*, 2 vols., London, 1891.
Stirling, Edward, *Old Drury Lane*, 2 vols., London, 1881.
Tolles, Winton, *Tom Taylor and the Victorian Drama*, 2nd edn, New York, 1966.
Vandenhoff, George, *Dramatic Reminiscences, or Actors and Actresses in England and America*, London, 1860.
Waitzkin, Leo, *The Witch of Wych Street: A Study of the Theatrical Reforms of Madame Vestris*, Cambridge, Mass., 1933.
Watson, Ernest Bradlee, *Sheridan to Robertson: A Study of the Nineteenth-Century London Stage*, Cambridge, Mass., 1926.
White, Eric Walter, *The Rise of English Opera*, London, 1951.
Williamson, Jane, *Charles Kemble, Man of the Theatre*, Lincoln, Nebr., 1970.
Wyndham, Henry Saxe, *Annals of Covent Garden Theatre*, 2 vols., London, 1905.
Yates, Edmund, *His Recollections and Experiences*, 2 vols., London, 1884.